D0765616

Controlling London's Growth

Controlling
London's Growth

PLANNING THE GREAT WEN 1940–1960

By Donald L. Foley

UNIVERSITY OF CALIFORNIA PRESS 1963

BERKELEY AND LOS ANGELES

University of California Press
Berkeley and Los Angeles, California

Cambridge University Press
London, England

© 1963 by The Regents of the University of California

Library of Congress Catalog Card Number: 63-19958

Printed in the United States of America

To Katharine, Thomas, William,
Margaret, and Judith—
CO-RESEARCHERS OF LONDON

But what is to be the fate of the great wen of all? The monster, called, by the silly coxcombs of the press, "the metropolis of the empire?" . . . The dispersion of the wen is the only real difficulty that I see in settling the affairs of the nation and restoring it to a happy state.

WILLIAM COBBETT, *Rural Rides,* Journal entry, December 4, 1821

Sixty years ago a great Englishman, Cobbett, called it a wen. If it was a wen then, what is it now? A tumour, an elephantiasis sucking into its gorged system half the life and the blood and the bone of the rural districts.

LORD ROSEBERRY, speaking as Chairman of the London County Council, March, 1891

The continued drift of the industrial population to London and the Home Counties constitutes a social, economic and strategic problem which demands immediate attention.

Report of the Royal Commission on the Distribution of the Industrial Population, January, 1940

The fundamental question is not "How can the growth of London be stopped?" but "How can London's abounding vitality be guided and directed for the general good through the medium of self-government?"

Report of the Royal Commission on Local Government in Greater London 1957–60, October, 1960

Preface

Problems reflecting the agglomeration of vast metropolitan super-communities, by no means confined to any few nations, are becoming increasingly acute. And despite the already serious manifestations—congestion, physical obsolescence at the center, rampant outer sprawl, political chaos, and fiscal crisis—we are confronted with the appalling realization that, if anything, the situation may be due to worsen. In general, our efforts to cope have been "too little and too late." To date the American record in effectively guiding metropolitan development has remained clearly discouraging. Problems are separately grappled with and ad hoc measures alleviate total breakdown, but we have lacked positive, comprehensive planning of metropolitan areas. This study reports and analyzes the tremendously significant and highly unique experience in seeking to fashion and put forcefully into effect such guidance for metropolitan London. Although directed primarily to an American audience—whether city planners, scholars, politicians, or interested citizens—standing to benefit from knowledge about the London "experiment," the book also offers an interpretative account of the planning for Greater London not previously available to British readers.

The report is built around two questions: What are the main social policies incorporated in the plans for metropolitan London? How effectively have these social policies been carried out in the face of subsequent development forces? The study is accordingly selective in several respects: it reports primarily on the advisory plans prepared in the 1940's and the degree to which their ideas have been carried into effect, it is mainly concerned with planning at the regional level, and it dwells on social policy considerations. It is neither a general commentary on British town planning nor a definitive history of the planning for London during recent years.

In the study I seek to show the influence of certain ideas, the crystallization of a reinforcing web of these ideas into doctrine, and the need to review this doctrine in the light of ongoing experience. Some of my interpretations may, in themselves, appear unduly critical. Let me hasten to make clear that I consider the plans for London, the planning system for carrying them out, and the accomplishments as singularly impressive pioneering. No single example of planning for any large American metropolitan area can match the London experience and results. The very uniqueness of this planning effort affords to this particular story an urgent significance.

I have undoubtedly brought to the study and its reporting more personal biases than I am able to recognize, and it may be appropriate to indicate some that I do sense. I am very fond of London and identify with the incredibly challenging task of respecting its traditional features while introducing needed changes. I greatly respect the integrity and the social maturity of the British leaders who have had the responsibility of planning for London. I appreciate the primary place assigned in Britain to political determination of major policy issues, yet also respect the importance of market-place decisions.

I have faith in physical planning and see an important place for leadership by planners as professionals, while also honoring their advisory relation to elected political officials. But I become impatient with traditional planning approaches if they remain unduly geared to preserving patterns reflecting earlier forces. Planning must permit—and, indeed, facilitate—growth and change. Undoubtedly I hold a bias, characteristically American perhaps, favoring growth and shunning policy deliberately restraining growth. Yet I have sought to be fair in my review of the London planning situation. I have tried to be openminded to the possibility that holding down London's growth may be a most appropriate approach in Britain even though such a policy might not be equally relevant for American metropolitan areas.

Residing within some four hundred miles of the great metropolitan experiment, Los Angeles, I cannot help but be impressed with the importance of the automobile and with the forces in motion making for much looser and decidedly less focal metropolitan spatial patterns than we have hitherto witnessed or thought desirable. But I also believe in the critically important role of public transit (and was, of course, delighted with the marvelous public transport system serving London). If we are to be effective in positively influencing the future patterning of large metropolitan areas, we must be ready in advance with guiding concepts that may depart from traditionally accepted precepts.

My acknowledgments are many and heartfelt. The necessary and wonderful 1959–60 academic year in London was made possible by a faculty research grant from the Social Science Research Council; a grant from the Institute of Social Sciences, University of California, Berkeley; and a sabbatical leave of absence from the University. I am indebted to the London School of Economics and Political Science, and particularly to Professor W. A. Robson, for extending full staff privileges, including an office amid already overcrowded conditions. My other British debts are numerous; with some fear that I may neglect persons also deserving to be mentioned, I particularly express my gratitude to Professor Donald G. MacRae, Mr. S. J. Gould, Professor Peter Self, Mr. J. R. James, Mr. J. F. P. Kacirek, Mr. A. G. Powell, Mr. Richard Edmonds, Mr. Brandon Howell, Mr. Lewis Keeble, Mrs. Ruth Glass, Mr. Wyndham Thomas, and Mr. W. L. Waide for their friendly counsel. To Mr. Derek Senior, Dr. Nathaniel Lichfield, Professor T. J. Kent, Jr., and Professor Catherine Bauer Wurster, who were stalwart enough to read and comment most helpfully on drafts, I am most grateful. Mr. Irving Silver, Mrs. D. J. Sinclair, and Miss Clare Cooper provided research and cartographic assistance.

Mrs. Howard Harawitz bore the main final typing responsibilities, Mrs. James Petras and Mrs. Philip Davis typed parts of manuscripts, and Mrs. Sallie Walker effectively handled many arrangements.

Material from my own previous articles in the *British Journal of Sociology,* the *Town Planning Review,* and the *Journal of the*

American Institute of Planners has been adapted, with permission. I wish also to express my appreciation to the University of Liverpool Press for permission to reproduce the MARS plan from the *Town Planning Review* and to George Allen and Unwin, the Macmillan Co. of New York, and Professor Robson for permission to quote from W. A. Robson (ed.), *Great Cities of the World: Their Government, Politics and Planning.* A much broader sphere of indebtedness is suggested by my rather extensive footnoting.

The responsibility for the opinions expressed and for the presentation and interpretation of the ideas and events reported remains my own.

D. L. F.

Berkeley, California
January, 1963

Contents

PART III. *Implications and Conclusions*

THE TOWN PLANNING PROFESSION

UNITARY PLANS, ADAPTIVE CONSENSUS, AND DE-
   VELOPMENT FORCES

REGIONAL PLANNING FOR LONDON: WHOSE RE-
   SPONSIBILITY?

Tables

Figures

PART I. *The Background and Formulation of the Plans*

Chapter 1

Introduction:
Focus and Context

London is a great and very special metropolis. It was probably the first of the world's cities to cross the million mark—and this by about 1800.[1] It abounds in tradition reflecting its venerable history, and its physical make-up, particularly in its central parts, preserves much character from earlier architectural periods. It has played a unique and dominant role in Great Britain and the British Commonwealth, and, with many Victorian touches, recalls the memorable period of the Empire. London commands a particularly warm place in the hearts of countless millions, British and non-British alike.

Reflecting its historical significance and long evolving physical environmental setting, London strikes one as singularly unplanned. Indeed, London's solid importance relates to a core of functional precincts that have evolved over the years—precincts characterized by tradition, historic continuity, workability, distinctiveness, and yet over all an amazing accessibility that collectively makes for metropolitan greatness. Men of importance in many fields of endeavor are readily able to be in face-to-face contact. London is so wonderfully complex that it can be tampered with only at great risk of upsetting a delicate ecological balance and a hard-come-by physical environmental heritage.

Yet one will do well to avoid a romanticism that belies the presence of serious problems. London's very age spells obsolescence of physical plant, and large sections of London provide but mean living conditions. Private cars intrude impatiently, aggra-

vating traffic congestion in street channels scarcely designed for
the twentieth century. And suburban growth, reflecting ability to
afford single-family homes and automobiles, threatens to despoil
charming countryside. Two developments—the release of the Barlow Commission report in 1940 recommending that employment
concentration in Greater London be halted, and the heavy bomb
damage during the early war years—led the British to initiate new
plans for metropolitan London while still in the throes of war and
subsequently to carry major parts of these plans into effect. It is
to the social purposes of these plans and to the ensuing implementation of the goals and programs set by these plans that this
report is directed.

The Unique Social Ideas of the London Advisory Plans

At the instigation of the central government, three long-
range plans—for Greater London, for the County of London, and
for the City of London—were prepared, released, and, except for
the City of London Plan, approved as policy between 1941 and
1946. The Greater London Plan in particular, with the other
plans complementary in spirit, proved to contain several revolutionary ideas and, further supplemented by other controls restraining new industry in the London area, provided a highly unique
approach to planning metropolitan development. Had these plans
restricted themselves to tidying up things in a manner more
characteristic of most town planning or city planning, they might
have lacked significance. But the Greater London Plan, reinforced
by the other plans and by industrial location controls, boldly proposed that *the growth of metropolitan London should be firmly
controlled* [2]—physically by halting uncontrolled suburban spread
and by limiting the density of development within particular districts, and socially and economically by preventing undue employment concentration. Several highly significant concepts and approaches—particularly a reliance upon a broad metropolitan green
belt to encircle London, a ring of new towns just beyond this
green belt, a determination to thin out central London, and a
system of broad controls for dispersing residents and jobs out of
central London and for decentralizing employment opportunities
to other parts of Britain—were combined with other planning,
reconstruction, and housing approaches to provide an interlocking

web of constructive ideas. The fashioning of this web, crystallized by the advisory plans, was creative social invention of high order. Once formed, it became the basis of social policy—and, in a more subtle fashion, the foundation of a highly influential body of doctrine[3] providing a durable nucleus for political and professional consensus in town and regional planning circles and among the members of an informed elite more generally.

The plans, and subsequent planning doctrine, incorporated various social goals as to what kind of London was to be developed, what pattern of physical environment and what sort of urban life were to be promoted. Perhaps more important, the plans relied upon certain fundamental devices or concepts by which these goals were to be translated into attainable physical patterns. This study seeks to identify the social policies associated with the London advisory plans and to interpret the ascendency of these particular social policies in the light of the social-political context within which they emerged.

Since the plans were quite literally advisory only, it remained for their proposals to be carried out by subsequent measures. Another form of plan—the development plan—more precise and more closely geared to a comprehensive system of planning controls, came to be relied upon. Further legislation was required. And, as might be expected, varied possibilities for gaps and failures between advisory plan proposals and final effectuation abounded. The present study reports on how faithfully the plans have been carried out. It especially describes and seeks to analyze the development forces that have been at work in the fifteen years since the policies of the advisory plans were accepted, and examines how effectively the approaches recommended by the advisory plans stood up to the test of changing conditions. Too, the study deals pointedly with the institutional framework by which policy and doctrine are kept under surveillance and, as necessary, modified. It raises the question whether doctrine so ably evolved during the wartime period of plan preparation and public political discussion has been adequately subjected to basic review in the period to date.

The setting from which the advisory plans and the postwar reconstruction efforts emerged includes various aspects of London's character and growth, national and local reform and social policy traditions, several pre-Barlow Commission developments regarding the planning for London, the central importance of the Barlow Commission recommendations, and the impact of the war. The brief review that follows attempts to deal with key events and factors only insofar as they relate to our main interest.[4]

London's Functional Importance and Pattern

London is at once a world metropolis, the heart of the British Commonwealth, and the political, financial, commercial, and cultural capital of Britain. To create an even approximate American equivalent we would have to merge the New York, Washington, and Chicago metropolitan communities into one overwhelmingly dominant metropolis, compared with which all other metropolitan centers in America would appear provincial. As William A. Robson has aptly put it, London

is the place where the sovereign resides, where Parliament assembles, and the Cabinet meets. It is the headquarters of all the great government departments and the centre of the judicial system. It is the financial and commercial hub of Britain, the home of famous institutions like the Bank of England, Lloyd's, or the Baltic Exchange. It is also a great manufacturing city. The port of London, with its thirty-six miles of quays, has the largest system of docks in the world. . . .

The cultural resources of London are immense. The great national collections housed there include the British Museum, the Record Office, the Victoria and Albert Museum, the National Gallery, and the Tate Gallery. The metropolis is the home of the Royal Society, the Royal College of Physicians, the Royal College of Surgeons, the Inns of Court, and many other learned bodies. Most of the leading hospitals at which teaching and research are carried out are located in London. The University of London is the largest university in Britain and the principal centre for post-graduate study and research, to which students come from all parts of the world. London is the principal domain in Britain of dramatic and musical enterprise, of the opera and ballet, of film production and broadcasting. It is the directing centre for book, newspaper and periodical publishing. Its arenas provide the setting for many great sporting and athletic contests of national or international interest.[5]

Despite the rise of other important cities in Great Britain, London has maintained a most powerful influence in every phase of activity. The growth of central government has added to London's political and economic base. Even the spread of various branch factories and regional offices of industrial, business, and financial firms to other parts of Britain and the growth of other British cities have enhanced the importance of the central offices in London charged with overseeing the national situation. London's importance as a gateway for international travel has increased with the growing British reliance on the London airport. Indeed, at both domestic and international scales, London's dominant position continues to be reinforced by the radial pattern of major transportation and communication channels converging on the capital.

London has historically enjoyed social and cultural advantages, with other British cities, in contrast, characteristically thought of as provincial. Even the climate of the London area is believed to be superior to that of, say, northern England. London has served as the great opportunity center for ambitious young persons, whether for clerical employment or more specialized careers. Granted important biases prevalent about the grimness of large cities, London has not fallen into the same class as industrial towns in Yorkshire and the Midlands. It is little wonder that there continue to be serious political objections to governmental policies that, even though indirectly, further improve London's position vis-à-vis provincial cities.

I have spoken loosely of London or Greater London. As a basis for portraying growth trends of and within London, it is essential that we recognize several Londons, and this will further serve to describe something of London's spatial and governmental structure. (See Figure 1.) The smallest—the ancient City of London—is but a square mile in area. Its government dates back nearly a thousand years, a charter having been granted by William the Conqueror in 1070.[6]

Since 1889 the County of London under the London County Council has constituted a much larger main unit of local government. Together with the City of London it forms the Administrative County of London, 117 square miles in area. The London

FIGURE 1

LONDON AND SOUTH-EASTERN ENGLAND

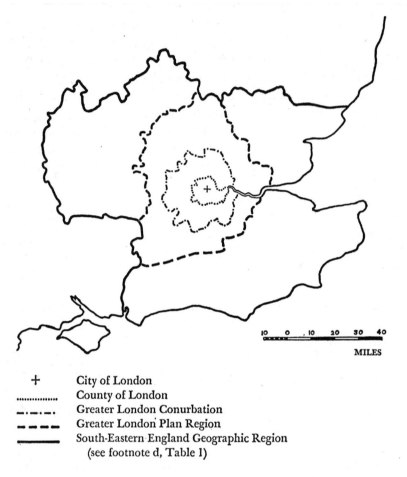

+	City of London
....	County of London
_._._.	Greater London Conurbation
____	Greater London Plan Region
▬▬▬	South-Eastern England Geographic Region
	(see footnote d, Table 1)

County Council constitutes a top-tier local government authority with strong powers, and within this lower-tier metropolitan boroughs and the City possess, or are delegated, lesser functions.

For census purposes, an area termed the Greater London Conurbation roughly delineates the main built-up part of the metropolis.[7] This Conurbation has a radius of some 12 to 15 miles from Charing Cross, covers 722 square miles, and is virtually coextensive with the Metropolitan Police District. The part surrounding the Administrative County, termed for this study the Conurban Ring, comprises 605 square miles.

Some considerations involve even larger areas, embracing more than the contiguous urbanized suburbs. The Greater London Plan Region for which Abercrombie prepared the 1944 Plan, for example, embraces slightly more than 2,600 square miles, with roughly a 30-mile radius from the center of London. The inner parts of this Plan Region are clearly urban or suburban, but the outer rural parts are also within commuting range of central London. Some current approaches would place the more realistic radius of a London region at 40 to 50 miles, the area within which daily functional ties to central London, particularly through commuting, are maintained. A South-Eastern England Region is the broadest geographical unit of all, comprising an area of a roughly 50- to 70-mile radius. As employed in this discussion, it includes twelve counties[8] and 10,558 square miles, 18 per cent of the area of England and Wales.[9]

London's Growth to 1939

Because the advisory plans sought to cope with problems of population and employment concentration in the London region, some pointed consideration here of major long-range population growth and redistribution trends relating to London is essential. Several aspects of these trends deserve mention. That both the Greater London Conurbation and the South-Eastern England Region have grown significantly is shown in Table 1. By 1939 the Conurbation had grown to 8.7 million and another 5.9 persons resided in an encircling Regional Ring. This amounted to an increasing concentration, to the point where in 1939 the Conurbation constituted fully one-fifth of the population of England and the South-Eastern England Region accounted for more than one-third. By way of contrast, the New York standard metropolitan area, with 12 million residents in 1940, comprised less than 9 per cent of the population of the United States.

Redistribution within the region and differential rates of growth also constitute important trends. In the two decades before World War II, the Conurban Ring gained 1.7 million residents and the Regional Ring gained 5.9 million, while the County of London

TABLE 1

THE POPULATION OF LONDON, SOUTH-EASTERN ENGLAND, AND ENGLAND AND WALES, 1801–1939

	Population (in thousands)					Percentage Distribution				
	1801	1851	1901	1921	1939[a]	1801	1851	1901	1921	1939[a]
County of London[b]	959	2,363	4,536	4,485	4,013	10.8	13.2	13.9	11.8	9.7
Conurban Ring	158	322	2,050	3,003	4,734	1.8	1.8	6.4	8.0	11.4
Greater London Conurbation[c]	1,117	2,685	6,586	7,488	8,747	12.6	15.0	20.3	19.8	21.1
Regional Ring	1,375	2,409	3,910	4,702	5,875	15.4	13.4	12.0	12.4	14.1
South-Eastern England[d]	2,492	5,094	10,496	12,190	14,603	28.0	28.4	32.3	32.2	35.2
Rest of England and Wales	6,401	12,834	22,032	25,696	26,857	72.0	71.6	67.7	67.8	64.8
England and Wales	8,893	17,928	32,528	37,887	41,460	100.0	100.0	100.0	100.0	100.0

[a] Mid-year estimate. No census in 1939. Other figures are census counts.

[b] The Administrative County of London, including the County of London and the City of London, with 1801 and 1851 figures adjusted.

[c] As defined in 1951 census, with earlier figures adjusted.

[d] The South-Eastern England Geographic Region comprises Bedfordshire, Berkshire, Buckinghamshire, Essex, Hertfordshire, Kent, London, Middlesex, Oxfordshire, Hampshire, Surrey, Sussex East, Sussex West, and the Isle of Wight, and is an area of from 50- to 70-mile radius from central London. This area, established in the 1931 census, is not currently reported. Other regional definitions will be used for postwar trends.

lost nearly a half million. The population losses within the very center, the City of London, are even more striking, down from about 130,000 in 1850 to 27,000 in 1901 to only 9,000 in 1937, although the City continued daily to accommodate several hundred thousand persons.[10]

To put oneself in the position of understanding what was happening during the 'twenties and 'thirties, it is well to examine the geographical distribution of population growth for the period. The Conurban and Regional Rings with a combined population of a fifth of England and Wales in 1921 accounted for four-fifths of the total net population increase in England and Wales, 1921–39. The London Conurban Ring was growing at six times and the Regional Ring at nearly three times their proportional shares had population growth been constant throughout the country. (See also Table 2.)

The Quest for Improved Living Conditions

Largely ineffectual reform efforts aiming to better what were judged to be deplorable living and working conditions in London and other industrialized cities marked the mid-nineteenth century. The fifty or sixty years before World War I, however, saw significant, hard-won advances. Environmental conditions were gradually improved—housing standards were formulated and enforced, sanitary sewers were constructed, streets were paved, refuse disposal was brought under control. And local government was put into a stronger position to cope with the filth, congestion, and overcrowding amid which disease and vice were rampant. By the early 1900's the worst conditions had been substantially bettered and, most important perhaps, the groundwork had been laid for an accelerated and far more effective attack on urban problems. Enlightened groping by a few gave way to a swelling movement of organized governmental and civic forces.

Several streams of reform and policy formulation bear on the social policy that was, in turn, to be further embodied in later advisory plans for London. Housing policy and the ideas promoted by the garden-city enthusiasts were particularly important and influential. Efforts to improve housing had many facets. Charitable trusts pioneered by investing in limited-profit, "reasonable" rental flats. Related to other public health measures, minimum housing

TABLE 2

POPULATION INCREASES FOR LONDON, SOUTH-EASTERN ENGLAND, AND ENGLAND AND WALES, 1921–1939

	Increase (in thousands)			Percentage Distribution of Increase			Indexes of Increase 1921 = 100	
	1921–1931	1931–1939	1921–1939	1921–1931	1931–1939	1921–1939	1931	1939
County of London[a]	−88	−384	−472	−4.3	−25.3	−13.2	98	90
Conurban Ring	816	896	1,712	39.8	59.0	47.9	128	157
Greater London Conurbation[a]	728	512	1,240	35.5	33.7	34.7	110	117
Regional Ring	560	613	1,173	27.2	40.3	32.8	112	125
South-Eastern England[a]	1,288	1,125	2,413	62.7	74.0	67.5	111	120
Rest of England and Wales	765	395	1,160	37.3	26.0	32.5	103	105
England and Wales	2,053	1,520	3,573	100.0	100.0	100.0	106	109

[a] Respective footnotes for Table 1 apply.

standards came gradually to be enforced. Reform literature in time had an educational impact, with the important result that political concern also evolved. What had previously been an elitist leadership passed along to, and was shared by, labor and consumer groups, vastly broadening the effective political support.[11]

Even before World War I, various local governments had moved to the point of providing municipal housing. The London County Council, after the Housing of the Working Class Act of 1890, embarked on a program of slum clearance and housing. By 1914 the Council had rehoused some 18,000 former slum residents and built 10,000 new cottages in the suburbs.[12] Urged along by a rising working-class movement, government assumed a growing responsibility for providing decent housing at subsidized rent levels.

From 1919 until the mid-'thirties, local authority housing and other state-aided construction accounted for about half of all new housing. More than a million housing units were built by the local authorities and another 430,000 units were built privately but with governmental financial assistance in the interwar period.[13] By the late 'thirties a major policy aim had emerged: to provide satisfactory housing for all at rents within their capacity to pay. Municipal housing, limited-profit developments by housing societies, rent controls, insistence on minimum standards—all these contributed along a broad front toward greatly improved housing.

Much of this housing was constructed as blocks of flats* at fairly high densities. But, partly to carry on the strong British tradition for the house-with-a-garden† as the most desirable housing, and partly to find raw land at reasonable prices, central cities, including the County of London, increasingly turned to outer suburban areas for their building. Private enterprise, too, added thousands upon thousands of houses. With a total volume of 4 million housing units of all kinds built in England and Wales from 1919 to 1939, it is not surprising that suburbanization made rapid headway. And with this trend, persons with town-planning and housing responsibilities came to be concerned lest the suburban developments sprawl unduly and fail to provide satisfactory, full community settings.

---

* We use the British *flat* rather than American *apartment* and *block of flats* rather than *apartment building*.

† We follow British usage of *garden* as the rough equivalent of American *yard*.

These concerns were not entirely new, to be sure. Earlier utopian reformers had considered whether a fresh start toward new communities outside the main city might be preferable on several counts to tackling the job of improving the central city. The attractiveness of the ideal of the country gentleman and the country house had long prevailed. Indeed, the British outlook has reportedly focused more on the country, perhaps even embracing a latent anti-urbanism, than is said to be true in other European nations.[14] Throughout the period of urban growth, various writers have romantically sought to recapture the virtues of the small balanced town.

Owen as early as 1799 had embarked on a model community at New Lanark and by dint of persistence kept it going for several decades. A series of new community undertakings followed: Buckingham's proposal for Victoria, the successful development of Saltaire, Cadbury's building of Bournville, Lever's Port Sunlight, and Rowntree's Earswick. Societies for building improved industrial villages appeared along with other housing societies.[15]

Following the publication in 1898 of his book, *Tomorrow: A Peaceful Path to Real Reform*,[16] Ebenezer Howard, with a practicality and intellectual leadership not previously mobilized, the next year founded the Garden City Association. Within a few years a site for Letchworth had been acquired and development, although destined to proceed slowly, was underway. Through the successful example of Letchworth and various other promotional activities, the Association provided the major ideas for town planning, which until World War I remained virtually synonymous with "suburban layout on garden city lines." [17] The first Town Planning Act of 1909; the first formal university program in town planning, the Department of Civic Design of the University of Liverpool, initiated in the same year; the founding of the Town Planning Institute in 1913; the formation, also in 1913, of the International Garden Cities Federation, which later became the International Federation for Housing and Planning—all reflected in considerable degree the garden-city notions of town planning.

Following World War I, the Association (after 1909 the Garden Cities and Town Planning Association), with F. J. Osborn and C. B. Purdom also becoming involved, propagandized for action on the housing and planning fronts and jumped into a second

major venture, the building of Welwyn Garden City. The organization moved into even more influential action in the late 1930s
and, as the Town and Country Planning Association (1941),
achieved its greatest impact on national postwar reconstruction
policies.[18]

The garden-city advocates proposed that large urban centers,
and London in particular, be decentralized by planning and developing small, satellite cities—garden cities. These were to be
relatively self-sufficient in their provision of industrial employment; they were to be set within an agricultural green belt so
as to preserve a sharp delineation between town and country.
Howard himself proposed that several satellite garden cities might
be set within a linked green space outside of a larger central city.[19]

It would be inaccurate to attribute the basic ideas of the Greater
London Plan exclusively to garden-city doctrine. Some plans for
redeveloping London date back to Wren, and even earlier, and
they have had their impact. The main ideas of postwar planning
can be seen as flowing so importantly, however, from the garden-
city movement that they deserve brief documentation.[20] The concepts of green belt (although at first a narrow and irregular one),
a ring road, and satellite towns evolved gradually, with new proposals building on parts of earlier ones.

Lord Meath, in 1901, suggested a green girdle to encircle all
London.[21] In 1909, D. B. Niven proposed a ring road and a depressed railway around London about ten miles from the center.[22]
This was followed the next year by George Pepler's suggestion of
a ringway around London, a parkway-type ring road in a green
belt.[23] Arthur Crow, in 1911, prepared what is probably the first
comprehensive modern plan for Greater London, featuring a
transport web and ten dormitory garden cities.[24] During World
War I, the London Society came up with a development plan
which proposed an irregular pattern of scattered but linked open
spaces.[25] Purdom, as secretary of the Garden City and Town Planning Association, developed a plan that showed possible sites for
about fifty satellite towns around London, and presented this to
the Minister of Health and to the London County Council.[26]
George Pepler, from the 'twenties on, favored green wedges of
open space rather than a circular green belt.[27]

In 1927, Neville Chamberlain, then Minister of Health, appointed a forty-five-member Greater London Regional Planning Committee. It was chaired by a prominent architect, Sir Banister Fletcher. Raymond Unwin was appointed as the Committee's technical adviser in 1929. A report issued later that year argued for the control of ribbon development along outer roads, for the amendment of the Town Planning Act, and for a regional authority for Greater London. Of particular substantive interest was Unwin's proposal for acquiring 206 square miles of open space, 63 for playing fields and 143 for additional areas.[28] These proposals were themselves modest; they included, however, an exploration of two alternative ideal programs: the provision of relatively small areas of open space within a background of built-up or potentially buildable land as against the acquisition of a great background of open space—a vast green belt—within which planned building areas could be controlled.[29] While Unwin's proposals were directed toward the former alternative, the idea of an open green belt of generous size was introduced. A second report, in 1933, rounded out the recommendations and, in addition to the ideas as to open space, proposed new satellite towns and improved roadways.[30] Funds ran low, and Unwin could not be retained; Major Hardy-Sims took his place and prepared a sketch plan that more nearly foreshadows the Greater London Plan of 1944 than any other plan developed.[31] But the London County Council withdrew its support, and the Committee died in 1936.

A. Trystan Edwards in 1933 and 1934 began to circulate the idea of "a hundred new towns" to be widely spread through the country and not merely close-in satellites of London. Edwards also proposed, for Greater London, green wedges between four wings of built-up areas in cruciform shape.[32] A Departmental Committee on Garden Cities and Satellite Towns, chaired by Lord Marley, issued a report in 1935 which generally reinforced the garden-city idea.[33] The London County Council the same year decided to embark on a program of purchasing outlying open space as a part of a green-belt system. For this it allocated £2 million, and by mid-1938 nearly 100 square miles had been acquired. Although this action has been criticized as *ad hoc* and timid, it represented a direct move toward implementing a green-belt scheme for Greater London.[34]

The Barlow Commission

Yet another significant influence on the character-to-be of the London advisory plans was the set of recommendations by the Barlow Commission in response to the extremely serious unemployment situation in Britain. The depression of the interwar years hit industrial Britain hard. Basic industries upon which the nation had traditionally relied so heavily, especially for exports —coal mining, cotton and wool textiles, shipbuilding and repairing, iron production, and the railroads—were plagued with severe and prolonged drops in employment. Unemployment was a most serious social burden, averaging 14 per cent for the period 1921–1939. And great as that average is, it blurs the even greater severity of the problem in regions in which the depressed industries were concentrated.[35] In short, the Royal Commission on the Distribution of the Industrial Population, appointed in 1937 and under the chairmanship of Sir Montague Barlow, was faced with hard, undeniable evidence of great differentials in unemployment, as summarized in Table 3. Whereas London and South-Eastern England had unemployment rates of 8 per cent, the percentages for less fortunate sections ranged from 16 to 25.

The Commission was charged with inquiring into past and possible future trends in the distribution of industrial employment in Greater Britain, the disadvantages of concentrating industry in certain large towns or areas of the country, and remedial measures which should be taken. The Commission focused mainly on the concentration of industrial employment in the London area and South-Eastern England. The Commission was not asked to, and did not, deal with problems of office employment or office space which were to reach crisis proportions during the 1950's.

The Commission's report, completed in August, 1939, but because of the outbreak of war not released until January, 1940, concluded that industry was significantly overconcentrated in the London Region. Evidence clearly pointed to more rapid growth of industrial employment in the London area than in other parts of Britain. With less than a quarter of all the employed persons in 1921, London and the seven surrounding counties cornered almost half the entire British increase in employed persons for the suc-

TABLE 3

DIFFERENCES IN THE EXTENT AND DURATION OF UNEMPLOYMENT
IN LONDON, SOUTH-EASTERN ENGLAND, AND OTHER REGIONS
OF GREAT BRITAIN, 1938 AND 1939

Region	Percentage Insured Workers Unemployed, 1938	Duration of Unemployment, Applicants for Insurance, May, 1939			
		All Appli- cants	Less than 1 Yr.	1–2.9 Yrs.	3 Yrs. or More
London	8.0	100.0	91.6	6.9	1.5
South-Eastern	8.0	100.0	92.1	6.2	1.7
South-Western	8.1	100.0	90.9	6.3	2.8
Midlands	10.2	100.0	80.1	12.4	7.5
North-Eastern	13.5	100.0	79.8	12.2	8.0
North-Western	17.8	100.0	73.7	14.8	11.5
Northern	18.3	100.0	66.7	17.1	16.2
Wales	24.7	100.0	66.9	17.1	16.0
Scotland	16.3	100.0	68.7	16.0	15.3
Average for Great Britain	12.6	100.0	77.2	13.0	9.8

SOURCES: Adapted from the *Report of the Royal Commission on the Distribution of the Industrial Population,* Cmd. 6153 (London: HMSO, 1940), p. 169; *Ministry of Labour Gazette* (July, 1939), p. 262.

ceeding ten years. A correspondingly disproportionate increase in insured workers (more indicative of manual and lower-income employment) also occurred, particularly for the period 1932 to 1937. (See Table 4.) Based on these findings, the Commission concluded that "The continued drift of the industrial population to London and the Home Counties constitutes a social, economic and strategical problem which demands immediate attention." [36] The Commission was probably more heavily influenced by the imminence of war, which pushed strategic considerations into the forefront, than the open and published evidence and final report suggest.

The Commission recommended creation of a national authority to act with these objectives: "Continued and further redevelopment of congested urban areas, where necessary. Decentralisation

TABLE 4
EMPLOYMENT INCREASES IN LONDON AND THE HOME COUNTIES AND IN GREAT BRITAIN, 1921–1937

	Employed Persons (in thousands)		Percentage Distribution		Increase (in thousands)	Percentage Distribution of Increase	Index of Increase (1921 = 100)
	1921	1931	1921	1931	1921–1931	1921–1931	1931
London and the Home Counties[a]	4,614	5,417	23.8	25.7	803	49.2	117
Rest of Great Britain	14,808	15,638	76.2	74.3	830	50.8	106
Great Britain	19,422	21,055	100.0	100.0	1,633	100.0	108

	Insured Workers (in thousands)			Percentage Distribution			Increase (in thousands)		Percentage Distribution of Increase		Index of Increase (1921 = 100)	
	1923	1932	1937	1923	1932	1937	1923–1932	1932–1937	1923–1932	1932–1937	1932	1937
London and the Home Counties[a]	2,421	3,027	3,453	22.4	24.4	26.0	606	426	38.5	50.5	125	143
Rest of Great Britain	8,405	9,373	9,791	77.6	75.6	74.0	968	418	61.5	49.5	112	117
Great Britain	10,826	12,400	13,244	100.0	100.0	100.0	1,574	844	100.0	100.0	115	122

SOURCES: *Top:* First four columns from *Report of the Royal Commission on the Distribution of the Industrial Population*, Cmd. 6153 (London: HMSO, 1940), p. 23. "Employed persons" equivalent to British "occupied population." *Bottom:* First six columns from *Ibid.*, p. 24. "The statistics for insured persons . . . cover the bulk of the population which is employed . . . in manual work or in work remunerated at a rate not exceeding £250 a year . . ." (*Ibid.*, p. 20). "Insured workers" equivalent to British "insured population."
[a] The Home Counties included Bedfordshire, Buckinghamshire, Essex, Hertfordshire, Kent, Middlesex, Surrey.

or dispersal, both of industries and industrial population, from such areas. Encouragement of a reasonable balance of industrial development, so far as possible, throughout the various divisions or regions of Great Britain, coupled with appropriate diversification of industry in each division throughout the country." [37] It recommended that in carrying out decentralization or dispersal, consideration should be given to such developments as "garden cities or garden suburbs, satellite towns, trading estates," or to "the development of existing small towns or regional centres." [38]

For all its recommendations and for all that has been made of the Barlow report in retrospect, it was in many ways an equivocal document. It recognized that large metropolitan size per se may not be disadvantageous.[39] And although the report showed that by most criteria the country remained healthier than the large city, it also pointed out great improvements in mortality and morbidity rates in cities and the existence or potentiality of superior medical and health facilities in cities.[40] Six of the thirteen members of the Commission, including Abercrombie, signed minority reports urging stronger recommendations. Sir Frederic Osborn has recalled that when he saw the report he was doubtful whether he should have the Garden Cities and Town Planning Association support it. He did, however, decide to urge support and, with Barlow himself, set about to make it into a turning point in policy.[41] Although the report did not achieve official Government approval in White Paper form until 1944, it did, meanwhile, in the preparation of the advisory London plans provide a basis for the important assumption that it would be Government policy to restrain increases in industrial employment in the London area.

The State of Demography

It is extraordinarily difficult to propel oneself back to the late 'thirties and early 'forties and to recapture the outlook that pervaded population forecasts of that period, to appreciate how deeply the mood of the times and the fresh impact of recent changes in fertility and mortality rates influenced the "science" of demography, and how the projections of that discipline came to take on an authoritative tone and to be uncritically accepted.[42] These population projections, as it subsequently turned out, indicated much lower rates of growth than eventually materialized. The acute need of policy advisers—including town and regional planners—for such data made them particularly susceptible, and the projections undoubtedly had an undue impact. Other presuppositions came to be woven around them; various policies were proposed so as to ensure meeting the needs of the expected population developments. The Greater London Plan leaned especially heavily on forecasts by the General Register Office.[43] Although the actual census counts for Britain for 1951 and 1961 respectively were to prove only about 3 per cent and 9 per cent higher than these forecasts, the distortion for the London Region was considerably greater.

Low projections were by no means confined to Great Britain. In the most authoritative textbook published in 1941 for American city planners, Ladislas Segoe, quoting from his own 1935 paper on the subject, stated:

The most competent authorities on population problems generally agree that there is to be a very pronounced slowing up in the growth of the population of the United States; that . . . maximum [total population] is likely to be reached within the next 30 to 40 years [i.e., by 1965 to 1975]; and that this maximum will probably fall between 140 and 145 millions. . . . It has been estimated that the urban population may reach 75 millions by about 1960 and may decline thereafter to about 67 millions by 1980, less by about a million than in 1930. . . . Therefore, whatever margin of error population prognostications are subject to, it is certain that, in comparison with the unprecedented growth of the past 30 years, in the next 30 years the Nation as a whole and the cities also will appear to be standing still in point of growth. A stationary or even a declining population within the next 30 to 50 years does not appear to be improbable. . . .[44]

By 1960 the United States Census reported 178.5 million, 25 per cent higher than the forecast maximum with 112.5 million urban population, 50 per cent above the urban forecast. (According to a newer definition of "urban," the figure for 1960 is 124.7 million, a full 67 per cent above the forecast.) Demographers and city planners in the United States proved to be far more seriously in error in underforecasting the growth of American cities than were their colleagues in Britain. What, we might ask, would have been the result of basing a major metropolitan plan (such as that for Greater London) on these seriously erroneous American projections?

Whatever that, the point here is to emphasize that British town and regional planners, like those in any country, have been heavily dependent upon population projections prepared by demographers; and, further, that, low as these British projections were, they were not nearly so far off as were the projections by American demographers. The Greater London Plan, based on the British projections, was, indeed, a reasonably foresighted and effective effort.

War and Its Impact

In addition to the forces already identified, it was, ironically enough, the war that brought planning to London and helped to shape the character of the national planning system of which London planning became an essential portion. Some attention to the character of the bomb damage and the wartime context of controls is warranted here.

The war damage was inflicted in three major phases. In the first, the

German Air Force struck at London on Saturday, 7th September 1940, with about half its total serviceable strength of bombers. . . . Except for one respite—2nd November—London was bombed continuously for seventy-six nights. Some 27,500 high explosive bombs, and many incendiaries, oil explosive bombs, parachute mines and delay-action bombs were employed. The East End, and particularly Stepney, received the heaviest blows in September. Although the attack continued to cover a very wide area, the main weight of bombing moved from the East End and the riverside boroughs in September to central London in October. More diffuse and lighter raiding followed in November.[45]

The last major raid by piloted aircraft occurred in May, 1941, ending the first battle of London.

Flying-bomb attacks started in June, and lasted for about three months, with more than 5,000 bombs having London as their destination. During the final phase, from September, 1944, until March, 1945, some 500 long-range rockets landed within the London civil defense region. All in all, "the alert was sounded on 1,224 occasions," an average of once every 36 hours for longer than five years.[46]

The total effects of these bombings are difficult to summarize. It is clear, however, that the "brunt of destruction fell . . . on London. Of all houses in the country completely wiped out, and of all 'damage incidents,' nearly sixty per cent applied to the London civil defence region. This area, with its 2,151,000 houses—or one sixth of the country's stock—took more than half the damage and destruction. At the heart of the capital, the county of London itself, only about one house in ten escaped damage of some kind. Nearer the centre still, in the sector of Bermondsey for instance, only four houses in every hundred came through the war unscathed." [47] Schools, hospitals, and other public buildings were also extensively damaged. Nevertheless, the damage was less serious and much more scattered than for the most severely bombed cities on the Continent, and did not provide the clear opportunities for large-scale reconstruction that may have been envisaged during the war.

The bombings threw all classes of citizens into shared dangers. Air-raid warnings came at unpredictable times. The British suffered a larger number of civilian air-raid casualties as related to total population than did any other Allied nation. About one person in every six (totaling 1.4 million) was made homeless during the 1940–1941 raids on the London Region.[48]

Evacuation from London during the period of the bombings also contributed to the common difficulties and shared experiences and had an over-all impact on population distribution within the London Region. Throughout the war people moved out and returned on their own as well as within the framework of the Government's program. Perhaps 1.5 million persons—mainly children, but also mothers, teachers, helpers, crippled persons—were evacuated during 1939; probably not more than half of these were official evacuees. The subsequent major bombings, in 1940 and in 1944, never forced as many to evacuate anew as left in 1939.[49] Nevertheless, the net accumulation of the evacuations dropped the County of London's population from 4.1 million in mid-1939 to 3.1 million in December, 1940, and to 2.3 million a year later. Population climbed only to about 2.5 million even by December, 1944.[50]

From this experience came strong feelings that full democratic
action must be pushed forward to provide homes, schools, and
shopping and other facilities for those who had been bombed out.
The necessity for military and defense planning and the accompanying wartime restrictions introduced Britishers to collective
action. Building materials and other resources could not be turned
loose for most civilian construction. This enforced moratorium
left those who were to be charged with planning a breathing space
to think out what would be the best approach. A surge of idealism
swept the country, with a concern for what the nation was fight-
ing for.[51]

The Early 'Forties

The inevitability of reconstruction coupled with the Barlow Commission investigation and report encouraged a number of
nongovernmental organizations to undertake plans or to make
recommendations for the future of London and the surrounding
region.[52] The efforts of the 1940 Council, the Social Reconstruction Survey of Nuffield College, and the Association of Planning
and Regional Reconstruction, and committees of the Royal Institute, and other national and professional associations were primarily national in scope. Three undertakings deserve our particular attention: the respective plans for London proposed by the
London Regional Reconstruction Committee of the Royal Institute of British Architects (the LRRC), the Royal Academy's Planning Committee, and the Modern Architectural Research Society
(MARS).

The LRRC plan was prepared by a committee of twelve members, all architects, with assistance from some outside experts. By
and large, this plan accepted the present structure of London,
with its main center and its radial transportation routes. It proposed the deliberate use of transportation and natural spaces as
barriers around self-contained communities; residential areas as
articulated communities; a great increase in the amount of open
space; the separation of industry from residential areas; and the
integration of all modes of transport. As one critic has suggested,
the plan was a "cosmetic approach," seeking to tidy up London
with any fundamental reorganization. It was committed to containing the growth of each of the many communities introduced.[53]

The Royal Academy Committee's plans were exhibited in three years—1942, 1943, and 1944. Chaired by Sir Edwin Lutyens, this Committee took as its main point of departure the 1937 Bressey London road plan. The proposals emphasized monumental architectural façades to be developed along these main roads (from Bressey). This plan was widely criticized as circumscribed and traditional, earlier ideas being given classical architectural treatment and new ideas lacking.[54]

The architect-dominated MARS group, having been at work as a study team since the 'thirties, came up with the most original of the three plans. This contemporary plan proposed an east-west spine with fingers of development growing off the spine at right angles. (See Fig. 5.) The plan featured a scheme for expandability, but ruthlessly reshuffled London as it had actually developed.[55]

Spurred by the heavy bombing raids, government efforts to prepare for postwar reconstruction unleashed a vigorous series of activities and proposals from the autumn of 1940 on through the rest of the war years.[56] Lord Reith was appointed to head the newly created Ministry of Works and Buildings in October, 1940. One of his first acts established the Consultative Panel on Physical Reconstruction. As proposed by the Barlow Commission, the Uthwatt Committee (Expert Committee on Compensation and Betterment) was appointed in January, 1941; it submitted an interim report in June of that year, and a final report in September, 1942. A third important policy exploration group, the Scott Committee (Committee on Land Utilization in Rural Areas), issued its report in August, 1942.

In July, 1942, town and country planning functions were transferred from the Ministry of Health to a newly organized Ministry of Works and Planning with Lord Portal as Minister. A system of regional planning officers was put into effect the same year. The emphasis directed toward planning was strengthened even more when a separate Ministry of Town and Country Planning was set into operation in February, 1943, with W. S. Morrison as the first Minister.

The year 1944 saw several major governmental moves. In May the Government issued the White Paper, *Employment Policy*,[57] asserting that the maintenance of a high and stable level of employment was to be a governmental responsibility, and that, as a

facet of this, the location of industries would be controlled so as
to encourage diversified employment in areas vulnerable to unemployment. This, then, was the Government's first official response
to the substantive recommendations by the Barlow Commission,
and was followed during the next year by the passage of the Distribution of Industry Act.

In June, 1944, an extremely important policy document, *The
Control of Land Use*,[58] was presented. This statement accepted
the purposes, although not the specific approaches, put forward
by the Uthwatt Committee. It outlined a general scheme for controlling development, acquiring land for public use, collecting
betterment charges, and paying compensation. This document
foreshadowed the passage of the Town and Country Planning Act
of 1944, which provided means for undertaking the redevelopment of bombed and obsolete areas and introduced various additional powers essential to an "activist" approach to planning.

These developments were but part of a larger ferment; other
aspects of reconstruction were also under consideration. A series
of proposals were being formulated that were in the postwar years
to provide Britain with expanded social services, health insurance,
retirement and unemployment insurance, a reorganized approach
to public education, and a set of nationalized undertakings—finance, transport, fuel and power, iron and steel, and others. The
Labour Party in particular was very active during this period in
shaping its own proposals; *Let Us Face the Future*, the policy statement released for the general election of 1945, provided an outline
of things toward which to strive.[59] When Labour was swept into
power in 1945 it was to give the idealism directed toward postwar
planning a directly Socialist flair.

Chapter 2

The Advisory Plans
and Their Main Ideas

In this wartime, depression-oriented context the British Government embarked on a most bold venture. It determined to divert the necessary energies and talents to preparation of advisory plans upon which to base postwar reconstruction. These advisory plans* were to be vehicles of physical development policy, dealing primarily with the physical environment and its spatial organization. Behind these concrete proposals were goals, programs, and approaches reflecting a larger sphere of social policy fashioned by the Government during the following World War II. We shall deal particularly with the web of approaches, compounded of assumptions as well as policies, which led to a major emphasis on containing London—both the physical delimitation and holding in of the built-up Greater London Conurbation, and the more general restraint of employment and population growth of the Greater London Plan Region as a whole.

Development of the Three Advisory Plans

In March, 1941, Minister of Works and Buildings Lord Reith asked the London County Council and the City of London Corporation, separately, to prepare plans for postwar development. The London County Council appointed Professor Patrick Aber-

---

* *Advisory plan* in the discussion that follows refers to the Greater London Plan, which carried the brunt of the proposals at the metropolitan regional scale; *advisory plans* also includes the County of London Plan, the City of London Plan, and such additional policy statements and approvals by the central government or local authorities in the London area as serve to augment and to clarify the three plans.

FIGURE 2

THE LONDON ADVISORY PLANS

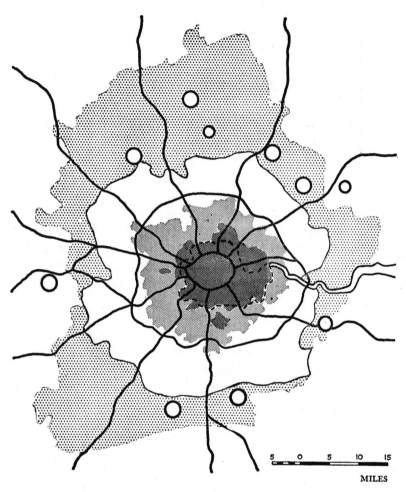

MILES

■ Inner Urban Ring (and the Administrative County of London, shown by dashed line)

▒ Suburban Ring

□ Green Belt Ring

⋮ Outer Country Ring

○ New Satellite Towns

— Arterial Roads

crombie as consultant to work with the Council's architect, Mr.
J. H. Forshaw. He assumed broad direction of preparing the plan,
but the County's staff, directly under Wesley Dougill (who, trag-
ically, died on the eve of the plan's completion), carried out the
work. Prepared under great pressure and despite difficult wartime
conditions, the plan was completed in two years, and was submitted to the London County Council for consideration in June,
1943, with the admonition "that the Plan submitted is provisional
only . . . [and] is in no sense a statutory plan." [1] The Council
approved the motion that the plan be transmitted to the Minister
of Town and Country Planning and to various other public authorities and be considered further when their views had been
received. Subsequently, the Town Planning Committee, chaired
by Lewis Silkin, recommended that "certain major decisions in
principle" be accepted "as a guide for works of redevelopment,
whether undertaken by the Council or by private enterprise." [2]
In July, 1945, the Council accordingly approved seven of these
major principles: [3]

1. Highways should be mainly three ring roads and a series of radial
   roads; highways should enclose residential communities and precincts where possible.
2. Three principal density zones should be established, averaging
   200 persons per acre in central districts and decreasing to 136
   and 70 persons per acre in successive outer districts.
3. Industrial location is a subject for national planning policy; local
   authorities should try to match housing and industrial employment.
4. Where industry is to be segregated from residential areas, it should
   be brought into industrial estates; some of these estates should be
   sited in outer parts of the County to provide local employment.
5. Open space should be provided, 4 acres per 1,000 population
   within the County and 3 acres per 1,000 County population outside the County.
6. Re-planning should seek to provide socially mixed and balanced
   communities; these communities should be broken into neighborhood units.
7. Amenities should be safeguarded by harmonious architectural
   treatment, by preservation of buildings of historical and architec-

tural importance, and by improvement in street furniture and public advertisements.

The County of London Plan, as published in 1943,[4] was given broad circulation and evoked many critical reviews, mainly laudatory.

Midway in the preparation of the Council's plan, in the summer of 1942, Professor Abercrombie was also appointed by the Minister of Works and Planning to prepare a comprehensive plan for the development of Greater London. This scheme was to embrace 143 local authorities and 2,599 square miles outside the Administrative County of London. Prepared directly under Abercrombie's direction, with assistance from representatives of various ministries and extensive consultation with the many local authorities, an initial version of this plan was submitted to the Minister late in 1944, and the final edition of the report, complete with colored plates, was published in 1945 as the *Greater London Plan 1944.*[5]

Meanwhile the Corporation of the City of London had reacted to Lord Reith's request by preparing its own plan, under the direction of City Engineer F. J. Forty. A draft plan was sent to the Minister of Town and Country Planning in June, 1943. A final report, issued in May, 1944,[6] was presented to the Court of Common Council of the City Corporation and forwarded to the Minister of Town and Country Planning and to other public authorities.

In July, 1945, the Minister, W. S. Morrison, informed the City Corporation that the plan was less than satisfactory, hinting at technical incompetence, and suggested a fresh approach. After much "fuss and fuming," the City Corporation appointed Professor William Holford and Dr. Charles Holden to prepare another plan. Their interim report was submitted in July, 1946, and their final report in April, 1947.[7] The report was duly circulated; a public inquiry was held in early 1948; and the plan passed to the Ministry for its formal approval.

The importance of these three advisory plans was not a matter of statutory status, for they were not legally binding schemes. Nor was it in the thoroughness of the analysis that went into them; they were prepared under relatively hurried and harried conditions, with no full census more recent than that of 1931 and no authoritative projections of likely postwar economic, demographic, and technological changes. The plans were significant because, in marked contrast to the limited and essentially restrictive planning schemes that had been (or could be) prepared under legislation to that date, they represented the movement of competent planners into an exploration of broad problems and new ideas, without restriction as to statutory requirements.[8] That they proved powerful idea generators and carriers is the main theme of our subsequent story.

Policy Statements by the Central Government

The Ministry of Town and Country Planning did not separately announce any formal policy approval of the County of London Plan. But when the Greater London Plan was being reviewed, it recognized the proposals of the County of London Plan as complementary in their impact. The review of the second City of London Plan prepared by Professor Holford and Mr. Holden carried well into the 1950's.

The Greater London Plan was prepared on behalf of the Standing Conference on London Regional Planning (created in 1937) and was referred to this Conference in late 1944. In October, 1945, at a conference convened by the Minister, a new Advisory Committee for London Regional Planning was established. Carrying out its mandate to review the Greater London Plan, it reported back in July, 1946.[9] The Committee concurred with the plan in most respects, but proposed that more persons be accommodated in the green belt, that new towns be built to house only 200,000 (rather than 415,000) persons, and that existing towns absorb most of the decentralizing population.[10]

An official interdepartmental committee composed of senior officials of a number of governmental departments was also created to review the Greater London Plan.[11] The report prepared by this committee was never published, but was made available to the Advisory committee.

In an important statement of policy to the House of Commons, March 5, 1946, Lewis Silkin, the Minister of Town and Country Planning, asserted:

Firstly, the overall growth of London's population and industry should be restrained. . . . Secondly, a planned program of decentralisation to the outer parts of [the] Greater London [Plan Region] should replace the uncontrolled sprawl of the interwar period. . . . Thirdly, it is proposed that the general lines of the decentralisation and re-settlement should broadly conform to the proposals made by Sir Patrick Abercrombie for dividing the area surrounding the County of London into four Rings. . . . But while the Government endorses the main principles underlying the Greater London Plan, they do not at this stage adopt a number of the individual projects for development recommended by Sir Patrick Abercrombie, such as the location and number of new towns and the proposals for highways. . . .[12]

Mr. Silkin also explained that this policy was in accord with the fourth and fifth conclusions of the Barlow Commission. In response to a question he explained that the policy proposed "to deal with industry and population side by side."

The Minister supplemented the Government's policy with respect to the Greater London Plan in a further brief oral statement in Parliament and in a written report reacting to the Advisory Committee's recommendations.[13] The Government reaffirmed the sanctity of the proposed green belt and rejected the Committee's proposal to house greater number of residents there. The Government also agreed on a system of arterial and subarterial roads in general accord with the Abercrombie plan but involving some changes and requiring further investigation of several routes. The Minister stated that the planning authorities would be expected to adhere to the Greater London Plan as modified by the Advisory Committee report and the Minister's memorandum on that report. Major feature by major feature—green belt, new towns, industrial redistribution, and population decentralization—the Ministry was offering official support for the proposals in the Greater London Plan.

The Social Policy of the Advisory Plans

The heart of the social policy associated with the advisory plans is to be understood in terms of three main social goals:[14]

1. *Best possible living conditions.*—Town planning has adopted as its primary goal the provision of decent residential conditions for all, including the working class and others who in the past have

particularly suffered from overcrowded housing in neighborhoods lacking ordinary amenities and decent community facilities.[15] In reaction to the grimness of industrial cities and reflecting a long British tradition, the amenities of civilized living have been judged to include, if humanly possible, comfortable housing with a garden for each family. And this provision implied that average net residential densities were to be kept relatively low. Residential districts were to be developed on a planned-community basis providing community facilities, open space, convenient access to employment opportunities, and freedom from dangerous traffic.

2. *Orderly and workable physical organization of the London Region.*—As the Greater London Plan put it, "it is the regrouping of population and industry that is the real task of this Plan for Greater London." [16] If the first goal of improved living conditions reflected humanitarianism and social reformism, this second goal emphasized the practical, design-related insistence upon workability. Accommodating port, commercial, governmental, industrial, and headquarters activities; arranging for the decentralization of people, jobs, and supporting activities to well planned communities in the outer parts of the Region; enhancing the transportation system and other functional systems essential to a great metropolitan area; reconstructing crowded and bombed central areas and facilities; planning for new outer growth; and guiding persons and firms to suitable locations in the outer areas—these were the responsibilities assumed by the town and regional planners charged with planning the Greater London Plan Region.

3. *Maintenance of full employment.*—This goal, quite unlike the other two, stemmed mainly from the central government's depression-oriented determination to ensure a steady and healthy level of employment in Britain. In particular, it reflected, as we noted in the last chapter, unduly heavy unemployment elsewhere, particularly in Northern England, in Scotland and in Wales, while, in contrast, the London Region and South-Eastern England and the Midlands generally continued to attract employment. Following the Barlow Commission's recommendations, the Government declared its support for encouraging and, if need be, requiring new or growing industrial firms to locate or relocate in areas of unemployment.[17] Conversely, it was judged that the London Re-

gion was growing too large and attracting too much employment, and that the growth of its industrial employment should, as a matter of policy, be restrained.

Other related goals, concepts, and approaches, in part derivative from and fully complementary to these major social goals, were also formulated. The web-like character of their total configuration is illustrated in Figure 3 (some relatively peripheral goals, such as the preservation of agriculture,* have not been included).

The major social goals become more meaningful when we examine the programmatic goals that flow logically from them. *Providing decent housing in a good neighborhood environment* had already gained strong political support, thus bolstering humanitarian and environmental-design concerns for improved living conditions. Even by the 'thirties Britain had committed itself to full governmental responsibility for constructing and managing good housing for families of low income by providing subsidies.[18] Unlike the predominant reliance in the United States on the private real estate market, the British governmental machinery had already succeeded in providing a considerable proportion of all new housing, and there was every evidence that housing had to become a major component of postwar planning. The strengthening of government involvement was to be in planning complete neighborhoods and communities to complement the housing.

Great stress on *providing community facilities and open space* followed logically. Neighborhood and community shopping centers, clinics, libraries, swimming pools, play lots, schools, and other public facilities were to be encouraged as integral features. Open space was to be retrieved in crowded central areas and to be given a guaranteed existence in newly developing outer districts.

Because of obsolescence and war damage, *reconstructing large sections of central London* was also granted very high priority. This provided opportunities for comprehensive planning for these areas and for bringing them up to adequate standards. Not only were better structures feasible, but greatly improved functional arrangements could be implemented. The full introduction of

---

* We may be understating the full importance of preserving agricultural land as a goal. We deal with it below in relation to the Metropolitan Green Belt, but do not list it separately as a major social or programmatic goal.

FIGURE 3

THE WEB OF APPROACHES COMPRISING DOCTRINE FOR PLANNING LONDON

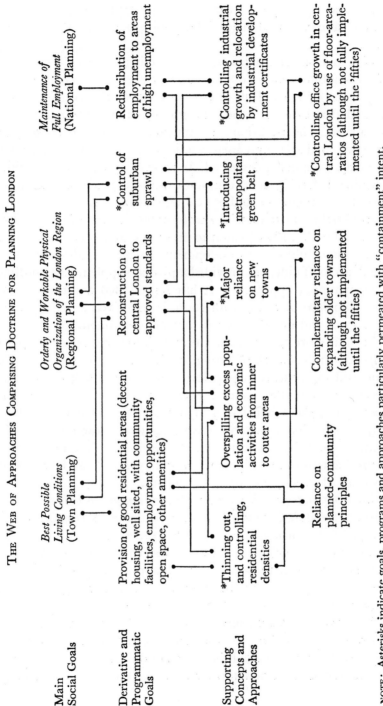

NOTE: Asterisks indicate goals, programs and approaches particularly permeated with "containment" intent.

amenities—open space, attractive shopping areas, safe walkways for children, and well-maintained public facilities—would be possible.

Like metropolitan areas elsewhere feeling the centrifugal impact of automobile usage, London has also been confronted with the major task of *controlling suburban sprawl.* The conviction crystallized that formless, land-consuming ribbon development must be curbed. The traditional separation of town and country was being vitiated and rural areas, whose conservation was judged vital by many, were being despoiled. As positive approaches for guiding peripheral development, the new-town and green-belt ideas have become indispensable and appealingly attractive.

Redistributing industrial employment opportunities from the Greater London Plan Region to other designated parts of Britain, by means of industrial development certificates administered by the Board of Trade, has provided a pivotal supplement to ordinary town planning approaches. It has represented a direct national incursion into planning with controls conceived amid depression conditions and handled by the central government.

Various more specific concepts and approaches have also played important roles in the planning for the Greater London Plan Region and its constituent political units. *Controlling densities* has become an essential feature. Provision of community facilities, open space, and a sufficiently high proportion of homes with private gardens has inevitably meant relatively low densities. The control of density has ensured an upper limit to the intensity and vertical extent of development. Indirectly, it has also bolstered the restraint of overall metropolitan growth.

Creating and maintaining a metropolitan green belt around the Greater London Conurbation has provided a practical device for controlling suburban sprawl and for preventing ribbon development along the major roads leading out from the Conurbation. It also has contributed to a containment approach by delimiting, and hence cutting down on, the area in which new development is permitted.

Building new towns, small cities created and nurtured in their entirety out beyond the metropolitan green belt, has been strongly supported for supplanting the spread of dull, ill-planned suburban development. Each new town was conceived as a separate city of about 50,000 inhabitants, designed and built by a single development authority or company. The new town was to provide its own employment, service, and cultural facilities for a diversity of income levels and family types. It typically featured a predominance of homes with gardens, although mixed development and some blocks of flats might also have been included. The new town characteristically was to be surrounded by a permanent local green belt, in turn linked with the metropolitan green belt.

Controlling Residential Densities

Residential development was expected to include as large a mixture of housing with separate gardens as the situation within a particular section of the metropolis justified. The impact of density controls would vary, depending upon the circumstances and the particular local precedents. In the suburbs and in the new towns, most houses, whether free standing or attached, were to have such gardens. Within the County of London this arrangement was in many areas not practicable, and fairly high proportions of flat dwellers were sanctioned. The London County Council has insisted, however, on low ground coverage and standards of space considerably more generous than previously obtained.

In fifteen central boroughs of the County of London, the proposed average density of 1936 would have resulted in an average decentralization of 39 per cent of the prewar population, leaving only three-fifths of the former population.[19] In Stepney, as a specific example, the 1938 net density was 186 persons per acre, and this was to fall to an average of 136 per acre according to the County of London Plan.

In 1939, a full two years before he was to become, under Abercrombie, the chief planner preparing the County of London Plan, Wesley Dougill said that the first most urgent requirement in town planning was "the thinning out of population densities in the centres of our cities and towns. . . ."[20] While engaged in work on both plans, Abercrombie explained:

Firstly, we must make up our minds as to whether we are going to aim at any real standards of requirements for decent, comfortable and happy living conditions. . . . If we decide on a reasonable standard of density, then it follows that we shall have large numbers of people

FIGURE 4

RESIDENTIAL DENSITIES RECOMMENDED BY THE LONDON ADVISORY PLANS

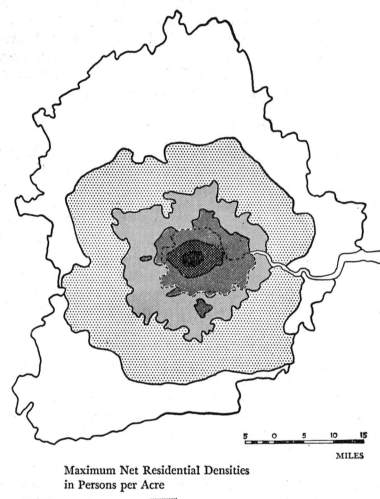

MILES

Maximum Net Residential Densities
in Persons per Acre

200   75

136   30–50

100

whom we shall have to take out of their existing towns and find accommodations for elsewhere. The standard set by 'Osborn' is 75 persons to the acre, exclusive of open space or industry. The existing populations in many of our industrial towns are between 250 to 300 to the acre, on the average. Between the ideal and the existing averages there is a considerable gap. Some places have decided they cannot go as low as 75, and 100 has been suggested. Whatever is decided, the figure must be much lower than the present one. . . .[21]

In addition to insisting on lower residential densities, the advisory plans also strongly advocated adequate community facilities. It followed that sizable tracts of land would be required for new schools, clinics, libraries, shopping centers, and additional open space. Since in central areas this land was available only if recaptured from previous built-up use, provision of these facilities implied further significant reductions in land available for direct housing use. Thus, the drop in gross densities (persons per unit of area, including community and open-space use) was greater than the lowering of net residential densities would indicate.

The problem of density was not only one of urban crowding. There was also a problem of preventing excessively low densities in suburban areas. The new town, proponents argued, assures a more compact community and somewhat higher densities than are common in unguided suburban development.

In general, the spatial pattern that characterized the various density zones recommended by the advisory plans was that of a central plateau of allowed residential densities surrounded by concentric rings of successively lower densities. (See Figure 4.) Permitted densities varied from 200 persons per net residential acre in the very central part of London to densities of 30 or fewer for residential settlements in the outer suburban areas. The density zones, in descending order, are shown on page 40.[22]

Unlike American zoning practice these density designations were not to restrict type of dwelling, and it was expected that a mixture of housing was to be encouraged and would result. Since housing types could be mixed in many combinations, the resulting density for a zone would be an average of a range of subzone densities. For example, dwelling units mixed 50–50 in low-density two-story terrace houses and high-density seven-story blocks of flats

Density District	Persons per Net Residential Acre	Equivalent Density, Including Open Space and Community Areas	Nature of the Residential Development
London County Council Central	200	97	Predominantly high blocks of flats
Intermediate	136	77	Mixed flats and houses
Outer county	100	60	Predominantly terrace and semi-detached houses
Selected outer districts	70	—	Houses of suburban character
Regional ring Inner urban ring	100 and 75	55 to 40	Same character as two outer county districts
Suburban ring	Maximum of 50	Maximum of 28	Predominantly detached houses
Green belt	About 30; some 22	20; 15	Garden-city type development
Outer country ring	—	—	Somewhat more scattered suburban development

would yield a middle-level average net residential density of about 80 or 90 persons. The typical mixture in the new towns, with some 10 to 15 per cent of the dwelling units in blocks of flats, was to average about 25 to 35 persons per net residential acre.[23]

By far the most important consequence of imposing strict density controls was the fostering of extensive decentralization of residents. Wartime evacuation had brought about a net outward migration of 1.5 million persons, dropping the County of London's resident population from about 4 million in 1939 to 2.5 million as of the end of 1944. The County of London Plan estimated that a half million persons would be displaced by lower density central reconstruction and would need to be rehoused outside the County.[24]

The County of London density proposals evoked varied reactions. Some critics felt that the London County Council was doing all that it reasonably could and that the plan represented a great step forward.[25] Others, outspoken in their disappointment, argued that voluntary out-migration following the war would probably produce these target densities anyway, and that stronger and more incisive controls should have been provided.[26]

New Town and Green Belt as Concepts

The most distinctive approaches introduced in the Greater London Plan—approaches given no special mention in the other plans—were those proposing eight new towns and a metropolitan green belt.[27] (See Figure 2.) These were introduced with no dramatic gesture and no defensive justification. Patrick Abercrombie took the position that these ideas were already well accepted and proceeded to apply them to the London Region.

The key place of these concepts in the planning doctrine was bolstered by their multipurpose character. New towns were conceived as providing fresh opportunities for building attractive new communities according to the best contemporary standards. They were to permit large-scale, well-organized construction methods. They were to reap the fiscal advantages of raw-land purchase and community ownership, with the resulting rising values accruing to the new town. The new town was viewed as a hard-headed way of achieving needed housing in a planned community setting.

New towns were related to a social policy seeking to create communities as optimal social and functional units for good living. The new towns were to be relatively self-contained, providing employment for most resident workers and a range of cultural and commercial facilities. Each new town was expected to attract a cross-section of income and class levels. While residents of a new town would enjoy the possibility of occasional trips to London to take advantage of its unique opportunities, regular commuting was to be discouraged. New towns were also envisioned as devices for siphoning off excess population and employment from inner, congested areas.

The Greater London Plan proposed to decentralize about 400,-000 residents to eight new towns. Each new town was to be built only to a maximum size of 60,000 population and to have its physical expansion bounded by a local green belt.[28] The new town and its encircling agricultural zone were to be conceived as a unit, with contrast and balance between town and country. The new town concept provided a way in which a reasonably compact and clearly contained community could be promoted, replacing prevalent trends toward a spread-out suburbia.

Supplementing the proposed creation of new towns, a selected number of existing communities in the outer portions of the London Region were also to be deliberately encouraged to grow. Such communities had already received heavy inflows of evacuees during the war and social ties between some residents of central areas and particular peripheral communities had thus been established.

The proposed metropolitan green belt was to be approximately five miles deep, ringing the built-up urbanized area of London 13 to 16 miles from the center. While it would include additional land purchases for public use, most of this ring, mainly in agricultural use, would be preserved in green-belt status by compensating owners for refusals to grant development rights. Some large green wedges extending in toward London from the main green belt would be encouraged. Local green belts around new towns or older communities, roughly a half-mile in depth, would be merged with the metropolitan green belt where possible.

The makers of the Greater London Plan saw in the green belt a strategic device for halting the continuing spread of undesirable suburban growth. Drawing specifically on Unwin's earlier proposals, Abercrombie asserted the importance of a concept of green background, publicly controlled, into which compact communities could be set, under careful control. The case for the green belt also relied on its potential availability for the enjoyment of London residents. Whether for active recreation or for passive visual enjoyment, it was to provide an attractive and contrasting open reserve, permanently accessible. Recreational use was actively supported.

The green belt was also to help in preserving good agricultural land conveniently close to London. After the experience of World War II, it was determined that agriculture be kept viable, by subsidies and by warding off urban encroachment. Abercrombie also stressed the values of ensuring agriculture as a pattern of living, respecting the symbolic and visual importance of agriculture as a traditional English pursuit. In the plan's words, "nothing is more attractive than a town hemmed in by the farming countryside." [29]

The green-belt and new-town ideas were mutually supporting. New towns could not be separated from the major course of urban expansion without an intervening green belt. And the green belt could not possibly be preserved intact if new outer growth were not to be significantly channeled into a limited number of compact new towns.

Support for the Plans

On at least three bases the advisory plans found general support; or, perhaps more accurately, they evoked no pointed opposition. Bombed-out quarters and blighted, obsolete physical environs urgently required reconstruction. Living conditions and the effective functioning of the metropolis called for a wide range of planning measures. London's main traditional features and spatial patterning as they had been evolving over time were to be respected and selectively preserved.

Many of the proposals of the advisory plans for the Greater London Plan Region were, indeed, within a sufficiently narrow range of choice so that no very marked alternatives, short of nonplanning, were realistic.[30] Major rehousing was imperative, new schools and other community facilities were urgently required, road improvements were in order, and planning controls over suburban sprawl were judged to be required. Some of these generally accepted proposals stemmed from the character of the situation; others reflected standard city-planning approaches for that period. Other ideas integral to the main approach as adopted were, however, more distinctive, and merit more detailed attention. Despite the considerable eclecticism of the Greater London Plan and the County of London Plan, these plans—and particularly the former —did carry and reflect a philosophy of approach.

The Greater London Plan drew upon major concepts deriving from the garden-city movement, and traceable to Ebenezer Howard, Raymond Unwin, Frederic Osborn and other main proponents. The Town and Country Planning Association and its spokesmen have ever been ready with their own interpretation of the best approach to amenity, backed by the conviction that theirs was the distinctive British preference.

As if to accept Rasmussen's description of the "character and tendency" of London and his prophecy that "London will continue to be a town of one-family houses," [31] the Greater London Plan placed highest priority on maintaining a large proportion of houses with gardens. Unquestionably, this advocacy of relatively low densities also found strong consumer support and corresponded with a strong tradition. But if the Greater London Plan accepted low-density, peripheral residential development as desirable (as did American planners in their acceptance of suburbanward trends), the plan also took a positive, virtually utopian turn in asserting impressively that it was fully possible to guide this outer growth into planned communities and to create a major encircling open belt that would halt sprawl. The new-town and metropolitan green-belt proposals were responses to the threat of uncontrolled suburbanization.

The new towns, per se, were clearly the result of decades of propagandizing by the garden-city spokesmen. They reflected the concerted determination of a handful of leaders—in particular, Frederic Osborn, Lord Reith, and Lewis Silkin—that this was the best way to resolve problems of deconcentration, suburban sprawl, and inefficient and disorderly community development.[32] The solution developed and tested by the garden-city sponsors also came to be endorsed by the Labour Government as a way by which improved living conditions could be promoted and by which social classes could be merged. The practical necessity to provide new housing for overspilled and suburban-interested families combined with an ideological interest in lessening the upper-middle-class exclusiveness that might otherwise characterize suburban developments.

The green-belt idea found important support from several highly influential conservationist groups, particularly the agricultural conservationists. These conservationists argued their case from various angles, not necessarily mutually supporting, but in their total impact amazingly effective. The Scott Committee (officially the Committee on Land Utilization in Rural Areas) provided strong leadership for the conservation cause. In its report of 1942, it stated:

We regard the countryside as the heritage of the whole nation and furthermore we consider that the citizens of this country are the custodians of a heritage they share with all those of British descent and that it is a duty incumbent upon the nation to take proper care of that which it thus holds in trust. . . . The countryside . . . must be farmed if it is to retain those features which give it distinctive charm and character. . . . Farmers and foresters are unconsciously the nation's landscape gardeners, a privilege which they share with the landowners.[33]

While the green-belt concept had the support of those seeking outdoor recreational opportunities for London residents (the London County Council realized that adequate space could not be acquired within the Administrative County of London), the scales may well have been tipped by the sympathetic advocacy of a conservative class which has traditionally respected a country-gentleman, landed-estate pattern of living combined with an elite responsibility for guardianship of the English countryside.

Nor should we overlook the appeal of the Greater London Plan and its companion County of London Plan on ideological and esthetic grounds. The plans contained an adroit mixture respecting the traditional and taming the unwanted. They reëmphasized the singular and dominant importance of the great center of London with its traditional functional precincts. The plans maintained the main transportation lines feeding into this center, and preserved the pyramid of residential densities stressing the distinct centrality of it all. On top of this traditionally monolithic and unitary pattern was added the reinforcing character of a circular green belt designed to offer contrast and to assure containment. By these plans, British citizens were offered the reassuring impression that the best features of London as they knew them could be maintained while forces at work to change the London they revered could be brought under control. This was a welcome and hopeful message.

Patrick Abercrombie himself exerted great professional and personal influence. Trained as an architect, experienced as a town planner, he had made his most distinctive professional contributions as a regional planner during a pioneering period when the potentials of regional planning were being uncovered. Having prepared other regional plans, he was accepted as a logical leader for preparing these two major advisory plans. He had long been active in and sympathetic to the garden-city movement. One of its founders, he had served for many years as President of the Council for the Preservation of Rural England. He accomplished the tremendously important job of adapting major planning approaches to the London situation and imaginatively developing the new-town and green-belt concepts beyond the point of previous application. He was without question single-handedly responsible for much of the vitality with which these plans were developed, presented, and advocated.

Although not on the planning teams preparing these plans, Frederic Osborn unquestionably provided much of the doctrinal leadership that carried the ideas to broad acceptance. He headed the organized promotional efforts of the Town and Country Planning Association and crusaded on his own as a policy adviser and practical man-of-action. Frustrated in his efforts to bring about national planning, he nevertheless successfully fostered the decentralization of London, the lowering of residential densities, and the building of new towns amidst a green-belt background. A vigorous and effective pamphleteer, he organized and edited a series of reconstruction booklets and, for several years, an annual volume summarizing the state of planning and housing. He persuaded Lewis Mumford to write his influential booklet, *The Social Foundations of Post-War Building,* which provided a philosophic rationale.

The Main Alternative Ideas

All told, major alternative proposals with realistic possibilities of acceptance were conspicuous by their absence. The unofficial proposals by the three planning teams already mentioned—the London Regional Reconstruction Committee of the Royal Institute of British Architects (the LRRC), the Royal Academy's Planning Committee, and the Modern Architectural Research Society —(MARS) group and other scattered ideas lacked the thoroughness and balance that might have afforded them serious impact. The plan by the Royal Academy committee merely dressed up the

Bressey London road plan with monumental garb and provided no convincing organizational ideas. The LRRC plan mainly conserved the character of London as it then existed, but proposed breaking London up into a number of physically separate and rather self-contained communities. It reinforced approaches subsequently introduced in the advisory plans, but lacked their comprehensiveness.

The MARS plan contained the only important alternative ideas as to how a metropolitan area might be spatially organized. This scheme was a "linear" plan.[34] It provided for a number of advantages that deserved serious consideration, but because it so ruthlessly disrespected London's existing features, most Londoners,

FIGURE 5

THE PLAN FOR LONDON BY THE MARS GROUP

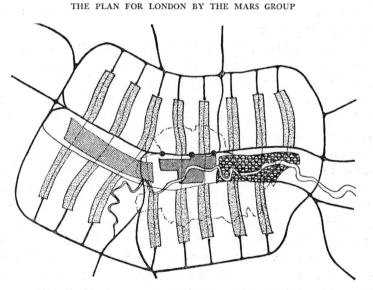

NOTE: This lineal plan concentrated commercial and industrial areas in a core paralleling the Thames and placed residential areas in strips of development perpendicular to the core.

SOURCE: *Land Use in an Urban Environment: A General View of Town and Country Planning,* a special issue of the *Town Planning Review,* XXII (October, 1961–January, 1962), Fig. 17, p. 175. By permission of the University of Liverpool Press.

and political leaders could not take it very seriously. Thus, although it provided a stimulating exercise in the design of a metropolis, in completely failing to recognize and to build from the here-and-now it also failed to serve as a responsible alternative for dealing with tradition-rich London.

The MARS plan features meriting consideration included a radical scheme for communication, with a main spine and offshooting minor spines at right angles providing what its members conceived to be a fully contemporary way of organizing a metropolis. It grappled with the problem of accommodating future growth. The linear plan allowed for metropolitan extension by lengthening the main spine and introducing more subspines. By and large, the plan recognized the functioning of the metropolis as of major importance, along with amenity considerations. It suggested a willingness to experiment with metropolitan forms adaptable to contemporary and future demands, and turned its back on a preservationist approach.

Probably the main additional spatial pattern that could logically have been explored was a finger plan, with axial extensions of linear growth extending out from the main urbanized area and with green wedges of open country interpenetrating these developed fingers. This was subsequently developed for Copenhagen and in 1961 was proposed for the Washington, D. C., metropolitan area. Theoretically such a pattern could have provided effective constraints on unwanted suburban growth, could have taken the best possible advantage of a limited number of main radial transportation lines, and could have provided full access to countryside brought in to the metropolitan area in bold green wedges. Such a form could have been far more respecting of existing central development patterns and existing transportation routes than the linear plan proposed by the MARS team. But this finger-plan approach was apparently never given serious consideration.

The green-wedge idea had been talked about and recommended during the 'twenties by G. L. Pepler. In his proposal, the green wedges were subsidiary, however, to a further idea of a narrow circular green belt. His areas of suburbanizing growth were much broader than fingers, assuming virtually a circular form.[35] Indeed, a circular form of urban and metropolitan development seems to have maintained so strong a hold on British town and regional planners that they never seriously explored noncircular patterns.

Major alternative residential densities might also have been possible, and this subject proved highly controversial. The County of London Plan accepted reasonably high densities in central areas, although generally greatly reduced from even higher levels in the past. The Greater London Plan generally followed the garden-city advocates in supporting rather low densities (albeit with a minimum level up to which outlying development would be brought). The new towns as proposed were to combine relatively low density, the deliberate delimitation of community size, and the separation of these communities from the main urbanized area. Their proponents held them to be very efficient, using proportionately less land than did the privately developed suburbs.

While Osborn and the Town and Country Planning Association held out for low densities together with the planning for compact satellite towns, a body of writing architects and architectural critics maintained that high-rise residential flats have a logical and desirable place in urban development. The editors of the *Architectural Review* and others argued that in many places it would be better and more economical for families to live closer to the metropolitan center, even if this meant somewhat higher densities.[36] These architects held, too, that high net residential densities might be offset satisfactorily by a greater massing of open space between residential clusters. The architects who favored higher-density residential development combined with agricultural preservationists in arguing that new towns would absorb excessive rural land.[37]

Political leaders, particularly members of the London County Council, the largest municipal landlord in the world, were faced with enormous pressures for housing, badly needed following the war. They were impelled to favor measures that offered the best promise of providing decent housing in quantity and at reasonable rent levels. They thus elected to compromise desirable density standards in the interest of providing a sufficient quantity of new housing units.[38]

Thus, while there was some questioning of new towns and other critical reactions to the approaches utilized in the advisory plans, there turned out to be little serious challenging of their major organizing principles for metropolitan planning. By and large, an amenity approach, concentrating on improving the residential areas, dominated the scene.

Chapter 3

Doctrine Affirmed
by the Plans

The advisory plans, as we have seen, integrated into a remarkably coherent web a great number of historical biases, social policies, and planning concepts; they were neither unimaginative nor tied exclusively to short-run practical expediency, but offered a compromise between facing up to urgent needs and recognizing ideal wishes. The carrying out of these plans and the institutional mechanisms for revising planning doctrine constitute the chief foci of the rest of this book. Before advancing to these topics, however, the present chapter digresses from the historical to analyze several features of the advisory plans and the doctrine they embodied which provides a basis for our interpretations of subsequent developments.

Idea, Plan, and Doctrine

Some concepts that fed into the advisory plans had been firmly accepted in advance of preparing the plans—for example, the main policy proposals of the Barlow Commission and the commitment to reconstruct central areas. Other approaches had for years been gaining some acceptance in various circles outside of government—particularly among the garden-city proponents and among town planners. The new-town approach falls in this category.

Still other approaches, while by no means new in their entirety, were introduced in the advisory plans. The full working out of these approaches—reduced central residential densities, overspill to the outskirts, and accommodation of this overspill in the suburbs and in new towns—represented creative invention. So, too, did the bold application of the idea of a large metropolitan green belt (as contrasted, for example, to the relatively small areas proposed by Unwin in the early 'thirties or acquired by the London County Council in subsequent years).

Some of the component ideas dealt with problem conditions and with trends to be reversed. Central blight and peripheral sprawl are examples. Concern about London's overgrowth and congestion was ever in the background. An important turning point was reached when feasible, constructive proposals for combatting or offsetting problem conditions were formulated and developed. Planned reconstruction became the positive approach to central blight; green belt and new town, the positive approaches to controlling sprawl; and a complete regional plan, the positive approach for dealing with London's growth.

The advisory plans came to take on the character of a single package—a policy bundle for containing London and guiding its controlled decentralization. The Greater London Plan, schematic and general in its graphic character and supported by a textual rationale, showed the main patterns and relationships to be sought. It converted ideas, otherwise disparate and utopian, into more specific, graspable spatial patterns and development goals. It reconciled these ideas with the historical character and the geographic realities of the community involved. And it provided an explanation for the main approaches so that they might be understood and defended.[1]

Without doubt the advisory plans paved the way for a consensus on development policy that would otherwise have been difficult to achieve. The plans thus provided a basis for firming up a widespread acceptance of a web of congruent approaches which came to assume a doctrinal character.[2]

Doctrine is to an activity such as town and regional planning what personal habit and philosophy are to individuals. It may not be completely written or codified and is, in fact, likely to be rather taken for granted by the participants involved. It is less self-conscious and less official than public policy per se. Doctrine defines the situation for participants, specifying which problems are to receive major attention, the solutions to be employed, and why alternative approaches should be ignored or discarded.[3]

It characteristically builds around seemingly self-evident truths and values and, in turn, bestows a self-justifying tone to its main propositions and chains of reasoning. It may embody a defensive air, providing simple replies to criticism or attack. While it may contain highly rational arguments, it is characteristically supra-rational in its over-all spirit. It may be comfortable and protective, contributing to the emotional security and self-confidence of the participant. While doctrine thus provides an essential kind of consensus supporting an activity, its self-evident and self-justifying nature may also contribute to a smug and traditional outlook and may discourage healthy self-awareness and skeptical reëxamination.

Since town and regional planning is a governmental function, its doctrine needs to provide a broad and attractive rationale for winning over and maintaining the allegiance of political leaders, appointed officials, and citizens. If it is sufficiently inclusive or even ambivalent, this may enhance the chances of wide-spread political support, including, for example, both conservative and liberal blocs.[4]

By the middle or late 1940's, ideas previously promoted as utopian proposals or suggested in technical, unofficial papers and reports had been lofted to the status of official policy and planning doctrine. In Britain, in particular, doctrine and official policy tend to be in close rapport.[5] Official reports and plans rather clearly spell out the rudiments of doctrine. And doctrine stands convincingly behind official policy.

Characteristically, doctrine embraces a web of reinforcing approaches. A given approach, such as advocacy of the metropolitan green belt, comes to be justified for various "intrinsic" reasons and also because by its successful effectuation it strengthens other approaches. Figure 3 has already suggested schematically a number of the interrelations involved in the advisory plans and the doctrine they crystallized.

Viewed broadly, two characteristics marked the London plans: their focus on containment and their unitary approach.

Containment as an Underlying Theme

The array of goals and approaches already reviewed (and depicted in Figure 3) made it readily possible for various interests to ascribe to the advisory plans distinctive interpretations. Like the proverbial blind men characterizing an elephant, the plans proved to be different things to different men. This "versatility" had important consequences, which will become evident in later chapters.

The elephant does, however, have an "objective" identity. Similarly, there is an underlying feature which ties together the diverse concepts and approaches proposed by the advisory plans: *containment* provides the unifying key to the plans and has a pivotal place in the doctrine represented in them.[6] Because this central idea—or set of associated, mutually reinforcing ideas—has not been more openly identified and analyzed, its importance has never been adequately explored. And because the interlocking features of assumptions and policy, of social goals and physical plans, and of planning for the region and planning for the conurbation have not been more clearly separated, the doctrine that has emerged is difficult to pin down.

Containment as used here refers to various approaches, both social-economic and physical, controlling London's growth. In part, containment implies deliberate policy to hold in the lateral physical expansion and the vertical intensity (*i.e.,* the density) of the growth of the main London Conurbation. Containment also implies policy to restrain the growth of employment and population in Greater London (with some difference of opinion, perhaps, as to whether this applies to the Greater London Plan Region as a whole or more particularly to the Conurbation). The containment concept is also allied with the demographic projections of the late 'thirties and early 'forties that posited future stability for the Greater London Plan Region.

Several of the main distinctions are suggested in Figure 6, which shows the social, economic, and demographic aspects and the physical planning aspects separately and indicates that the containment and population growth within the Greater London Plan Region or to the Greater London Conurbation. In general, the upper, left-hand box indicating restraint of industrial employment growth

FIGURE 6

VARIOUS APPLICATIONS OF THE CONTAINMENT CONCEPT

	As applying to the Greater London Plan Region	As applying to the Greater London Conurbation
Social, economic, demographic aspects or goals	Restraint of industrial employment growth in the Region so as to maintain, or to restore, better balance between the Region and the rest of Britain. (Barlow Commission report) Corresponding restraint of population growth—partly assumption and partly policy. E.g., "accepted target population." (Barlow Commission and subsequent government policy)	Control of suburban sprawl. (Greater London Plan) Preservation and maintenance of reasonably low residential densities; control of the growth of the Conurbation. (Greater London Plan)
Physical plan aspects	Redistribution of population and employment within the Region, mainly by overspilling from inner areas to new towns and to other approved settlements in outer parts of the Region. (Greater London Plan)	Lateral containment of the Conurbation by a metropolitan green belt. (Greater London Plan) Vertical containment of the Conurbation by density controls and planning standards. (Greater London and County of London Plans) Reconstruction of central areas to approved standards. (County of London and City Corporation Plans)

NOTE: For physical planning purposes, it was assumed that (a) the distribution of industrial employment would be accomplished through national planning efforts and (b) a slackening of natural population growth would result in a virtually static population level. (See text, however, for discussion of ambiguity between assumptions and policies.)

and population growth within the Greater London Plan Region as a whole and the lower, right-hand box showing more specific physical planning policy for the lateral and vertical containment of the Greater London Conurbation are the most important. The Greater London Plan dealt mainly with the lower right-hand box in translating the social policy advocated by the Barlow Commission, which finds its place mainly in the upper left-hand box.

The Unitary Character of the Plan and Doctrine

The Greater London Plan and the other advisory plans relied heavily on an architect-planner approach. They viewed the metropolitan community as having a spatial, physical form that could be grasped and reduced to maplike graphic presentation. In line with this outlook, they viewed planning as an activity dedicated to establishing a scheme for a future physical-spatial form and to fostering such other development and control measures as would best ensure realizing desired future form for the community. We may term this a *unitary* approach to planning, for it builds around a single comprehensive design for the entire urban community.

Such a unitary view reflects a design orientation. Implicit, too, is the assumption that there will be a reasonably centralized governmental authority to prepare, approve, and carry out the plan. Planning becomes a matter of political leaders and advising designers firmly recommending what they believe to be desirable and then working to convert this to fulfilment. The program therefore stresses the primacy of striving toward a positively stated future spatial form as physical environmental goal-product. The plan is characteristically presented for a hypothetical future point or period in time.

What we may term as an *adaptive* approach to planning, in contrast, focuses on the complex interaction of the diverse and functionally interdependent parts of the urban community and on the processes by which that community develops over time. This approach to planning seeks, as its main purpose, to influence the direction of development through the selective application of public policy, rather than planning for a future spatial form as goal-product.

The adaptive approach is by no means nonplanning or an evasion of planning commitment, although it may be so interpreted by devotees of the unitary approach. Rather, it places great faith in decentralized decisions arrived at through market mechanisms and incremental decisions emerging from the political process.

Western free-enterprise tradition heartily supports a view of the city or the metropolitan community as a complex process and framework, constantly in flux, with the main overall changes lying beyond the control or comprehension of most residents, developers, or governmental officials. In making their various decisions, these persons tend to adapt to the ever-changing context around them in terms of their understanding of how it works and the direction in which it seems to be moving. These actions, viewed one at a time, are by no means tantamount to planning in any broad public sense, and yet collectively they comprise a decision-making process of great sensitivity and flexibility, and, insofar as the various adaptive actions are rational, a planning mechanism of importance.

But the adaptive approach may also place faith in our capacity to gain scientific understanding of the processes at work and of the impact of possible public actions. It is fully consistent, therefore, to assume that governmental leaders can be provided with greater knowledge and with a greater capacity to uncover the best means by which to attain stated desired goals. If carried to an extreme, this approach assumes a technocratic tone. It would seem to place the knowledgeable specialist in a sounder position to recommend public policy than the elected political official.

The two approaches surely can be—perhaps ideally should be —complementary in character.[7] The Greater London Plan and the County of London Plan provide almost classic examples of the overwhelmingly unitary approach to planning. A greater balance between the two approaches might have had distinct merit, as we shall demonstrate at the end of this report. On the other hand, some outlooks that have been gaining influence in the United States in recent years may well lean too far toward the acceptance of the adaptive approach.

Despite the "advisory" status of these London plans, they served to crystallize and to communicate widely a single, forceful, integrated set of ideas. Assuming projections of but limited population growth, positing a firm national policy of restraining the growth of industrial employment in the Greater London Plan Region, and offering a simple future spatial pattern as a goal, the Greater London Plan and the other associated plans packaged potentially powerful ideas. Born in a highly unusual wartime context of utopian goals and a climate of acceptance of governmental planning controls, the advisory plans carried high (but necessarily reserved) hopes for the future.

The image of a desirable Greater London provided by the advisory plans—an image built around a single major design for the metropolis—embraced these features:

A simple concentric-ring pattern of residential densities, with a low plateau in the center, falling off to much lower densities in most of the suburban areas.

Maintenance and reinforcement of a dominant main center within the metropolis (no strong proposals for major, competing, new sub-centers).

Pattern of radial and ring highways; radial rail routes maintained, but with modifications of central routings and terminals.

Large portions of the central area to be rebuilt to new standards; some industry to be relocated.

Metropolitan green belt surrounding the built-up portion.

A series of new towns to be created just outside, or in the outer part of, the green belt.

The size and lateral growth of the London Conurbation to be controlled.

The London advisory plans sought, then, to view London as a single city, with a single dominant center, and a single circular green belt, while also providing for evolution toward a more diffuse, more spread out, multi-centered metropolitan region.[8]

PART II. *Implementation and Modification*

■

Chapter 4

Carrying Out the Plan:

■
■ *Governmental Machinery*

Organization for Land-Use Planning

The land-use planning system in effect in England and
Wales since 1947 and the governmental organization for land-use
planning in the London Region have had considerable impact on
the application and adaptation of the advisory plans for Greater
London. The comprehensive system for planning and controlling
land use development in England and Wales resulted mainly from
the 1947 Town and Country Planning Act, supplemented by the
1953, 1954, and 1959 Acts.[1] Under this system, and in contrast to
city planning coverage in the United States, land throughout
England and Wales has been brought under integrated national
planning control. At the central governmental level, the main
responsibility for administering the system has been lodged in the
Minister of Housing and Local Government,[2] although various
responsibilities have also been given to other ministries and departments. At the local level, the main responsibilities have been
placed with the 62 county councils and 83 county borough councils, with certain specified requirements for ministerial review of
local proposals or actions.

This nationwide physical planning system provides for the
preparation of development plans by county and county borough
councils; the administration of planning controls by these same
councils, with every prospective developer applying for permission; the inauguration of a system of compensation and betterment (subsequently largely dismembered by a changed govern-

ment); the creation of organizational mechanisms for building new towns and carrying out redevelopment; and the assignment of important responsibilities to the Ministries of Housing and Local Government, Transport, and Agriculture, the Board of Trade, and other central departments.

During the war and postwar periods in which the planning system was being designed and put into effect, the initiative for land development was mainly governmental. This reflected an assumption of responsibility for positive action by government—related to socialist tendencies of recognizing social commitments—and a wartime priority system strongly favoring governmental undertakings. The planning system sought, then, mainly to coordinate governmental efforts, giving heavy reliance on public schemes for construction and reconstruction. To be fully effective in such a situation, the planning system had to control—or at least strongly influence—the proposed activities of many governmental authorities, both local and nonlocal; to count on extensive public acquisition of land; and to secure sufficient financial backing. As we shall see, the decade of the 1950's was to bring difficulties on all three counts.

Development Plans

Before the 1947 Act, Britain had various kinds of local plans. Some areas had completed and instituted compulsory, official plans, which were often judged to be overly rigid. Once approved, they were difficult to modify. Many areas were regulated by schemes in preparation, a situation revealingly termed "interim development control." Nearly a hundred advisory plans for urban areas and a half dozen regional plans (including the Greater London Plan) for metropolitan areas were prepared during the period from 1939 to 1951.[3] But none of these had official status as a basis for administering planning controls or designating land for public acquisition. And unfortunately, a considerable part of the country had no effective plans prepared by which development might be controlled.

The 1947 Act introduced the requirement that each local planning authority—that is, each county or county-borough council— was to prepare an official development plan, providing a view of what development forces and trends were expected and invoking public policies for guiding physical development.[4] "The purpose is to present the broad picture of the expectation which the authority has for the development of this area, by public and private enterprise, for a period of approximately twenty years in the future." [5]

In marked contrast to the long-range, virtually timeless span of the typical advisory plan, with its distinctly unitary character, the development plan was to be limited to expectations that were financially feasible and politically attainable, and was to provide an amendable, and hence a deliberately flexible, set of proposals. In general, the development plan was not to show proposals beyond a twenty-year period, was to focus on probable developments rather than portray semi-utopian possibilities, and was to devote much of its attention to a succession of five- or seven-year periods for the first of which, in particular, concrete public improvements were to be designated. Every five years, following a re-survey, necessary amendments to this plan were to be prepared and submitted to public hearing and governmental review. Proposals were also to be added so as to round out a new twenty-year period. While the development plan made use of map-like presentations, and in this sense assumed a unitary tone, its focus on the unfolding and amendable process of development proved more in line with an adaptive approach to planning. Instead of concentrating on communicating major design ideas, it assembled public projects and stated the probable character of planning control decisions.

The new system required that prior to preparing a development plan the planning authority conduct a thorough survey of the area: to take into account *inter alia* the physical features, population and economic trends and social structure, land use status and trends, and the projects being developed by various governmental authorities. The report of this survey, while not an official legal part of the plan, has been required along with the plan, and has tended to provide not only background information regarding the present situation and the problems to be faced but also a sense of the rationale behind the plan.[6]

The actual development plans are prepared at various scales to reflect the characteristics of the area. For each county borough (and, because of their highly urban character, for London and Middlesex Counties) a development plan of three parts has been

required: a *town map* (at 6″ = 1 mile) showing areas for residential, business or industrial development, areas for major public
use and new public projects, and areas covered by supplementary
special or detailed maps comprising part of the plan; a *programme
map* (same scale) showing separately what proposals are planned
for the first five years and for a subsequent fifteen-year period;[7]
and a *written statement* precisely listing and describing specific
proposals to be accomplished as part of the plan, including areas
to be acquired for public use and areas to be comprehensively developed.

For each county the development plan also has three similar
components, except that the town map is replaced by a *county
map* (at the much smaller scale of 1″ = 1 mile) showing the relative growth of various communities anticipated and to be planned
for, the future pattern of community facilities within the county,
and areas covered by town maps and other supplementary maps.
In addition town maps are prepared for the towns within the
county (excluding the county boroughs).

Additionally, a local planning authority may include a *comprehensive development* area map* (at the fairly large scale of 25″ =
1 mile), accompanied by a programme map showing phasing and
a written statement detailing how a comparatively small area is to
be rebuilt, and a *designation map* (also 25″ = 1 mile) showing
land to be acquired within the area of comprehensive development by various governmental authorities or public utilities.† Certain standards have also been fashioned to supplement the development plan, but are invoked at the discretion of the authority and
do not have the character of ordinances. Controls over building
bulk, for example, have been found to be important (these will
be described in subsequent sections).

How effectively has the development plan served as a device for
crystallizing, conveying, and modifying major development policy?
The answer varies from one political jurisdiction to another, depending upon the existence and forcefulness of a previous advisory
plan and upon the initiative and vigor of the elected officials and
the technical offices. There is considerable evidence that while the

---

* Perhaps more appropriately termed *redevelopment* for the American reader, but
we follow British usage.

† We use the American term *public utility* for the British *statutory undertaker*.

development plan has fulfilled certain legal necessities, it has tended to be an uninspiring, technical sort of document.[8] It has communicated guidelines for the future, has indicated the shape of public projects planned for the immediate future, and has shown what areas must be procured for public use. In requiring full consultation with local district councils, with the Ministry of Housing and Local Government and with other governmental authorities, plus a series of public hearings, the preparation and airing of a development plan pulls differences and objections out into the open, works toward their resolution, and establishes a picture of what governments intend to do and what general policies they will use in administering applications for development.

The main initiative for preparing and amending a development plan lies with the local planning authority. But the system includes the prior statement of various broad policies (*e.g.*, regarding population targets) and even specific suggestions (as with the London metropolitan green belt) by the Minister of Housing and Local Government and other departments, and "advice" throughout its preparation which reflects the Government's attitudes. Finally there is review and approval of the plan by the Minister of Housing and Local Government, who must then also take into account local objections and representations. The Minister typically insists on revisions in development plans. Moreover, other ministries, important *ad hoc* governmental bodies, and public utility authorities all have power to acquire land and to undertake projects, over which the local planning authority sometimes exercises no formal approval authority, at most—if indeed at sufficiently early stages —merely being consulted. The vacuum is filled—theoretically at least—by the Minister of Housing and Local Government, who thus assumes a most important coördinative role.

Planning Controls

The development plans provided logical vehicles for stating policy and for showing proposed patterns of development. They might be expected (particularly under the typical American reliance upon law) to have comprised the major tool by which planning was to be accomplished. But this was not the case. The crux of British planning lies in the control exercised over development. This probably constitutes the most complete mechanism for such control ever enacted into law in any Western industrial mixed-economy nation.

Under the 1947 Act everyone who proposes to undertake development must apply for permission. "[Development] may be considered to comprise all substantial changes in the use of land, except from one kind of agriculture to another, and of buildings and the erection of all buildings, except minor ones. Control extends to the design and appearance of buildings and even in some cases to the fences, etc., which enclose their sites." [9] Moreover, it encompasses "the carrying out of building, engineering, mining or other operations in, on, over or under land or the making of any material change in the use of any buildings or other land." [10] A minister's order set forth eighteen classes of land use. Any change that falls completely within the same general class (*e.g.,* a change from a nursing home to an institution for children) is exempt from control.[11] So, too, are changes that are relatively slight.

Not only must private developers who contemplate nonexempt developments apply for permission; so, too, must local governmental authorities and public utilities. In the case of an application by a district council or a borough council (as, for example, to build a housing project) or by a public utility (*e.g.,* to extend water mains), the approval may be granted by the local planning authority. An application by a local government that is also a planning authority must be approved by the Minister of Housing and Local Government. A central government ministry is not required to apply for permission, but is expected to consult with the local authority within whose jurisdiction it proposes to proceed with some new undertaking or a significant modification of one already developed.

An essential feature of the planning control system is the right of applicants to appeal decisions by local planning authorities to the Minister of Housing and Local Government. Furthermore if a local planning authority wishes to sanction an application which is a material departure from its own plan, it must ask for prior ministerial review and judgment. And the Minister retains the privilege—rarely invoked—of "calling in"cases he judges to be of national or important local concern, thus taking them out of the hands of the local planning authority. By these methods the Minister is able to keep a firm hand on the situation and may wield considerable influence. Planning authorities and potential developers watch carefully how decisions on appeals are running.

This system, reflecting the administrative discretion characteristically allowed in Britain, makes for considerable flexibility in interpretation as specific cases arise. It permits some change over time in the policy line to be pursued—with respect to firmness of control, relative priorities, definitions of standards, etc.—as suggested by modifications in ministerial outlook or by changes in a local authority's own viewpoints. It also encourages a certain leeway in interpreting density standards and other classes of regulations. A subtle and pervasive shift in interpretations with time may, cumulatively, build up to the equivalent of policy modification. Given the pragmatic spirit with which much British administration works, this system of planning controls encourages a sort of muddling along (in contrast to a clearer broad-gauged approach to policy amendment). It probably to some extent reflects and perpetuates a basic problem: that with thousands of development-application decisions being settled in so dispersed and unpublished a manner, it is difficult for any local authority or developer, or even the Ministry, to be fully and clearly informed about the policy interpretations and modifications taking place.[12]

Compensation and Betterment

Integral to the new land-use planning system was the provision in the 1947 Act that all development rights be nationalized —a most revolutionary feature. In return for owners' surrendering the rights to, and hence the increased values accruing from, future improvements to their properties, the Government agreed to compensate them on a once-and-for-all-time basis from a "global fund" of £300 million.[13] This compensation to owners was proportional to what they would have stood to gain had the land-use restrictions of the 1947 Act not gone into effect. The Government was also empowered to levy betterment charges, collecting from owners the equivalent of what they could be expected to gain by being allowed to proceed with development. Henceforth, every applicant for planning permission had to purchase development rights from the State. The betterment charge was to "equal 100 per cent of the anticipated increase of land values which would flow from a particular planning permission." [14] It was hoped that as a result of this system land would change hands at values related to its current rather than its potential use.

This complex legislation was designed to make it possible for sweeping substantive planning proposals to be favorably considered and put into effect without the limitations which had traditionally dogged all such efforts. And vigorous planning has indeed meant a marked shift in land-use patterns and firm controls to achieve them, often involving important land acquisitions and development by governmental authorities. If full compensation had to be paid every time land values were adversely affected by planning controls and every time government needed land for open space, schools or other civic uses, the pressure to limit proposals would be extremely great. But paying at one fell swoop for all rights to future development and levying 100 per cent betterment charges cleared the way for bold and comprehensive planning.

These compensation and betterment provisions were misunderstood and often unpopular, and, probably far more serious, removed the incentive for land development by the private owner and investor. The new government which came into power in 1951 proceeded to engineer several major modifications that virtually dismembered these crucial financial features.[15] The idea of compensation from a global fund was withdrawn and compensation for loss of development values resulting from planning controls was greatly restricted; the betterment charge was completely eliminated. Private development was thus returned to a more nearly free-market status (except for the recognition that land-use controls could still be imposed). In the case of compulsory purchase of land by governmental authorities, the owner was to be compensated on a basis reflecting the agreed share of the £300 million global fund. By a 1959 Act, such compensation to the property owner was brought up to full current market value whenever the government proceeded with compulsory acquisition. The effect of these amendments has been to pass back the major initiative to the private developer and land owner, and seriously to impede planning authorities in achieving the full benefits of a comprehensive planning system.

Public Schemes

The British planning system has stressed the close relations between plans and their implementation. And, shaped as it was in the context of conditions and political outlooks of the 1940's, the system has particularly looked to government as the major builder—in constructing (or reconstructing) housing, schools, recreation areas, and other community facilities. Hence, coördinating the development efforts of the many governmental authorities was especially emphasized, even if not entirely successfully achieved.

Coördination has been especially "natural" where the same unit of local government that serves as the local planning authority also carries out the public schemes. The London County Council has been exceptional in this regard, being also responsible for housing (concurrently with the metropolitan boroughs), for education, and for a number of health, welfare, and other public services. In other parts of England and Wales, housing has been a responsibility of county borough councils and of borough and district councils. Education has been county administered or county controlled, but in some cases county district councils have also been delegated responsibilities. Highway construction has been carried out by various levels of government, depending upon the class of highway.

But much of the physical development in Britain has been by governmental units other than local government. The various Ministries of the central government acquire and develop land and, as has been indicated above, are not directly subject to local planning control. There have also been created, over the years, numerous special-function districts and authorities, and this number has increased with the socialization of functions previously in private hands or organized as public utilities. Some of these districts function only in specific metropolitan areas; some are organized on regional bases. Their proliferation and the irregularity of their districting contribute not a little to the difficulties of full coördination and effective planning.

Sparked by the need to rebuild war-damaged areas and recognizing that other areas, too, needed to be comprehensively redeveloped, the 1944 and 1947 Planning Acts established full powers for local authorities, the various ministries, special governmental authorities and public utility authorities to acquire land for these purposes, through compulsory purchase if necessary.[16] At the local level, the county district councils and the county boroughs were given this broad land-acquisition power, although the designation of the areas to be redeveloped was accomplished through the local planning authorities' development plans. (The London County Council, always the exception, was also granted these powers.) Land so procured could either be leased (only in exceptional circumstances, sold) for private development or retained for direct public use or development. Once Ministry approval was obtained, the local authority could obtain generous financial assistance from the central government.[17]

The New Towns Act, 1946, empowered the Minister of Town and Country Planning to designate sites for new towns, to set up development corporations to build and manage these new towns, and to request from the central government financing for them after satisfying himself that the developments envisaged were likely to secure a reasonable financial return. The corporations of these new towns were given important powers to acquire land, to plan comprehensively, and to carry out construction. They were also expected to manage the new towns once built. The corporations were to be independent governmental units in the conduct of their affairs, subject to ministerial approval as to their main plans and to appropriate consultation with adjacent local authorities.[18]

As a complementary program, the 1952 Town Development Act sought to promote the planned expansion of various outlying towns as reception areas for overspilling population from overly congested cities. This scheme depended upon negotiations between the central city and each outlying town, and was supported by modest grants from the central government and by designated charges borne by the exporting city.[19]

Central Government's Responsibilities

The Ministry of Housing and Local Government, as that part of central government mainly concerned with town planning, has come to have major powers and responsibilities. As has been noted earlier, it establishes broad policies to be followed by the local planning authorities, reviews development plans prepared by these authorities, judges appeals by prospective developers when local planning authorities have refused to grant them planning permissions, establishes new towns, and administers the compensation-betterment system.

The Ministry has generally been more ready to carry out its review functions than to take strong initiative. It has never pushed ahead to prepare a national physical plan, and it has been admittedly weak in its regional planning. Moreover, the Ministry, as a relatively new and hence "junior" governmental unit, has found itself hard put to exercise the kind of coördination within central government that some planning supporters in the 1940's might have expected.

In the years up to about 1946, technical officers within the Ministry were in a position to exert considerable leadership. As the years went by, however, the Ministry's administrative officers rose to positions of greater power. The Ministry has tended during the past decade to reflect a Conservative philosophy that planning is by no means to have a capital "P."

To the Board of Trade, a "senior" ministry concerned with production, was given the responsibility for administering the industrial dispersion policy. Any industrial firm seeking more than 5,000 square feet of new floor space was required to apply for an industrial development certificate. The Distribution of Industry Act of 1945 and the Town and Country Planning Act of 1947, under which this control was inaugurated, empowered the Board of Trade to determine whether proposed industrial construction should be allowed within Greater London or within other large conurbations, or whether such development should be refused in order to encourage locating in areas where employment needed to be bolstered.[20] The application for such a certificate precedes, and is distinct from, a firm's planning application; the Board of Trade passes only on whether the firm may locate within its area of choice, while the local planning authority considers the merits of the particular siting within any location previously blessed by the Board.

Highway planning falls within the province of the Minister of Transport, although highways are also shown on development plans and are subject to full discussion regarding their relation to other land-use proposals. The Ministry of Transport has direct responsibility for overseeing highway construction, and exercises control by authorizing grants for varying portions of construction costs to local governments which, in turn, are responsible for constructing and maintaining designated classes of roads. The grants range from 100 per cent for trunk roads down to 50 per cent for Class III roads.

Other ministries also carry responsibilities impinging on the local planning scene. Thus, the Ministry of Education sets standards with respect to, and makes grants for, schools; the Ministry of Health, for medical facilities; the Home Office, for fire services and child-care services; the Ministry of Aviation, for maintaining various major airports and guiding the operation of others. Still other governmental authorities, such as the British Transport Commission and the London Transport Executive, also play significant roles in planning and development.

The British sense of partnership between central and local government is very real—and, in an intriguing sense, elusive. One is told, on the one hand, that central government is the only real policy-determining body and that local governments only execute this policy. But one also discovers that, in actuality, many of the more active local governments (and the London County Council again poses a very special example) exercise considerable initiative. Indeed, the Ministry of Housing and Local Government may wait for local government to propose developments, knowing full well that the Minister and his representatives can wield great influence by approving or disapproving permission and by granting or withholding funds.[21]

Organization for Planning within the Local Authority

The American reader may benefit at this point from a description of the rudiments of planning organization at the local level. The basic structure, as was noted earlier, comprises the 62 county councils and 83 county borough councils which have been constituted by the local planning authorities and which prepare development plans and administer planning controls. But who carries out the day-to-day work?

As a rule, most of the work of each county or county borough council is carried on by a number of committees, each responsible for a particular "function" such as education, health, roads, or finance. Each council appoints a planning committee responsible for its planning functions, "that is, the preparation of the development plan for the area and the supervision of day-to-day planning administration and planning control." [22] Unlike the American planning commission that is insulated from the city council by its distinctive composition and by its traditionally "nonpartisan" character, the British county or town planning committee is a direct arm of the council. The committee is charged with recommending policy and programs for council consideration and with carrying out delegated aspects of such, once approved, on behalf of the council. The committee is composed of council members (the council itself is usually large enough to permit such deployment), and in some cases up to a third of the committee members may be coöpted from outside the council. The chairman of the planning committee assumes particularly heavy responsibility.

A planning department, under the direction of a planning officer, usually provides technical services. The planning officer serves as an adviser to the committee, although he also may, in fact, assume considerable initiative and, in the spirit of what he understands to be committee and council policy, carries out various administrative affairs on behalf of the committee. The typical working relation between the planning officer and the committee chairman is close, with the exact balance of initiative and leadership reflecting personalities and local circumstances.

This general mode of organization applies most directly to counties, where in fact county planning departments and county planning officers are the rule. In county boroughs, on the other hand, most "planning officers" are either subservient to other officers or bear different designations. Titles such as "borough engineer," "borough surveyor," "architect and planning officer," or "engineer and surveyor" abound. Only a handful of county boroughs have initiated separate town planning departments, with distinct planning officers in charge, since the 1947 Act. But, following a breakthrough in Newcastle in 1960, some other county boroughs are now following suit and are establishing separate planning officers and departments.

Distinctive Features of Government in Greater London

As we have seen, there are many Londons and a variety of definitions of Greater London and the London Region. For present purposes, it is convenient to introduce and to use the review area assigned to the Royal Commission on Local Government in Greater London for its recent inquiry. This area is slightly larger than the Greater London Conurbation and considerably smaller than the Greater London Plan Region used by Abercrombie in his plan.[23] The differences are summarized here:

	Area in Square Miles	Estimated Population in 1959 (in thousands)
Greater London Conurbation (for census purposes)	722	8,205
Review Area for the Royal Commission	840	8,714
Greater London Plan Region (for Abercrombie's plan)	about 2,600	10,420

By way of perspective we may break down the Greater London review area further:

	Area in Square Miles	Estimated Population in 1959 (in thousands)
City of London	1	7
County of London	116	3,199
Administrative County of London	117 (14 per cent)	3,204 (37 per cent)
Remainder of Review Area (roughly the Conurban Ring)	723 (86 per cent)	5,510 (63 per cent)
Review Area	840 (100 per cent)	8,714 (100 per cent)

The main local governments—those that are also constituted as local planning authorities—comprise six counties (London, Middlesex, Hertfordshire, Essex, Kent, Surrey) and three county boroughs (East Ham, West Ham, Croydon). Within the Administrative County of London, in addition to the hallowed City Corporation, are 28 metropolitan boroughs. Outside of the County of London and within parts of five surrounding counties (only Middlesex is completely within the review area) we find 42 municipal boroughs, 28 urban districts, three rural districts and six parishes. Including the counties and county boroughs, 117 local governments operate in Greater London.

Within the Administrative County of London, the County

FIGURE 7

LOCAL GOVERNMENTS IN GREATER LONDON

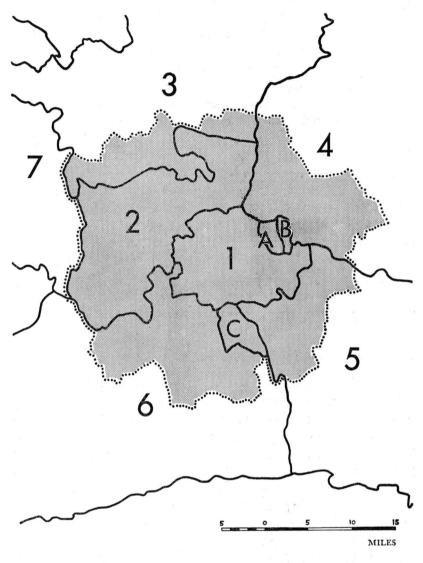

1 Administrative County of London	
2 Middlesex County	6 Surrey County
3 Hertfordshire	7 Buckinghamshire
4 Essex County	A West Ham County Borough
5 Kent County	B East Ham County Borough
	C Croydon County Borough

——— County and County Borough Boundaries

••••••••• Review Area of the Royal Commission on Local Government in Greater London

Council has been given the main planning and development responsibilities, the metropolitan boroughs playing distinctly lesser roles. Outside the County of London, with considerable county-to-county variation in some matters, the borough or urban or rural district councils are given a relatively more important share of local governmental responsibilities than the metropolitan boroughs.

Because of Greater London's enormous size and importance, it is also overlayered with a number of other governmental units, mainly special-purpose authorities. Some reflect the central government's direct concern for London as the national capital. Among the more important of these are the Metropolitan Police Commission, with the Commissioner responsible to the Home Secretary; the Metropolitan Water Board, its members indirectly elected; the Port of London Authority, indirectly elected by various governmental authorities and business interests; the London Transport Executive (formerly London Passenger Transport Board), operating the underground and buses, and appointed by the Minister of Transport although not formally under his direction; and regional boards or authorities for gas and electricity, for hospital service, and for higher education.[24]

Planning for Greater London

Although there is a Greater London Plan, there has never been any single planning authority for Greater London. Planning powers were given to the six counties and the three county boroughs, each being charged with preparing and periodically revising a development plan. Each is responsible for administering planning controls, although some delegation has been made to district councils and borough councils. An interested but restrained Ministry of Housing and Local Government oversees the plan preparation and the administration of planning controls by the several local governments.

Abercrombie, in his plan for Greater London, advocated a Regional Planning Board for Greater London, appointed by and responsible to the Minister. He envisioned this Board as reviewing all planning schemes for the area.[25]

In November, 1945, Lewis Silkin, as Minister of Town and County Planning, appointed an Advisory Committee for London Regional Planning, under the chairmanship of Clement Davies, which reviewed the substantive proposals of the Abercrombie Greater London Plan and, in July, 1946, reported back to the Minister. In March, 1946, the Minister appointed a second group, the London Planning Administration Committee, also under Clement Davies' chairmanship, to advise "on the appropriate machinery for securing concerted action in the implementation of a Regional Plan for London as a whole." [26] This group had difficult going. The passage of the 1947 Act disrupted the Committee's deliberations, forcing it to abandon approaches previously developed. A serious split in members' outlooks further impeded work. Finally, in February, 1949, the majority report recommended as an interim measure the establishment of a regional advisory committee with an independent chairman named by the Minister, and also the investigation by a local government commission of possibilities for governmental reform for the London Region. The minority report recommended that a joint planning board be formed as the local planning authority for the region, but rejected the advisory committee proposal as ineffectual.[27] No action in designating a regional planning mechanism of any sort was ever taken, although a governmental reorganization study was to be undertaken in the late 'fifties by a Royal Commission. The Ministry has not exercised its 1947 Act powers of forming new joint planning boards among different authorities.

Only two means of achieving regional coördination have remained. Informal consultation among local planning authorities has been encouraged by the Ministry of Housing and Local Government but has been relatively ineffectual. There also exists the coördinating role of the Ministry in its capacity to establish policy, its review of development plans, and its review of planning appeal cases. Related to this, the use by the Ministry of regions for planning administration and analysis deserves brief mention.

Arising out of the wartime need to decentralize national administration in case of invasion, a set of administrative regions came into use in England. From the mid-'forties until 1951, regional offices of the Ministry of Town and Country Planning served as intermediaries between the Ministry and the local authorities in their respective regions. One of the ten planning regions was a London Region corresponding closely to the Greater London Plan area. The London regional office included about 35 technical staff members who carried out regional planning studies, and reviewed proposals not in conformity with the Greater London Plan.[28] But this office was not charged with preparing or revising a regional plan, and it represented, by and large, merely a convenient administrative breakdown of the country rather than an area for which a regional plan, *per se,* was to be prepared.[29] During the 1950's, regional offices were weakened and finally eliminated altogether, although the Ministry continues to assume a responsibility for overseeing the planning of the London Region.

Much has hinged on the Ministry's interest and resources in coordinating planning for the London Region. The Ministry undoubtedly continues to exert some leadership—in carrying out trend studies, identifying problems, and recommending policies and programs. The local authorities have tended to expect policy direction from the Ministry, and the standard arguments for the *status quo,* as pled before the Royal Commission on Local Government in Greater London, were that the Ministry could hold things together. Yet the Ministry, in turn, tends to rely rather heavily on local authority initiative.

Public Development Projects in Greater London

The London County Council is unique among county authorities in combining at the same level both planning and major public construction and development responsibilities. It handles housing concurrently with the metropolitan boroughs and the City Corporation. It assumes the main responsibility for central area redevelopment, with the City of London also active in redevelopment within its limited area. The responsibilities for road construction and for traffic management are complexly distributed between the County Council and the metropolitan boroughs.[30]

Outside of the Administrative County of London and the county boroughs, public development is carried on by both the county and district councils, while major planning responsibilities are retained by the counties. In such situations, the split between a county as planning authority and the smaller governments as public developers makes for some problems and impedes coördination.

Some important functions and responsibilities for capital investments are vested in the various special governmental authorities—the London Transport Executive, the British Transport Commission, the Port of London Authority, and the London and Gatwick airports operated directly by the Ministry of Transport. Throughout the London Region, other ministries also carry out public schemes.

Within the London Region, eight new town development corporations have been established, responsible for the planning, construction, and maintenance of new communities.[31] Coördinating these corporations' plans and the plans of surrounding local planning authorities has posed a great challenge.

Conclusions

A vivid contrast emerges. On the one hand, a single strong, competent town planner, Patrick Abercrombie, was commissioned by the Government to prepare a plan for metropolitan London. On the other, divers responsibilities were assigned to nine local planning authorities, to a Ministry committed to reviewing local plans and planning-control decisions but cool to national or strong regional planning, and to a multiplicity of sundry governmental authorities, some decidedly powerful in their own right. Serious splits in planning and development initiative and responsibility have followed. It is little wonder that, in such circumstances, the Greater London Plan proved able, at best, to provide ideas and grand policy but did not become the nucleus of the vital, comprehensive planning many desired.

Chapter 5

Carrying Out the Plan:
Programs, Trends, and Results

Although their value as inspirational, informational, and policy-suggesting instruments should not be underestimated, the advisory plans certainly were not prepared as ends in themselves. The real test has been their impact in guiding the growth and reconstruction of Greater London. How faithfully, then, have the advisory plans been followed?

The Socio-Economic Context of Postwar Planning

The Greater London Plan assumed that neither population nor industrial employment would grow significantly within the area around London. This conclusion derived from two basic assessments: that Britain would not make great gains in its economy or in its resident population, and that Greater London could be prevented from continuing to draw industry and population from the rest of Britain.

In short, the Greater London Plan was built upon the fundamental preconception that London was not to be subjected to forces of growth so strong that they could not be contained. This, in general terms, has proved not to be the case. Britain has, in fact, enjoyed economic prosperity, relatively full employment, a rising standard of living, and a considerable growth in population.

The economy has thrived. In marked contrast to the depression years, postwar Britain has had a national unemployment rate generally under 2 per cent. (Some areas, notably Scotland, Northern England, and Wales, have been plagued with higher unemployment, while London, the Southeast, and the Midlands have had less.) Manufacturing production, upon which Britain so strongly depends, has risen significantly, although it has by no means kept pace with growth rates in Western Germany and the United States. Correspondingly, despite postwar increase in living costs the typical household has had a more adequate and a steadier income. While the incomes of the wealthy have been heavily taxed, the broad base of workers has gained greater purchasing power. This, as we shall see, has spelled important implications for consumption behavior in the realms of housing, automobiles, and other items for which prewar differentials between middle-class and working-class purchasing ability were so marked.[1]

The London Region has benefited very much from this economic growth and general wellbeing. Increased nationalization has augmented employment within national offices, mainly in London. The growth and consolidation of major industrial and business firms has led to greater importance for their headquarters offices —also mainly in central London. And the rise of new industrial activities has encouraged an incubator role for London, as, for example, with the burgeoning electronics industry.

Underlying London's position, moreover, has been its continuing central importance in finance, insurance, shipping, publishing, and other sectors of activity traditionally concentrated in the metropolis. The Port of London now handles 20 per cent more shipping than in 1938, and from 1950 to 1959 alone its share of all United Kingdom shipping tonnage rose from 17 per cent to nearly 21 per cent. The London airport has grown to outstanding importance, with an eightfold increase in passenger traffic from 1950 to 1959 and the rise of the airport district to an employment subcenter for 30,000 employees.[2] Any increases in trans-Channel contacts will further augment London's importance as the main contact point between Britain and the rest of Europe.

In the depression context of the 'thirties, with falling birth rates taken as an inevitable trend, demographers envisioned only a modest population growth within Britain. The Greater London Plan assumed that from 46 million population in 1937, Britain would grow merely to 47.2 million by 1960 and would then drop to 46 million again by 1970. As things have turned out, the level of population has moved upwards steadily and at 51 million (as of

1960) was nearly 4 million higher than forecast for that date. While this reflects but 8 per cent more than the 47.2 million projection, it represents five times the amount of growth expected— 5 million rather than 1 million.

Even more important than the population growth itself has been its changing distribution. Households have dropped in average size—particularly in inner London—so the growth in population has generated an even higher rate of growth in households. From 1951 to 1961, the population of England and Wales increased about 5 per cent, but households increased 12 per cent. The Greater London Conurbation gained 61,000 households, despite population loss of 176,000 (see also fuller discussion and Table 10 below).

Moreover, the continuing redistribution of income has brought higher living standards to an ever enlarging proportion of households. In contrast to the 12 per cent increase in households, private dwellings gained 21 per cent for the decade to 1961.[3] Thus the modest increase of 5 per cent in population during the past decade, buttressed by other factors, has led to a significant increase of over a fifth in private dwellings. These additional dwellings have created heavy site demands on available land in and around large urban centers. And it is probable this trend will persist. More households will undouble (move from shared quarters into separate quarters) and will seek and obtain better dwellings.

The changing standard of living is also strikingly evident in the marked rise in car ownership which has come to Britain, accelerating mainly during the latter part of the 1950's.[4]

	Private Cars in Great Britain (in thousands)	Private Cars Per 1,000 Population		British Ratio as Per Cent of U. S. Ratio
		Great Britain	United States	
1938	1,944	42	194	22
1951	2,380	49	278	18
1960	5,526	108	341	32

This increase may appear inconsiderable as compared with American auto usage, yet Britain has been moving into a new era in which many more people can live at increased distances from employment and shopping centers. Since the Britisher has so typically sought after a house with a garden, the car gives him the chance to get to and from this house, even if distant from established public transport routes. The availability of cars has encouraged the building of single-family detached houses and the suburbanization and exurbanization of metropolitan areas.

The Labour Government's policy, following the war, was for government to assume the major role in constructing and managing housing. The central government provided financial aid to local governments for this undertaking. Because of material shortages, private builders were permitted only a limited volume of construction. As of 1951, for example, only about a tenth of all housing units were being provided for private ownerships. But the formation of a Conservative Government and the easing of materials shortages brought forth greatly expanded construction of private housing during the remainder of the 'fifties. By 1955 about half of all units were for private owners, and in 1960 this had risen to over three-fifths. (See Appendix Table A2.) Correspondingly, the Government's policy has been to decrease the volume of general housing provided by local housing authorities and to restrict government's role essentially to housing for special groups such as the elderly and persons being relocated following slum clearance or other public improvements, and those being exported under overspill schemes.

All in all, then, distinct elements of consumer sovereignty, abetted during recent years by the Conservative Government's encouragement of a private-enterprise approach to building, have unleashed forces potentially more at variance with, and certainly less directly under the control of, town and regional planning policies and directives than those foreseen by developers of the advisory plans or by high governmental circles devoted to fashioning a planned social economy for Great Britain.

These evolving forces have strongly encouraged the suburbanization of the largest conurbations. As we shall see, they have worked to bring about more dispersion within the London Region than could have been envisaged, thus serving to accomplish the decentralization aims of the Abercrombie plan—but without imposing such strong controls as were generally anticipated. But the very suburbanward forces that have been unleashed may also be much less amenable to the sort of lateral containment that the metropolitan green belt was supposed to provide.

Employment in the London Region

The advisory plans assumed that employment opportunities in Greater London would not be permitted to increase. Following the focus of the Barlow Commission recommendations, they directed attention to industrial employment in particular. The Greater London Plan very explicitly stated "that no new industry shall be admitted to London and the Home Counties except in special cases." [5] Both the Greater London Plan and the County of London Plan assumed that national controls would force relocation of industry to other sections of Britain, particularly to areas with high unemployment. And, except for discussing the prospects for decentralizing industries to various local districts within the Greater London Plan Region and building up a case for the feasibility of decentralization, neither of these major plans attempted any systematic forecasts of national and regional employment trends.

It is striking indeed that no central concern was shown for the likely future character of Britain's economy and London's vital place in it. How does one account for the fact that, at the very time economic planning was being shaped for Britain, no closure was attempted between broad economic forecasts and the particular development problems confronting the Abercrombie planning teams? [6]

One possible answer is that essential data were highly incomplete. It is still extremely difficult to procure full and comparable statistics on employment for the London Region that start well before the war and carry up to the present; at the time the advisory plans were being prepared the available statistics were even more meager. But this circumstance does not fully explain the situation, for statistics are collected only in response to a purposeful appreciation of their utility. The question is, then, whether there was even a sensitive notion that they were important for urban and metropolitan planning in Britain at that time.

In any event, the advisory plans gave no projections as to likely or desirable employment levels at designated postwar dates; they fostered only a general idea that industrial employment should not be permitted to grow in the Greater London Region. Hence, no comparisons can be made between the planned distribution of employment within this region and the distribution that has actually occurred.

But it is evident that overall employment within the Greater London Region has not been held constant. How significant the increase has been is, however, subject to various interpretations.[7] The data per se can be grouped conveniently into three main periods: the prewar period (up to 1939), the war and immediate postwar period (from 1939 to the late 'forties), and the decade to 1960. Unfortunately, no single time series can be constructed.[8]

We have already reviewed briefly the prewar employment trends. (See Chapter 2, especially Table 4.) The changes during the war are, like the earlier ones, inadequately documented. Insured employment figures, incomplete as they were prior to full national insurance, are shown in Table 5. From 1939 to 1948 those parts of the County of London outside the central area lost more than 350,000 insured workers; the Conurban Ring gained a quarter million workers; and the Conurbation as a whole lost 100,000 workers, a decline of 3 per cent. During this same period, the rest of England and Wales gained 900,000 workers, a 9 per cent gain. It is difficult to interpret just what this shift indicates, for insured employment underrepresented important segments of London employment (e.g., insured employment represented only 66 per cent of all employment in the County of London, while it accounted for 78 per cent of employment in the rest of England and Wales). Much employment necessarily moved from inner London during the war, and many workers were unable to return or were not interested in returning after the war. These figures do not tell us how rapidly employment was reconcentrating in central London when peace returned.

If we bypass the late 'thirties and rely only on the 1921, 1931 and 1951 censuses, our information is somewhat better. (See Table 6.) Two qualifications must be kept in mind, however, when considering these figures: the 1931 data are incomplete, and dealing with changes from 1921 to 1951 buries prewar, wartime, and immediate postwar adjustments in a single set of 30-year shifts.

The region of London and the Home Counties showed little

TABLE 5

INSURED EMPLOYMENT IN SECTIONS OF THE GREATER LONDON CONURBATION AND IN ENGLAND AND WALES, 1939–1948

	Employment (in thousands)		Increase (in thousands)	Percentage Distribution			Index of Increase (1939 = 100)
	1939	1948	1939–1948	Employment		Increase	1948
				1939	1948	1939–1948	
Central Area[a]	659	667	8	5.0	4.8	1.0	101
Rest of County	1,322	962	−360	10.1	6.9	−44.7	73
Administrative County of London	1,981	1,629	−352	15.1	11.7	−43.7	82
Conurban Ring	1,401	1,649	248	10.7	11.8	30.8	118
Greater London Conurbation	3,382	3,278	−104	25.8	23.5	−12.9	97
Rest of England and Wales	9,745	10,655	910	74.2	76.5	112.9	109
England and Wales	13,127	13,933	806	100.0	100.0	100.0	106

SOURCE: *Administrative County of London Development Plan 1951: Analysis* (London: LCC, 1951), pp. 65, 67. Insured employment particularly covers workers in manual and lower-income positions. The 1948 total for England and Wales, 13,933,000, was only 77 per cent of the 18,180,000 employed persons subsequently identified in 1948 under the full coverage of the new National Insurance Scheme. These 1939 and 1948 figures cannot be directly compared with the employment figures in Tables 6, 7, and A3.

[a] Those labor exchanges representing the City, Westminster, Holborn, Finsbury, and parts of St. Pancras and St. Marylebone.

TABLE 6

PREWAR AND POSTWAR EMPLOYMENT TRENDS IN THE LONDON REGION
AND IN ENGLAND AND WALES, 1921–1951

	Employment (in thousands)			Percentage Distribution			Indexes of Growth (1921 = 100)		Employment per Thousand Population		
	1921	1931	1951	1921	1931	1951	1931	1951	1921	1931	1951
Administrative County of London	2,685ᵃ	n.a.	2,605	15.6	n.a.	12.8	n.a.	97	599	n.a.	778
Conurban Ring	936ᵃ	n.a.	1,760	5.5	n.a.	8.7	n.a.	188	312	n.a.	352
Greater London Conurbation	3,621ᵃ	n.a.	4,365ᵃ	21.1	n.a.	21.5	n.a.	121	484	n.a.	523
Rest of London and Home Counties	993	n.a.	1,523	5.8	n.a.	7.5	n.a.	153	389	n.a.	402
London and the Home Counties	4,614ᵇ	5,417ᵇ	5,888	26.9	28.7	29.0	117	128	460	486	485
Rest of England and Wales	12,564	13,436	14,448	73.1	71.3	71.0	107	115	451	467	457
England and Wales	17,178	18,853	20,336	100.0	100.0	100.0	110	118	453	473	465

SOURCES: Except as separately footnoted, employment figures are from 1921 and 1951 Census reports.
ᵃ Centre for Urban Studies, *Statement of Evidence to the Royal Commission on Local Government in Greater London* (London: Centre for Urban Studies, University of London, December 4, 1959), Table 4, p. 35.
ᵇ From Table 4, p. 19 of this book. The Home Counties include Bedfordshire, Buckinghamshire, Essex, Hertfordshire, Kent, Middlesex, and Surrey. (See also note b, Table 4.)

change in its share of national employment from 1931 to 1951. Within the Home Counties, however, a decided dispersion of employment was underway. From 1921 to 1951 employment rose 88 per cent in the Conurban Ring and 53 per cent in the rest of the Home Counties region, but fell 3 per cent in the Administrative County of London. Without a 1938 or 1939 benchmark, the timing of the growth cannot be established definitely. But it is clear that employment in proportion to population was on the rise in the London Region; and most of this increase appears to have taken place between 1921 and 1931 rather than later.

Table 7 summarizes the entire period from 1921 to 1960 in two pairs of comparative figures, 1921/1951 and 1952/1960; comparisons are possible within each pair, but not between pairs. The earlier pair reveals (as did data on insured employment) that dispersion was underway within South-Eastern England, and that, overall, this area's gain in employment was larger than that of the rest of England and Wales.

TABLE 7

SUMMARY OF EMPLOYMENT TRENDS FOR SECTIONS OF THE LONDON REGION, FOR SOUTH-EASTERN ENGLAND AND FOR ENGLAND AND WALES, 1921-1960

	Employment (in thousands)[a]				Percentage Distribution				Employment Increase (in thousands)		Percentage Distribution Employment Increase		Indexes of Increase		Employment per Thousand Population			
	1921	1951	1952	1960	1921	1951	1952	1960	1921–1951	1952–1960	1921–1951	1952–1960	(1921=100) 1951	(1952=100) 1960	1921	1951	1952	1960
Central Area[b]	1,175e	1,252e	1,229	1,402	6.8	6.2	6.6	7.0	77	173	2.4	12.6	107	114	1,992	3,303	3,234	4,006
Rest of County	1,510e	1,353c	1,335	1,365	8.8	6.6	7.1	6.8	-157	30	-4.9	2.2	90	102	388	456	448	480
Administrative County of London	2,685	2,605	2,564	2,767	15.6	12.8	13.7	13.8	-80	203	-2.5	14.8	97	108	599	778	762	866
Conurban Ring	936	1,760	1,838	1,827	5.5	8.7	9.8	9.1	824	-11	26.1	-0.8	188	99	312	352	368	364
Greater London Conurbation	3,621	4,365	4,402	4,594	21.1	21.5	23.5	22.9	744	192	23.6	14.0	121	104	484	523	526	560
Regional Ring	n.a.	n.a.	889	1,310	n.a.	n.a.	4.8	6.5	n.a.	421	n.a.	30.8	n.a.	147	n.a.	n.a.	319	315
London Region[d]	n.a.	n.a.	5,291	5,904	n.a.	n.a.	28.3	29.4	n.a.	613	n.a.	44.8	n.a.	112	n.a.	n.a.	449	477
Rest of South-Eastern England	n.a.	n.a.	2,021	2,069	n.a.	n.a.	10.8	10.3	n.a.	38	n.a.	2.8	n.a.	102	n.a.	n.a.	417	401
South-Eastern England[e]	6,057	7,730	7,312	7,973	35.3	38.0	39.1	39.7	1,673	651	53.0	47.6	128	109	449	470	440	455
Rest of England and Wales	11,121	12,606	11,386	12,103	64.7	62.0	60.9	60.3	1,485	717	47.0	52.4	113	106	456	462	417	429
England and Wales	17,178	20,336	18,698	20,066	100.0	100.0	100.0	100.0	3,158	1,368	100.0	100.0	118	107	453	465	425	439

SOURCES: Table 6, Census volumes, and Table A3, except as otherwise noted.

[a] This table contains two pairs of figures, 1921–1951 and 1952–1960, with comparability within each pair but not between the pairs. The 1921 and 1951 figures are "occupied population" at workplace, from the respective Censuses. They include employed persons 12 and over, fulltime students 18 and over, and retired workers. The 1952 and 1960 figures represent a different series, "employed persons," from national insurance records. They exclude employers and those who work for themselves. Note that the 1952 total for England and Wales, 18,698,000 is 1.6 million (3 per cent) less than the 1951 total, 20,336,000.

[b] The City and Finsbury, Holborn, St. Marylebone, St. Pancras and Westminster metropolitan boroughs or their closest equivalents in labor exchanges. For source see Table 6, footnote b.

[d] As defined by the London Technical Branch (Research Section), Ministry of Housing and Local Government (abbreviated as MHLG in subsequent footnotes). See also note c, Table A3.

[e] The London and South-Eastern, the Eastern, and the Southern standard regions combined. Figures prior to 1960 adjusted for boundary changes in the Southern region.

The more reliable recent figures provide a more conclusive picture of a continuing rise in employment. The London Region as defined by the Ministry of Housing and Local Government (similar to the Abercrombie region at the north and south, but extended to roughly circular shape to the west and to the east) shows a considerable increase of 613,000 employees during this eight-year period. By any of several comparisons, this is highly significant. It represents about 45 per cent of the national increase in employment, despite the Region's having had only 28 per cent of the employment of England and Wales in 1952. The Region's proportion of national employment rose from 28.3 to 29.4 per cent during the same period. The concentration of employment relative to population also rose, from 449 to 477 employed persons per 1,000 population, an increase in this ratio of 8 per cent (with the comparable national increase less than 3 per cent).

Some general conclusions about the total employment situation within the London Region are warranted. First, there has been an extremely important increase in employment in the six central boroughs of London, particularly in the West End. The modest gain of 77,000 employed persons during the entire 30-year period prior to 1951 has been followed by the substantial increase of 173,-000 during the brief eight-year period following 1952. This increase in central employment is largely of an office type.

Second, the outer ring of the Region—outside the Conurbation—has shown much larger employment increases than were envisioned by the Abercrombie regional plan team. In but eight years, this ring gained 421,000 employed persons, a rise of nearly 50 per cent. And the greatest employment growth has been moving steadily outward. What is clear—and effectively emphasized by a number of recent reviewers[9]—is that even the Greater London Plan Region must now be recognized as too small a geographic area to embrace all persons and activities maintaining daily interaction with central and built-up London.

Third, these two great loci of employment increase, the very center and the outer ring of the region, have more than offset the tendency for most of inner London—i.e., the County of London outside of the central area and the close-in sections of the Conurbation beyond the County—to stabilize or even to lose employment. Indeed, their increase has been so great that, despite only very modest increases in employment in the rest of South-Eastern England, the total region of the South-East continues significantly to increase its share of national employment. From 1952 to 1960, employment in the London Region gained 12 per cent and in South-Eastern England as a whole 9 per cent, but in the rest of England and Wales only 6 per cent. Jobs continue to become available in the Region, particularly in the central area of London, at a rate of 15,000 to 20,000 per year, and, correspondingly, a steady in-migration of workers to the South-East has been underway.[10]

Industrial and Office Employment: Trends and Controls

Two aspects of the employment situation and governmental controls directed to them have special importance. The first is the matter of dispersal of industrial employment, hinging mainly on the success with which manufacturing plants have been guided to locate or relocate outside of the London Region. The second is the phenomenon of office employment, with emphasis on the effectiveness of governmental controls over the construction of office buildings in central London.

Following Barlow Commission recommendations, the central government adopted a policy of preventing undue concentration of industrial employment in the London Region and steering it to areas with employment needs.[11] The Board of Trade has administered the issuance of industrial development certificates in order to carry out this policy. How effective has this system of controls been?

A. G. Powell has concluded that "the operation of industrial controls by the Board of Trade in the London area is almost as tight as public opinion in a democratic society is prepared to accept." [12] McCulloch has sought to demonstrate that the controls by the Board of Trade compelling industry to go to what he terms the "unfortunate regions" were strong from 1945 to 1952, were noticeably weakened from 1953 to 1959, and have been considerably tightened again since 1959.[13] In any event, the control system has had notable loopholes. Factories under 5,000 square feet and extensions of up to 10 per cent of existing space have not needed certificates. The Local Employment Act, 1960, has stipulated that only floor space actually used for an industrial development process is relevant, so office space in the same building is not counted.[14]

Local planning authorities have also sought to restrict industrial expansion in various sections of the London Region, but they have not been armed with the control available to the Board of Trade. The London County Council has, within its fiscal and legal limitations, actively striven to relocate industries. It has taken over, in the past ten years, about 100 acres previously devoted to industry. Up to 1959, the Council had spent more than $6 million and was prepared to continue spending about $1.4 million a year to acquire nonconforming industrial plants. An Industrial Centre established by the Council has helped industrialists to relocate successfully. The area zoned for industrial use within the Administrative County of London has gradually been contracted.[15]

Presumably industrial expansion within the London Conurbation has been slowed if not halted. Inner London is reported to have a quarter million fewer factory jobs than in 1939.[16] Dame Evelyn Sharp has observed that "the big increases are mainly accounted for by office employment; the distribution of industry policy has been relatively successful. For every 5 new jobs in the London conurbation only one has been in a factory requiring an industrial development certificate." [17]

Industrial expansion in the Regional Ring outside of the Conurbation has been significant, however. Thomas (presumably using Ministry figures) reports that 60 per cent of the increased employment between 1952 and 1959 for the entire Region was in manufacturing.[18]

But a serious shortcoming of the emphasis on controlling the location of manufacturing plants is that so significant a proportion of new jobs are not in manufacturing at all, but are in service-type and particularly in office-type activities. The Town and Country Planning Association in a recent policy statement explained: "In the entire conurbation . . . factory employment now represents only a third of the 4½ million jobs." [19]

The number of employees in central London, mainly in offices, continues to grow at about 15,000 per year (or 1.5 per cent, "a rate of increase almost twice as great as the average rate for England and Wales"). "There has been a striking shift of activity from the City to the West End, for about 50% more work in the West End than before the War, and about 20% fewer in the City . . ," [20]

The increase in central area jobs has probably totalled 100,000 merely since the middle 'fifties. From the end of the war to 1960 about 38 million square feet of new office space have been completed and another 11 million square feet approved in central London.[21] Office space is estimated to be expanding at about 3 million square feet per year.[22]

Neither the central government nor the London County Council has had any direct powers of control over office-type employment per se. The only controls have been over the erection of office buildings or their conversion from other uses. It was not until 1956 that full recognition was given to the office growth problem. As of that date, nearly 42 million square feet of new or converted office space for London's central area had been approved since the war. The full impact of lifting the embargo on office-building construction in 1954 was not accurately anticipated. From 1956 through 1960 only 8 million additional square feet of space were approved, for new controls were put into effect—and strongly supported—by the Minister of Housing and Local Government. But there were difficulties in enforcement. For example, an earlier law permitted an owner to erect a new building with up to 110 per cent of the volume of his previous building. Since new buildings make more efficient use of volume (with lower ceilings, etc.), this sometimes has entitled existing owners to increase their floor space by considerably more than 10 per cent.

The Greater London Plan's presupposition that industrial employment could be held constant has probably materialized within the Greater London Conurbation, although significant increases in manufacturing employment in the Regional Ring outside the Conurbation have occurred during the past decade. Industrial employment has constituted but a fraction of all employment expansion, however, and the very considerable increases in office-type employment, particularly in central London, have more than offset losses in manufacturing jobs in inner London and have contributed to the overall picture of continuing rising employment in the London Region.

Population in the London Region

From a population of some 10.3 million immediately before the war, evacuations and mobilization into the armed forces had by 1943 dropped the civilian population in the Greater London Plan Region to about 8 million. Development of the Greater London Plan assumed, as has been noted, that projected low rates of natural increase and limitations of future employment would lead to no population increase for the Region. The plan even proposed some reduction, to a target level of 9.8 million,* with population dispersal to towns outside of the Region encouraged.

While the development plans were being prepared, from 1948 until their submission between 1951 and 1953, the Region was already regaining population rapidly—back up to 9.6 million in 1946 and 10.2 million, virtually the prewar figure, by 1952.† The development plans clearly reflected this climate of growth. They provided for a total 1971 population of 10.6 million for the Region, 423,000 (8 per cent) larger than the target figure previously established in the Greater London Plan. As Cullingworth has observed: "It seems . . . likely that the Abercrombie policy of reducing the total population of the Region has been replaced by one which accepts a significant increase." [24]

The actual population trends to date show significant differences within the Region. Inner London has been losing population. From 1939 to 1961, the central area (the City of London, Westminster, and four contiguous boroughs) lost 150,000 persons. The rest of the County of London lost some 300,000 residents. In total, these combined portions of inner London fell from a 1938 figure of 6.0 million to 4.8 million, a level comparing closely with Greater London Plan and County of London Plan proposals for 4,718,000, and development plan forecasts for 1971 of 4,847,000. (See Table 8.)

As Greater London has lost residents from its inner portions and has added residents to its suburban periphery, it has witnessed an ever outward growth. At earlier periods this growth was most

---

* From this point we rely upon the Greater London Plan Region adopted for statistical purposes by the MHLG, smaller by 200,000 to 300,000 than the plan region used in the original Greater London Plan report.

† Most published population figures for the postwar period are for *home* population, comprising civilian population, members of the armed service, and certain other categories of persons; our figures are from published sources. The MHLG and local planning authorities, on the other hand, are able to use unpublished *civilian* population figures not available to outside researchers. Our figures may therefore vary from those occasionally released by the MHLG and the local authorities. [23]

TABLE 8

POPULATION OF THE GREATER LONDON PLANNING REGION, PLAN PROPOSALS, AND TRENDS
(In thousands)

	Mid-Year Estimates			Greater London Plan (4)	Development Plans 1971 Forecasts (5)	Development Plans Over Greater London Plan (5-4)		1961 Population Over Greater London Plan (3-4)		1961 Population Over Development Plans (3-5)	
	1938 (1)	1952 (2)	1961 (3)			Number	Per Cent	Number	Per Cent	Number	Per Cent
County of London	4,063	3,347	3,180	3,326	3,150	−176	−5.3	−146	−4.4	+30	+1.0
Inner Urban Ring	1,911	1,776	1,620	1,392	1,697	+305	+21.9	+228	+16.4	−77	−4.5
Suburban Ring	2,366	2,672	2,698	2,399	2,749	+350	+14.6	+299	+12.5	−51	−1.8
Green Belt Ring	977	1,332	1,661	1,288	1,567	+279	+21.7	+373	+29.0	+94	+6.0
Outer Country Ring	833	1,027	1,400	1,377	1,410	+23	+2.4	+23	+1.7	−10	−0.7
Greater London Planning Region[a]	10,150	10,154	10,559	9,782	10,573	+791	+8.1	+777	+7.9	−14	−0.1

SOURCES: Columns 1 and 2 from *Report of the Royal Commission on Local Government in Greater London 1957–1960*, Cmnd. 1164 (London: HMSO, October, 1960), p. 291; column 3 calculated from the Registrar General's annual estimate for 1961. The 1952 population figures are for civilian population; the 1938 figures are reported in their source to be civilian population but may be resident population; the 1961 figures are for home population (including members of the armed services in the country). Strictly speaking, therefore, there is some lack of comparability among these figures. The forecasts in columns 4 and 5 are from *Report of the Ministry of Housing and Local Government for the Year 1956*, Cmnd. 194 (London: HMSO, June, 1957), p. 74. They are presumably civilian population. This table relies upon the "rings" proposed in the Greater London Plan, so as to compare 1961 population estimates with 1971 population forecast by the Plan. These rings from the Plan do not correspond to the concentric rings used throughout the other tables dealing with population.

[a] This is for the region that resembles, but is somewhat smaller than, the area originally covered by the Greater London Plan. This region's boundaries also reflect the necessity of using complete local authorities as bases for available statistics.

pronounced in the ring outside the County of London but within the Greater London Conurbation limits. From 1939 to 1948, for example, this Conurban Ring gained more than 200,000 persons and was the only part of the Conurbation to grow.* But as the growth has swept farther out, even the Conurban Ring in recent years has been losing population. This Ring lost 25,000 persons between 1956 and 1961, a sizeable contribution to the overall loss of 118,000 for the Conurbation.

The Suburban Ring established by the Greater London Plan was that part of the Conurban Ring between Inner London (as dealt with above) and the so-called Green Belt Ring also established in the plan. The Suburban Ring contained about 2.4 million persons in 1938. The Greater London Plan expected it to hold at about that figure, but the development plans forecast growth to 2,749,000 by 1971. The population in 1961 was 2,698,-000, already within 50,000 of the development plan forecast. Most land anticipated as available for residential development in the 'sixties has already been absorbed for residential construction.

The Green Belt Ring has come under the greatest growth pressure. As defined for statistical purposes, it comprises complete political units, and thus includes more than the Green Belt as such. Some residential extensions into or through the Green Belt are significant urban places, and many smaller villages have inevitably invited further development. Most of these have been allowed some growth through an "infilling" process. This Ring contained 977,000 residents in 1938, and was to be allowed 1,288,-000 under the Greater London Plan. This latter figure was boosted by 22 per cent, to 1,567,000, by the development plans. By 1961 Green Belt Ring population had in fact risen to 1,661,000, 373,000 in excess of the Greater London Plan level and 94,000 more than the 1971 forecasts in the development plans. This vigorous, difficult-to-control growth has mainly reflected private residential construction, with only about 100,000 residents (14 per cent) in housing provided by governmental authorities.[25] Most of the Green Belt as proposed has been brought into existence, but nibbling at edges adjacent to established communities has been a

---

* Our dependence upon published figures—*resident* population for 1939, *civilian* population for 1948, *home* population for 1950 and later—makes for difficulties. We are reporting somewhat smaller increases from 1939 to 1948 and larger increases from 1948 to 1952 than truly comparable figures would show.

TABLE 9

POPULATION TRENDS: SECTIONS OF THE LONDON REGION, SOUTH-EASTERN ENGLAND, AND ENGLAND AND WALES, 1939–1961

	Population (in thousands)[a]			Increase (in thousands)		Percentage Distribution					Indexes of Population Growth				
						Population			Increase		(1939 = 100)			(1952 = 100)	
	1939	1952	1961	1939–1952	1952–1961	1939	1952	1961	1939–1952	1952–1961	1952	1956	1961	1956	1961
Central Area[b]	488	380	337	−108	−43	1.2	0.9	0.7	−4.3	−1.9	78	75	69	96	89
Rest of County	3,525	2,983	2,843	−542	−140	8.5	6.8	6.2	−21.8	−6.9	85	82	81	97	95
Administrative County of London	4,013	3,363	3,180	−650	−183	9.7	7.7	6.9	−26.1	−8.3	84	82	79	97	95
Conurban Ring	4,734	5,001	4,972	267	−29	11.4	11.3	10.8	10.7	−1.3	106	106	105	100	99
Greater London Conurbation	8,747	8,364	8,152	−383	−212	21.1	19.0	17.7	−15.4	−9.6	96	95	93	99	97
Regional Ring	2,791	3,417	4,308	626	891	6.7	7.8	9.3	25.1	40.3	122	134	154	110	126
London Region[c]	11,538	11,781	12,460	243	679	27.8	26.8	27.0	9.7	30.7	102	104	108	102	106
Rest of South-Eastern England	4,333	4,841	5,231	508	390	10.5	11.0	11.3	20.4	17.6	112	115	121	103	108
South-Eastern England[d]	15,871	16,622	17,691	751	1,069	38.3	37.8	38.3	30.1	48.3	105	107	111	102	106
Rest of England and Wales	25,589	27,333	28,475	1,744	1,142	61.7	62.2	61.7	69.9	51.7	107	108	111	101	104
England and Wales	41,460	43,955	46,166	2,495	2,211	100.0	100.0	100.0	100.0	100.0	106	108	111	104	105

[a] Mid-year estimates; 1939, resident population; 1952 and 1961, home population. For details on definitions, sources, etc, see Table A4, from which this is derived.
[b] The City, Finsbury, Holborn, St. Marylebone, St. Pancras, and Westminster.
[c] As defined by the London Technical Branch (Research Section), MHLG. See esp. A. G. Powell, op. cit. (note 2, this chapter), p. 82. We have used the same regional definition for all years to maintain comparability.
[d] The London and South-Eastern, the Eastern, and the Southern standard regions, with figures before 1960 adjusted for boundary changes.

constant temptation for developers and their demands on local authorities have posed difficult planning-control decisions.

The commitment to preserve a wide Metropolitan Green Belt has reduced the amount of land available for residential development and has forced much development to jump the Green Belt in search of the next best in accessible sites. As a result, the Outer Country Ring—the outermost, according to the Greater London Plan—which had a 1961 population of nearly 1.4 million, already exceeds the Greater London Plan forecasts—this in an area that was to have been a reserve for future growth. Five thriving—and planned—new towns fall within this Ring, contributing a residential increase of 173,000, although this has been but 30 per cent of the total 1938–1961 increase. From 1952 to 1961 alone, this Outer Ring has increased by an amazing 36 per cent.

The Greater London Plan sought to promote decentralization not only within the Plan Region but also proposed two new town sites outside. Bracknell and Crawley, accounting to date for 65,000 population increase, were built on this basis (although on different sites).

What was largely unanticipated, however, was the degree to which population growth, more affluent living standards, and increasing use of private automobiles would combine to encourage residential development in a ring outside the original Abercrombie Plan Region. Most of South-Eastern England has been affected. Correspondingly, at the lead of the Ministry of Housing and Local Government, larger statistical regions have been brought into use for analyzing London's spreading growth. In subsequent discussion, the London Region is the London Region of the Ministry's use, a circular region extending out to about a fifty-mile radius. The Regional Ring labels that part of the London Region outside the Conurbation, and thus, roughly, outside the Green Belt. The Outer Country Ring, already dealt with, makes up an inner part of this larger Regional Ring. (See Figure 8.)

This Regional Ring in 1961 contained nearly 5 million residents, having gained 1.5 million since 1939. In short, it was half again as large at the end of the 22-year period as before the war. This growth was initially spurred by wartime evacuation. It has been continued by the creation of new towns and a planned expansion of several old ones. Residential construction, particularly

FIGURE 8

THE CONTEMPORARY LONDON REGION

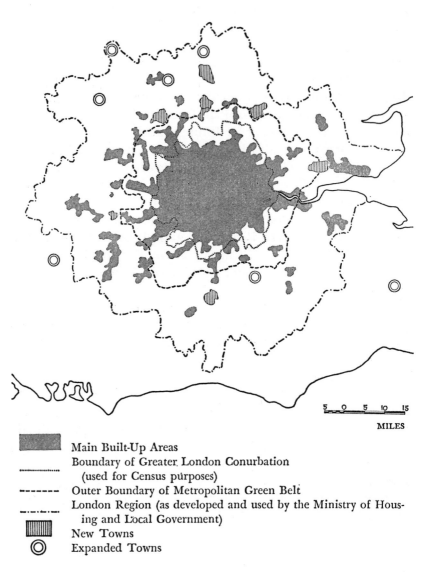

5 0 5 10 15
MILES

Main Built-Up Areas
Boundary of Greater London Conurbation
  (used for Census purposes)
Outer Boundary of Metropolitan Green Belt
London Region (as developed and used by the Ministry of Hous-
  ing and Local Government)
New Towns
Expanded Towns

during the past decade, has been predominantly of the private, single-family home variety.

There has also been a considerable population gain within the ring-like band, uneven in shape, outside of the London Region but within the broadly defined South-Eastern England Region ranging from East Anglia to Hampshire. From 1939 to 1961 this outer ring gained by 21 per cent while the rest of England and Wales recorded but an 11 per cent increase. Although the prewar population of the Regional Ring and this outermost ring constituted but a sixth of the population of England and Wales, together, the area has accounted for fully half of England and Wales' total population increase. The outer portions of the extended London Region are showing by far the most significant growth in all of England and Wales. Only the continuing lowering of population levels in inner London prevents overall growth of the London Region from being far greater. To be sure, much of the growth in the outer rings has resulted from spilling out of migrants from the inner areas.

How one assesses the record of London's growth depends on which outer boundary of London is used and which outer ring is included. The Conurban Ring is no longer growing and the inner parts of Greater London are losing residents. But the Ring of the new London Region has been growing in recent years at roughly five times the national growth rate for England and Wales. Redistribution within the London Region is being accomplished— and appears, in fact, to be abetted by suburbanizing forces not dissimilar from those at work in America.

The larger London Region and South-Eastern England in its fullest regional sense are, without question, continuing to grow at more rapid rates than hold for the remainder of England and Wales.* From 1956 to 1961, the Regional Ring and the rest of South-Eastern England outside the London Region amassed gains of 827,000 as against the loss of 118,000 residents from the Conurbation proper. At no time were the planners and political leaders responsible for the advisory plans sufficiently astute crystalgazers to envision the full force of the growth during the 'fifties to which the London Region was to be subjected.

Household Formation: Trends and Implications

Both employment and population growth have, in various ways, exceeded the expectations set by the advisory plans. Popula-

---

* Nevertheless, this growth of the London Region has proceeded at a considerably lower rate than holds for the largest metropolitan areas in the United States. In contrast to the 5.7 per cent growth rate of the London Region from 1952 to 1960, the five largest American metropolitan areas (all over 3 million) grew by an average of 23 per cent from 1950 to 1960.

tion in some sections of the London Region has surpassed even the forecasts established by the more recently prepared development plans. Employment increases have slightly outrun population increases in the London Region, a result, most likely, of selective migration trends such that the more active, working-force population has comprised a disproportionate segment of the influx.

Selective migration has also helped to make for differences in average household size within the London Region. The smallest average household * is to be found in the County of London; a somewhat higher average, in the Conurban Ring; and the highest average, in the rest of South-Eastern England. (See Table 10.)

Even more important as a pervasive trend during the past several decades has been a decline in average household size throughout England and Wales. Such a drop has been mainly related, as Cullingworth in Britain and Winnick in the United States have clearly shown,[26] to a change in the general age structure of the population in each country, for relatively fewer children and relatively more adults, and especially older adults, have come to be represented. Headship rates (*i.e.*, the number of household heads per 100 persons) vary strikingly by age, with rates higher for older persons. The 1951 rates in England and Wales, for example, were 22.4 for the age group 15–39, 48.5 for those 40–59, and 56.9 for the group 60 years and over.[27] As the population has aged, the number of households has increased more rapidly than total population. Correspondingly, average size of household has dropped.

But the modest gains in population in London during recent years have been accompanied by increases in households quite out of proportion to the population trends. In those parts of inner London in which population has declined, the drop in the number of households has been considerably smaller. Indeed, a 1951–1961 decrease of 23,000 residents within the Conurban Ring was accompanied by an increase of 72,000 households. For the Conurbation as a whole, there were household increases of 22 per cent and

* Throughout this book, the term *household* is the equivalent of *private household*, defined in the 1951 Census as "comprising single persons living alone or groups of individuals voluntarily living together under a single menage in the sense of sharing the same living room or eating at the same table." Boarders, domestic servants, and visitors are included; lodgers having or sharing separate accommodations or living in boarding houses are excluded.

TABLE 10

INCREASES IN HOUSEHOLDS AND POPULATION, SECTIONS OF THE LONDON REGION, SOUTH-EASTERN ENGLAND, AND ENGLAND AND WALES, 1931–1961

| | Increase in Population (in thousands) | | | | Increase in Households (in thousands) | | | | Average Household Size | | | Average Household Size as Ratio, England and Wales = 100 | | | Indexes of Change in Average Household Size, 1931 = 100 | |
| | 1931–1951 | | 1951–1961 | | 1931–1951 | | 1951–1961 | | 1931 | 1951 | 1961 | 1931 | 1951 | 1961 | 1951 | 1961 |
	Number[a]	Per Cent	Number[a]	Per Cent	Number[a]	Per Cent	Number[a]	Per Cent								
Administrative County of London	−1,049	−23.9	−153	−4.6	−69	−5.8	−11	−1.0	3.69	2.99	2.88	95	90	92	81	78
Conurban Ring	1,181	30.9	−23	−0.5	550	55.7	72	4.7	3.87	3.25	3.09	99	97	99	84	80
Greater London Conurbation	132	1.6	−176	−2.1	481	22.1	61	2.3	3.78	3.14	3.00	97	94	96	83	79
Rest of South-Eastern England	1,594	24.5	1,378	17.0	671	39.1	607	25.3	3.79	3.39	3.16	97	101	101	90	83
South-Eastern England[b]	1,726	11.7	1,202	7.3	1,152	29.6	668	13.2	3.78	3.26	3.09	97	98	99	86	82
Rest of England and Wales	2,079	8.2	1,112	4.1	1,732	27.3	917	11.4	3.98	3.38	3.16	102	101	101	85	79
England and Wales	3,806	9.5	2,314	5.3	2,885	28.2	1,585	12.1	3.90	3.34	3.13	100	100	100	86	79

SOURCES: Census volumes. Average household size derived.
[a] Because of rounding, figures may not add to exact totals.
[b] London and South-Eastern, Eastern and Southern standard regions combined. Figures before 1961 adjusted for shift in boundaries.

2 per cent for 1931–1951 and 1951–1961, respectively, although population stayed nearly constant.

The gain in the number of households, then, has increased the demand for housing; and, with rising income, the ability of households to undouble has further contributed to housing demand. The rising numbers and proportions of small households require distinctive matching housing.

Density Controls: Thinning Out the Central Area

One major aspect of containment has been control of the intensity of development, particularly in central areas where residential densities have been very high historically. The advisory plans proposed a pattern in which relatively high densities would be allowed in the central part of the County of London and somewhat irregular concentric zones of successively lesser densities would proceed out from the center.

Within the County of London the 1951 development plan, as approved by the Minister of Housing and Local Government in 1955, followed closely the recommendations of the County of London Plan. Four main density districts, in which average net residential densities were to be 200, 136, 100, and 70 persons per acre, were approved. A number of small districts allowing only from 30 to 50 persons per acre were also inserted into the development plan by the Minister. The overall effect was to reduce "ultimate" population capacity from the 3,326,000 of the County of London Plan to 3,250,000 according to the 1951 development plan as approved. The 1971 forecast of this latter plan was 3,150,000, for as explained in the development plan report, "This [lower level] is mainly because there are large areas within the County which are occupied by fairly recent development at much lower densities than those zoned." [28]

As a result of the first review of the County of London Development Plan, reported to the Minister in 1960, further modifications in the density districts, have been made. These enlarge the higher density districts, introduce a number of districts of 170 persons per acre, and, particularly in the South-Eastern portion, expand considerably the area of 50 persons-per-acre density and correspondingly reduce the 70-per-acre district. The effect has been to raise ultimate capacity slightly, to $3\frac{1}{3}$ millions, the capacity earlier proposed in the advisory plan. But the 1960 revision also estimates that, with a continuing modest rate of natural increase, the 1972 population in the County will be only 2.9 million. The County Council envisions that once the improvements of the next ten years make the County more habitable, the way may be cleared for a period of some recentralization. At such a point, the County's population might be expected to rise again toward its ultimate theoretical capacity.[29] But it is likely that the County's population will for a considerable future period remain somewhat below the expectations of the advisory plans.

In contrast to this, the initial development plans of every other planning authority in the Plan Region allowed for population increases greater than those foreseen in the Greater London Plan. The increases range up to an absolute excess of nearly 300,000 for Middlesex County and a percentage increase of 23 per cent for Croydon. In all, the forecasts for those portions of the nine planning authorities' development plans within the Greater London Plan Region, exclusive of the County of London, totaled 967,000 (15 per cent) in excess of the target population assumed by the Greater London Plan.[30] Images of the development that could be allowed have gradually altered so as to meet the increased population.

Subsequently, some of the original forecasts of the first group of development plans have also been revised upwards. Surrey County assumed a 1971 population of 1,426,000 in its 1953 development plan, but by 1958 a revised report was forecasting 1,510,000.[31] The mid-year actual home-population for 1961 was estimated at 1,477,000, some 51,000 in excess of the earlier forecast for a decade later. Buckinghamshire, only part of which is in the Greater London Plan Region, forecast in its 1951 development plan an increase of 100,000 by 1971. When the planners came to prepare their first five-year review, submitted in 1959, they found that natural increase from 1948 to 1957 had been nearly 24,000 and they raised their estimate of natural increase to 49,000 for the 20-year period, 1954–1974.[32] This new estimate is almost $2\frac{1}{2}$ times the natural increase forecast in 1951.

In a number of the outer counties, 1971 forecasts had already been nearly reached by 1961.* For example, Essex County's 1,341,-000 resident population in the London Plan Region portion was in 1961 only 10,000 less than the earlier 1971 forecast level; Kent County, with a 1961 estimated population of 743,000 within the Plan Region, was also only 10,000 short of 1971 forecasts; and Croydon's 252,000 estimate for 1961 compares with a 1971 forecast, as of 1951, of 266,000 and a 250,000 target figure for 1971 held as late as 1960.[33]

In central London density controls per se have been actively supplemented by comprehensive development proposals (loosely similar though not in precise social purposes and mechanics of operation to American redevelopment). A program of replanning and rebuilding has been restoring bombed areas to active use and replacing slum structures with new ones, all within controls insisting on new lowered densities and on criteria for well-planned community areas.

Since the war, more than six square miles (some 4,000 acres) within the County of London have been or are being comprehensively redeveloped,[34] with nearly 24,000 slum dwellings cleared.[35] In addition to new housing, by far the largest item of reconstruction, coördinated sets of community facilities have also been programmed. New schools have been built, open spaces provided, public buildings constructed, shopping centers rebuilt, roads improved, and industry relocated or rehoused locally.

The scale of this comprehensive development and the thinning out accomplished can be illustrated by the 1,300-acre Stepney and Poplar comprehensive development area. This area in 1939 provided housing, such as it was, for 217,000 persons. Large numbers of these residents were evacuated during the war and many never returned. As of 1951, the census counted only 107,000 residents. Gradually, this district is being almost completely rebuilt, starting with bomb-damaged areas and proceeding on to the replacement of slum structures. The planned population target is 97,000, but more probable 1970 or 1975 projections suggest about 78,000. Complex and scattered as the reconstruction has been, it involves in scale and in facilities the equivalent of two new towns. Since

* The forecasts were typically of civilian population only; the 1961 data represent total home population estimates which include armed forces personnel; but the statistical differences clearly cannot be attributed to the different bases alone.

the war, 9,600 new dwellings have been provided, nine new schools have been constructed, a few acres of new open space have been readied for use, and starts have been effected toward providing other facilities. Over the 20-year period covered by the development plan, 221 acres (or 17 per cent of the area) will be converted to use for schools, hospitals and other public buildings, and major open space. More than 16,000 persons, 15 per cent of the area's 1951 population, will have been displaced in the course of clearing sites for these new buildings.[36]

Whether the scope and pace of comprehensive development in the central area of London has kept up with the expectations suggested in the advisory plans is difficult to appraise. Brenikov has concluded that "In practice the amount of comprehensive redevelopment—as distinct from rebuilding—that has taken place in the central areas of the conurbations has been trifling." [37] But he is speaking of conurbations in general, and the London County Council is no ordinary local government.

Creating the Metropolitan Green Belt

The Greater London Plan proposed that clear outer building limits be designated and that beyond these a green-belt zone be created within which, except for controlled infilling of existing communities, new building would be prohibited.[38] The belt would constitute a permanent open area, mainly agricultural, providing a distinct visual change from built-up cities, opportunities for recreation, and a block to sprawl.

In 1950 the Minister of Town and Country Planning prepared and circulated to the planning authorities in the London Region a memorandum and a map defining a recommended green belt in precise terms. He suggested some modification in the Greater London Plan boundaries, and additional modifications emerged as the planning authorities incorporated the Minister's recommendations into their respective draft development plans.[39]

As of 1960 the Metropolitan Green Belt that had been firmly established, with Ministerial approval, by the development plans and by continuing planning controls was approximately the same for about half of the ring and somewhat wider (i.e., extending farther out from London) for the other half than had been proposed by the Greater London Plan.[40] In a number of cases the

Metropolitan Green Belt does not extend as close in to central London as originally proposed. Examples include sections of the Hornchurch and Thurrock Urban Districts in Essex, part of outer Croydon, and a large area in Middlesex in the vicinity of London airport.

Since the late 'fifties, however, Hertfordshire, Bedfordshire, Buckinghamshire, Berkshire, Surrey, Kent, and Essex have been considering major outward expansions of the Green Belt.[41] Should they materialize, they would widen the Green Belt from its present four- to twelve-mile width up to a maximum of twenty miles in some places, extending it, particularly in the northwestern and western sectors, well beyond the outer boundaries of the Greater London Plan Region. How much the more important towns (including new towns) would be permitted to grow within this widened Green Belt is not at this point clear. These proposals are, at least in part, in the process of Ministerial review.

Inspection of maps of existing land use shows that the Metropolitan Green Belt is by no means a solid or regular ring. It is crossed or penetrated by some 22 railway lines, five underground lines, and 16 major radial highways, all of which provide direct access to central London. Historically, communities have developed along these various routes, and some now represent sizable urban concentrations, as in the case of Watford, which extend solidly out from main, built-up London. Even by 1951 census counts it was clear that there was extensive commuting to central London from communities in and even beyond the Metropolitan Green Belt. With improvements in rail service, the commuter band has since been pushed out farther, so that the "containment" role of the Green Belt tends to be offset by radial transportation lines crossing it.

Control of development within the Green Belt has generally been firmly enforced. The green belt idea has apparently appealed to many of the governmental elite. Duncan Sandys, as Minister, exerted particularly outspoken leadership in promoting maintenance of the belt. A key nontechnical civil servant in the Ministry some years ago is alleged to have asserted that the Green Belt was the one goal he could readily understand and work toward with conviction.

There have nevertheless been variations in the thoroughness

with which, in specific local instances, building has been prohibited within, or immediately adjacent to, communities within the Green Belt.[42] In line with the general development philosophy of judging each case on its own merits, criteria and their respective weightings differ from jurisdiction to jurisdiction and from one time to another.

But direct major inroads on the Green Belt have been staved off. If anything, planning controls have become stricter in recent years, and the proportion of appeals approved by the Ministry has fallen.[43] Nonetheless, there is in some circles an uneasiness that development pressures are becoming unduly serious and that reaffirmation to hold the line may not in itself be sufficient.[44] Population within the Green Belt area continues to mount more than seems fully consistent with the principle of Green Belt maintenance.

Building New Towns, Expanding Old Ones

The Greater London Plan proposed ten new satellite towns to absorb some 400,000 persons from central London. Only two of the original sites, Stevenage and Harlow, were specifically accepted for subsequent development, but a total of eight new towns (six on different but equivalent sites) were constructed. Progress was slow at first: by the end of 1950 only 451 dwellings had been completed in five new towns. But development proceeded at a much more rapid pace during the 'fifties, and by the end of 1961 more than 79,000 dwellings had been completed and nearly a quarter million additional persons had been accommodated. With some allowances recently introduced to accommodate natural increase, the capacity of the London new towns is currently set at 545,000, nearly 200,000 more than present resident population and pointing toward a total increase of 446,000 (in addition to 99,000 original residents).[45]

In most respects the new towns have materialized in full accord with expectations. More than 80 per cent of the newcomers are reported as from the London Conurbation;[46] that is, the new towns have furnished overspill destinations for 200,000 or more residents who might otherwise still be living within the Conurbation. Nearly 73,000 jobs have been added in factories and about 5,800 in new offices.[47] Nearly 30,000 jobs have also been added in various service establishments.[48] Most workers who reside in the respective London new towns find employment in them. Some commute to London. And now, increasingly, the new towns are themselves becoming regional employment and service centers for somewhat larger areas. As of 1958, for example, there were approximately 19,000 persons employed in Crawley New Town— 12,000 in industry, 5,000 in non-industrial lines, and 2,000 in building and civil engineering—and of these an estimated 3,500 lived outside the town and commuted to work.[49]

Shops, schools, and other community facilities within the new towns are generally impressive, although there was some discontent about the slowness with which these were provided. As of 1961, each of the new towns around London could boast on the average 18 new schools, nearly 200 new shops, and various other services —fire stations, post offices, clinics, libraries, and perhaps a cinema and a dance hall. Housing and neighborhood development have generally respected high standards.

Some critics have commented that the new towns have not gone far enough, that they have not been able to absorb overspill from London at a sufficiently rapid rate, that they are unduly limited in number (one forceful criticism suggests the London Region needs another 10 or 12 new towns within 80 miles[50]), and that they should be tied in to an effective and continuing program of regional planning.

Others have held that the new towns are too small, isolated, and dull. Several new towns have, in fact, been encouraged to grow larger than the 50,000 maximum originally envisaged. The latest proposal is for Basildon, for example, to reach 100,000 or more. Harlow, Hemel Hempstead, and Stevenage are each expected to grow through natural increase to about 80,000 persons.[51] The London County Council designed and unsuccessfully sought permission to build a new town at Hook, in Hampshire, that would have been compact and urban in character, with about 100,000 in population.[52]

The Greater London Plan also called for the controlled expansion of selected towns in the Outer Country Ring and in other more distant sections of South-Eastern England. This complementary program aimed to relocate more than 400,000 persons—even more than the new towns.

Immediately following the war the London County Council, responding to great political pressures, built a series of housing projects out of the County but generally within, or in an extension of, the Conurbation (some were questionably sited in the Green Belt Ring). But it was not until the passage of the Town Development Act of 1952 that the expanded town program was formally inaugurated. The mechanics, involving joint responsibilities by the counties and districts within which the expansion was to occur and by the counties (particularly the London County Council) from which families were to be exported, proved cumbersome and things moved discouragingly slowly during the 'fifties. Sympathetic critics have held that insufficient money and legal controls were available for attracting industrial employment to the towns being expanded.[53]

Nevertheless, the program has been gaining momentum. Basingstoke, for example, under an agreement between the London County Council and the Hampshire County Council, is to raise its population from 24,000 to 74,000 by providing new housing and by encouraging light industry and new offices.[54] Some dozen or more similar schemes for decentralizing London are in operation, and, all told, negotiations have been underway in some 17 counties.[55]

How much have the new-town and the expanded-town programs contributed to the controlled deconcentration of population and employment from inner London? Much of the emptying out of central London and the migration to the suburbs would have occurred anyway. Only about two-fifths of the increase in population of the Outer Country Ring from 1952 to 1961 was accounted for by the five new towns there. (See Table 6.) Perhaps the importance of the new towns is more in controlling the form of suburban development and in purposefully decentralizing industrial employment than in absorbing overspilling population from the center.

The Greater London Plan envisaged a total dispersal or overspill of $1\frac{1}{4}$ million persons. This was to be distributed roughly as follows:[56]

Into the Green Belt Ring: for quasi-satellite communities, mainly by the LCC		125,000
Into the Outer Country Ring or into Ring within 40–50 miles from the center of London		1,025,000
8 new (satellite) towns	385,000	
Planned additions to existing towns	425,000	
Individualistic movement	215,000	
Dispersed beyond the metropolitan influence		100,000
Total		1,250,000

Abercrombie anticipated that about five-sixths of the redistribution would be by planned means and only about one-sixth (the 215,000 "individualistic" figure) would be private in character. This reflected the then prevalent outlook that dispersal to the outer suburbs was to be accomplished predominantly by direct, planned efforts.

The following summary of the kinds and magnitudes of decentralization that have actually taken place relies particularly upon A. G. Powell's succinct accounting for 1952–1958; estimated figures for the postwar period through 1960 are the writer's. The estimated decentralization beyond the Greater London Conurbation but within the larger London Region follows:

	1952–1958[57]		1945–1960[58]	
Planned schemes		175,000		295,000
New towns	120,000		180,000	
LCC estates beyond the Conurbation	45,000		105,000	
Expanded towns	10,000		10,000 (with agreements to accommodate 82,000)	
Private development		180,000		285,000
Total decentralization		355,000		580,000

Clearly, an impressive amount of decentralization has taken place. Of striking importance is the much larger role for private housing than was anticipated in the Greater London Plan; it has provided nearly half the new units. Correspondingly, planned decentralization has accounted for slightly over half of the total. New towns have accommodated only 31 per cent of the decentralized population, although three-fifths of the planned overspill.

Transportation and Commuting

Proposals for improving the transportation system for Greater London have been almost uniformly orthodox—more or less *ad hoc* extensions of the prewar system whose details need not be elaborated here. The transportation system is highly relevant to this review, however, for the deconcentration proposals with which we have been dealing relate directly to its general features and to the pattern of daily trips depending on it.

Under the rationale of improving living conditions, it was held that employment should be conveniently accessible. The new towns, as we have explained, were to be rather self-sufficient, providing full employment opportunities for local workers. Abercrombie made the point forcefully in a paper prepared in the midst of his work on the two plans: "The chief object of planning should be to reduce the daily travelling backwards and forwards to and from work. The less travelling to work the better." [59]

Although the bulk of the proposals relating to transportation were long delayed or never carried out at all, particularly because limited public funds were judged to be more urgently needed for other purposes, some improvements have been carried to completion. Several of the main line railways have been electrified or are undergoing electrification; trackage has been added to handle a greater volume of traffic. At least one underground line has been lengthened. These changes have somewhat added to passenger capacity and schedules on radial lines to and from the center of London.

Major road improvements have been limited, particularly in the inner parts of the Region. The two arterial rings proposed in the advisory plans have never been built. Virtually none of the planned arterial radial routes have been constructed. One motorway* from Birmingham has been completed, but only to the outer limits of the Greater London Conurbation, and connections into central London are lacking. Construction of a second motorway from the west is underway. Neither of these was recom-

---

* *Motorway* is the equivalent of American *freeway* or *expressway*.

mended in its present form by the Greater London Plan, although radial connections in one pattern or another were recognized as necessary for full access between London and other parts of Britain. Road improvements or not, the relentless increase in the use of automobiles has brought highway travel increasingly to the fore, and automobiles also provide a supplementary mode of travel between home and public transport station.

The full force of this increasing reliance on cars was not adequately anticipated by the advisory plans. The County of London Plan did assume that "within a few years" the ratio of cars to population would be two or three times the 1938 ratio of 1 to 22.[60] This would have been 1 to 11 or 1 to 7. By 1960, the actual ratio was about 1 to 9 for Britain as a whole, but about 1 to 5 within the London Region. The Greater London Plan made no forecast, but suggested that trends were "not likely in the long run to lead to a reduction in the number of cars . . . ; it is probable that speed and numbers will both be increased." [61]

The road improvements of the Greater London Plan were characteristically of the by-pass variety. Even the major system of radial and ring arterial roads was designed particularly to keep traffic from having to travel through London if it could be shunted around the outside.* All in all, the advisory plans by no means communicated any sense of urgency as to what was to hit the London Region within twenty years.

The suburbanization of resident population, already profiled, was accompanied by a considerable dispersal of employment opportunities. The new towns provide the most dramatic examples of planned industrial dispersal, but employment has grown at rapid rates in other outer communities as well. To a considerable degree, then, the Abercrombie goal of decentralizing both workers and jobs was being accomplished.

But what was not counted on was the marked rise in employment in central London, mainly in office buildings that were being constructed in significant volume. Centrally located jobs could be linked with suburban residents only by lengthening commuter trips. And lengthen they have. Mrs. Ruth Glass has stressed that up to 1951, at least, almost 70 per cent of all workers living in the

---

* This was also a bypass period of freeway and highway design in the United States.

County of London worked in their own borough or an adjacent one and that 62 per cent of workers in the rest of the Conurbation were similarly employed, thus indicating a preponderance of short-trip commuting;[62] but it is also evident that a heavy and growing volume of workers flow into central London every workday and that this is taxing already overcrowded transportation facilities to the utmost. From 1921 to 1951, the number of workers commuting into central London from outside of the County of London rose from about 400,000 to more than 600,000—from a third to one-half of all employed centrally[63]—and, although 1961 Census findings are not yet available, the trend seems to be continuing.

Moreover, various shifts have occurred in the shares borne by the several modes of transportation handling this mass of commuters. Comparable prewar figures are lacking; the situation from 1952 to date is summarized in Table 11. In the nine years to 1961,

TABLE 11

PERSON TRIPS INTO CENTRAL LONDON 7–10 A.M.,
BY MODE OF TRANSPORTATION, 1952–1961
(In thousands)

	1952		1956		1960		1961	
	Number	Per Cent	Number	Per Cent	Number	Per Cent	Number	Per Cent
British Railways	382	32.2	414	33.6	453	35.0	478	36.2
Underground	453	38.1	469	38.1	506	39.1	514	38.8
Buses	286	24.1	259	21.1	215	16.6	208	15.7
Total Public Transportation	1,121	94.2	1,142	92.8	1,174	90.7	1,200	90.7
Automobiles	45	3.8	65	5.2	87	6.7	92	7.0
Other[a]	24	2.0	24	2.0	33	2.6	31	2.3
Total Private Transportation	69	5.8	89	7.2	120	9.3	123	9.3
Total	1,190	100.0	1,231	100.0	1,294	100.0	1,323	100.0

SOURCE: Planning Office, London Transport Executive. Pedestrian entrants not included.
a "Other" in 1952 included 8,000 by motor cycles and scooters and 16,000 by bicycles; in 1961, 21,000 by motor cycles and scooters and 10,000 by bicycles.

the average number of British Railways passengers into central London during the three morning peak hours increased by nearly 100,000, from 32 to 36 per cent of all persons transported into the center. The underground increased its daily load of entrants by about 60,000, but held essentially constant the proportion it carried. Buses have reduced their passenger loads and have registered a significant proportional loss, from 24 per cent of all entrants in 1952 to 16 per cent in 1961. Entrants by automobiles, as might be expected, doubled in the course of nine years; but, since the number of automobile entrants was small initially, this reflected an increase of only a little over 20,000 and a percentage increase from less than 4 per cent to 7 per cent.

Rail transportation—the railways and the underground together —strengthened their carrying record, from about 70 per cent in 1952 to 75 per cent in 1961. This reaffirms other indications that the number of long-distance commute trips to the center has been markedly on the increase. Private transportation increased its share slightly, from about 6 per cent to over 9 per cent. Considering the great gain in automobile ownership in the London Region, the modesty of the commuting share suggests that congestion and parking problems in central London have discouraged greater reliance on the private car.

A Summary Review

Considering London's vital importance as a metropolis, it is natural enough that the forces impinging on its postwar development were to prove so powerful. Full employment, affluence, population growth, and London's attractiveness for business, government and households—these and other forces have been relentlessly translated into demands for space in the London Region. Similar forces and space demands, it might be noted, have also been at work in the United States and other western industrialized nations.

The advisory plans sought to crystallize and to synthesize various policies bearing on London's pattern of growth. The plans and policies approved by central government and passed on for local authorities to carry out were to serve as guides for channeling the diverse development forces. As things have turned out, much of the thinning out of inner London was helped along by attractive pulls to the suburbs. If anything, the advisory plans underestimated the force of such trends. In contrast, however, other highly significant patterns have gained in prominence—trends that by no means conform to the assumptions and the policies outlined by the advisory plans. These deserve brief restatement.

1. The outer ring of the Greater London Plan Region and the remainder of an even larger ring comprising a functionally more realistic contemporary London Region have gained in both population and employment on a scale and at a rate clearly in excess of that envisaged by the Greater London Plan. From 1952 to 1960 the total Regional Ring gained 421,000 employed persons, an increase of 47 per cent; from 1952 to 1961 this Ring added 891,000 residents, a 26 per cent gain.

2. An even larger, irregularly shaped, outer band comprising the rest of South-Eastern England gained, during this same nine-year period, an additional 390,000 population. While only an 8 per cent increase, this represented a rate double that for England and Wales exclusive of the South-East. Employment, however, did not increase for this South-Eastern England Ring as rapidly as in the country as a whole.

3. A marked and unanticipated increase in employment in central London, accompanying a rash of office construction, amounted to 173,000 additional employed workers in the eight-year period to 1960.

4. These selective increases in residents and employed persons —selective because large parts of the Greater London Conurbation actually lost population and employment—have contributed to net increases for the London Region and for South-Eastern England as a whole that clearly fly in the face of assumptions and policies very much at the heart of the advisory plans. In the past eight or nine years the London Region has gained more than 600,000 employed persons and nearly 700,000 residents. The employment increase seems even more significant when the Region's 12 per cent rise is viewed against a national rate of 7 per cent and a rate of 6 per cent for England and Wales outside of South-Eastern England.

5. The outward residential movement reflects, in part, the proposals of the advisory plans for planned overspill. Nearly 300,000 persons have been moved in accordance with various planned schemes to portions of the expanding London Region outside the built-up districts of the Conurbation. But it also reflects a much higher volume of private residential construction than was planned for—nearly half of all decentralization in contrast to the sixth suggested in the Greater London Plan. Neither the private resi-

dential developments nor the London County Council housing estates provided as much employment opportunity as had been hoped for; these new residents became commuters to employment centers, many of which remained within the Conurbation and even in central London.

6. This divergence between residential out movement and employment distribution was, in fact, compounded by the loss within the County of London of some 180,000 residents. In consequence, already differing ratios of employment to population have been even further exaggerated, as shown by these ratios:[64]

	Employees Per 1,000 Population		1952–1960	
	1952	1960	Change in Ratio	Per Cent Change
Administrative County of London	762	866	+104	+13.7
Conurban Ring	368	364	−4	−1.1
Regional Ring	319	315	−4	−2.7
Rest of South-Eastern England	617	401	−16	−3.8

7. This development has been accompanied by an increase in commuting trips from suburban areas to central London. Passengers entering the central area of London between 7 and 10 each morning increased by more than 100,000 from 1952 to 1960. The most important increases were accounted for by users of trains and private automobiles, tied to longer commuting trips. Even as early as 1951, more than 100,000 central-area workers lived outside the Conurbation, and this number has been on the rise.

8. The continuing build-up of employment opportunities in central London and in the Conurbation more generally has supported population growth and consequent heavy pressures for additional residential development within the Conurbation or beyond the Metropolitan Green Belt where land is more readily available. Proposals in the past several years to extend the Metropolitan Green Belt outward have raised afresh questions as to the function of the Green Belt. And there remain difficult questions as to how this new development in the outer rings of the London Region and the South-Eastern England Region shall be organized. We shall return to these questions later.

Chapter 6

Modifying Major Plans
and Policies

Constructive changes in plans and programs depend on accurate forecasts of the direction and magnitude of the socio-economic changes they refer to. With shifts in the conditions assumed, forecasts in turn require modification. And these changing conditions and altered forecasts, together with the fresh identification of problems, may lead to revisions in policies and plans. How do such revisions come about?

Development Plans as Vehicles for Policy Revision

The major device for accomplishing periodic resurvey of conditions and review and modification of plans and policy in Britain is the five-year review of the development plan. This review was stipulated in the 1947 Act and has, accordingly, been administered by the Ministry of Housing and Local Government. The essentials of the review process are coming to be well understood, for all of the local authorities in the London Region either have submitted their first five-year reviews or are in the process of so doing.[1]

There are limits, however, to what a revision of development plans can reasonably be expected to accomplish. Unquestionably, it is valuable for a local authority to restudy its situation and to revise and clarify its development plan. Changed indicators of trends, shifting priorities of the relative seriousness of problems, altered policies on the part of the central government, changing outlooks by officials and citizens in local areas—all of these can be taken into account in the course of reëxamining the present and probable future state of affairs.

But perhaps the most serious deficiency is at a metropolitan regional level, at which the Greater London Plan (in complementing the County and City of London plans) was designed to be operative. Since the London Plan Region is divided into nine local planning authorities, the advisory plans and central government's policy pronouncements provide the integrative backdrop. If the development plans are generally to follow overall policy limits as prescribed by the Ministry and largely crystallized by the advisory plans, then is merely revising the development plans an adequate substitute for carefully reconsidering the advisory plans as such?

The Ministry's initial statements of expectations regarding the first five-year reviews were not reassuring. The local authorities were to keep within the time period of the initial plans. A local authority was not necessarily to make an entire resurvey, being admonished to focus on those parts of the resurvey most relevant to the main problems of the area.[2] The Permanent Secretary of the Ministry in the autumn of 1959 stated:

We do not expect these first reviews to suggest any revolutionary alterations except where the pressure of events or some major local change has thrust on the planning authority the need to revise its ideas now; though we do expect some additions to be made to the first Plans in the way especially of town maps for overspill areas, and green belts round some of the larger provincial cities. But we do not believe that the first review could or should be the occasion for a complete re-examination of the foundations of the Plans.[3]

If modest revisions were the order of the day, this was not to preclude more thorough-going reviews at later dates.

By 1960, however, the Ministry realized that development pressures were rapidly growing more serious. Local authorities were directed to extend their plans up to 1981 and were thus indirectly encouraged to undertake more thorough-going reviews.[4] Some planning authorities have, as a result, been involved in more radical revisions than had been contemplated under the earlier Ministry directives.

In some respects the development plan lends itself to being an effective policy crystallizer and communicator. If the written statement is clear, it can communicate main policies. For example, the statement submitted by the London County Council as a portion of its first review is admirably lucid. It stresses main principles. And, by a distinctive printing that shows additions and deletions in full, the reader learns exactly what is being changed in the text of the statement. After repeating the three main parts of national policy for London—*i.e.,* restraining London's population and industrial growth, instituting a planned program of decentralization, and patterning this decentralization in accord with advisory plan principles—the Council's statement offers the following amendment of major policy:

The proposals for the first review are intended to secure the further implementation of this policy. However, the restraint of office development, particularly in the centre of London, has come to be considered at least as important as the restraint of industry. It is the Council's intention to implement further the policy of decentralization by exercising its powers of planning control, and encouraging dispersal throughout the region, so as (a) to restrict the further growth of employment opportunities in the congested centre, and (b) to encourage the retention and creation of residential accommodation in the heart of London.[5]

This paragraph, standing out in italics, states the rising concern about office development in no uncertain terms, and provides an example of a major modification and clarification of the Council's proposed policy.

The development plan also gains strength as a policy carrier—and hence as a prospective policy reviser—because it is prepared only after careful consultation with officials in the Ministry and after taking into account all Ministry directives and other releases for clues as to current policy lines. The subsequent Ministerial review provides still another opportunity for ensuring modifications in line with central governmental policies. In short, the development plan is a joint product of local authorship and design and Ministerial guidance, approval and modification.

One further technical feature of the development plan may be noted. In counties other than the County of London, two levels of development plan are customary: the county map and the town map. The county map (at $1'' = 1$ mile) becomes an overall regional plan for that county, serving "as a broad instrument of policy, a backcloth against which the day-to-day control of applications to develop are measured and compared." [6] The county map provides an opportunity for determining and communicating "in which towns and villages extensive development is intended to take place" [7] without indicating the precise pattern of land use within towns. This county map is intermediate in its generalness, and is supplemented by more detailed town maps (at 6″ = 1 mile) for urban areas within the county. Each town map indicates with far greater precision what land uses are to be developed or allowed on which portions of land.

But in other respects the development plan appears ill-suited to its role as policy carrier. Its standardized and technical symbols tend to be stilted and jargonish. It is very much a legal instrument. Even the county-map plans carry this tone, despite their greater generality. One may look in vain at a county development plan or an assemblage of such plans for a larger region for a broad impression of big ideas.

Within the Ministry, it is readily possible, and to some degree customary, to assemble contiguous development plans for an entire region such as that around London. Studies and the reports based on them tend, however, to be technical and often confidential. They are rarely circulated to political leaders and interested citizens. The Ministry, for example, has the full picture relating to the entire Metropolitan Green Belt and the exact status of proposals for expanding it. The citizen sees but one development plan at a time or a much simplified Green Belt diagram adapted for publication.

The Relative Initiative of Central and Local Government

Central government in Britain is expected to lay down, and periodically to revise, policy as to directions and standards to which local governmental plans and programs are to adhere.[8] By and large it is agreed that the local authorities will assume the main initiative. The Ministry's role is to examine planning and development proposals once they have been formulated.

Each local unit of government understandably proceeds in terms of its own interests and problems, and it becomes the central government's responsibility to exercise policy leadership, to inform local governments as to policy matters, and to discuss possible implications of these policies for the local area in question. As Dame Evelyn Sharp put it:

There is two-way traffic in this. I do not want to imply that [initiative] is purely for local authorities, and the Ministry can sit back until the local authority comes up with something. Plainly that would not be so. Even if you had a perfectly shaped local governmental organisation for this purpose the Ministry would still have an important contribution in making suggestions to the local planning authority for reconsideration of the way the policies were developing, which would entail some revision of the plan at the Ministry end as well as at the other end. . . .[9]

While a tradition of local initiative is encouraged, central government's own leadership responsibilities are recognized.

The construct of central government as policy formulator and of local government as initiator is, in effect, a model of benevolent partnership. How does the relation work out in practice? What are the respective responsibilities for altering significant planning policy?

A central government ministry seldom openly declares that it is proposing a major shift of policy in advance of specific problem situations requiring resolution in terms of such policy. Ministry officials tend, instead, to distribute suggested alterations in procedures, to drop hints that the minister would look favorably upon such-and-such proposal coming from a local authority, and, through considerable reliance on informal consultation, to discuss changed conditions and their implications for the authority in question. Thus, somewhat indirectly, the ministry may be instrumental in suggesting to a local authority that it prepare and submit a formal proposal or request. This informal consultation tends to blur the respective responsibilities of central and local government, and each level of government can claim, if it wishes, credit for recommending a policy direction.

Initiative for exploring needed policy revision varies, at the local level, with the authority. The London County Council, unique among local governments in its size and technical competency, has undoubtedly been a driving influence, self-confident in its know-how, convinced of the maturity of its policies, and eager to explore new ideas for controlling development. Other authorities have a far less effective record of initiative.

The role of the Ministry of Housing and Local Government, on the other hand, has undoubtedly varied over time. Some outside observers have suggested that the Ministry has been less vigorous in its initiative during the 'fifties than it had been in the tumultuous 'forties, and that on some matters the Ministry has tended to sit back, merely reacting to proposals and pressures from elsewhere.

The Case of Office Development in Central London

The respective reactions of the Ministry and the London County Council to the serious, unanticipated problem of controlling office development in central London illustrate the relationship of their recent roles in a situation of great concern to both.

As we mentioned earlier, the heavy bombings which demolished many office buildings and wiped out six million square feet of office space in the one-square-mile City of London alone, forced many office-based organizations to move out of central London.[10] In the years during and immediately following the war, building controls, mainly related to material shortages and to construction priorities granted to housing, factories, and schools, prevented the rebuilding of offices. Some bulk-zoning and daylighting controls were also fashioned after the war. Both plot-ratio controls (regulating the ratio of floor area within a building to the ground area of its plot) and daylighting controls (prescribing a method for testing the position, height, and massing of a proposed building to ensure sufficient daylight to its faces and those of adjacent buildings) were put into effect.[11]

As of mid-1954, when building controls were removed, a general policy of restricting London's growth was in effect but lacked firm supporting restrictions on the central construction of new buildings and the growth of office employment. At the time, this did not appear to be of any general concern; almost no speeches, papers, or reports explicitly identified or dealt with this major loophole in the control system by which London was to be contained. A few mild or indirect warnings had been sounded before 1954: the Holden-Holford reports in 1946 and 1947 to the City

Corporation stressed the necessity for controls; the *Advisory Handbook on the Redevelopment of Central Areas* published by the Ministry in 1947 also recommended the use of a floor-space index. Internal memoranda by the London Technical Branch of the Ministry in 1953 and 1954 warned that nonindustrial (office-type) employment in London was likely to increase at a scale not known.[12]

The staff of the London County Council's Town Planning Division was also beginning to sense that a problem might be imminent. One member of the staff, Walter Manthorpe, in June, 1954, completed a thesis dealing with this subject in the Department of Town Planning, University College, University of London, which he then condensed into an article in the November issue of the *Journal of the Royal Institute of Chartered Surveyors*.[13] He stressed that increase in office employment would, unless controlled, vitiate the overall policy for containing London's growth. He recommended thorough study and a program of firmer controls to prevent the overconcentration of offices, through licensing and plot ratios, and the encouragement of planned dispersal. Presumably the article enjoyed wide circulation. At about this time, the Ministry, feeling its way, prevailed upon the City Corporation to survey the amount of office space already approved for construction, and findings were reported back to the Ministry in the spring of 1955.

During this period, the County of London development plan, submitted in 1951, was still formally before the Minister. A public inquiry had been held and some 7,000 individual objectors had been heard. It remained for the Minister to issue his approval of the plan, with such amendments as he considered necessary in view of the objections heard. Meanwhile, it was not practicable—because of the Minister's quasi-judicial position vis-à-vis the public*—for the Ministry to discuss with the London County Council the implications of the new office-space problem, which materially affected that development plan.

When the Minister issued his decision on the plan early in 1955, he did, however, draw attention to the major problem which was

---

* The Minister must temper his advocacy of principles and programs by fairly passing judgment on possible disputes or differences between local authorities or between a local authority and citizen interests.

building up in central London, and made such limited modifications to the plan as he could reasonably do at that late stage. He notified the chairman of the Town Planning Committee that he had transferred some 380 acres of land allocated for industrial, commercial, or office use to residential zoning, and would insist on strict restraints against changing residential property to other use (particularly in the Mayfair portion of the central area). The Town Planning Committee and the London County Council appear to have received the Minister's modifications in good grace.[14]

Then followed a series of negotiations between the Ministry and the London County Council from June through October, 1955. In these were involved Mr. Sandys, the Minister; various administrative officers from the Ministry; Mr. Kacirek, the Ministry's technical officer for the London area; Mr. Fiske, the chairman of the County Council's Town Planning Committee; Mr. Lane, the newly appointed Town Planning Officer for the County Council; and officers from the County Clerk's office. The Ministry proposed that both the County Council and the Ministry would benefit greatly from a full study of the situation, so as to project more accurately the likely volume of proposed office construction and the estimated employment this would represent. The local officials agreed to the study and proceeded with it.

At least two further important, confidential technical memoranda from the London Technical Branch within the Ministry followed, stressing the seriousness of the emerging trend in office growth and exploring the points at which controls could best be tightened. Revocation of some planning applications for office construction that had already been approved was considered, but top-level discussion between the County officers and the Minister and his officials demonstrated that the central government was not in a position to offer financial compensation to the firms affected (the normal compensation for revocations coming from local authority sources), and the idea was dropped. Tightening could apply only to applications yet to come.

Mr. Sandys, attacking the problem in earnest, made two significant policy speeches, one at the Annual Conference of Municipal Corporations in September, 1955, one before the Town Planning Institute's annual dinner, March, 1956.[15] The Minister's support of office decentralization was unequivocal.

Concurrently, as the London County Council's survey findings became known early in 1956, the Town Planning Committee of the Council, keeping the Ministry informed, decided to revise administrative controls. Plot ratios in the central area were to be generally reduced, but within certain West End districts higher plot ratios might be granted if the additional accommodation were for residential purposes. For example, if the reduced plot ratio were $3\frac{1}{2}$:1 (representing the nonresidential floor space permitted), a further $1\frac{1}{2}$:1 of residential floor space might also be permitted, to bring the total bulk up to 5:1. The Town Planning Committee also recommended reducing the area zoned for office building by 23 per cent; this reduction was in fact introduced as part of the first review of the development plan submitted in 1960.*

When Mr. Edmonds replaced Mr. Fiske as chairman of the Town Planning Committee in May, 1956, he jumped into the problem with zest. His Committee reported to the County Council in July that nearly 42 million square feet of new or converted office space had been approved between 1948 and 1955 and that firm measures would be needed to restrain further office construction and to reintroduce additional residential development.[16] Controls were refined, plot ratios were tightened, and the scheme of dual plot ratios was devised—these revised controls being approved by the County Council in July 1957.[17] At this time, having been cleared in advance with the Ministry, an explanatory report, *A Plan to Combat Congestion in Central London,* was given wide distribution by the London County Council.

The new line on this aspect of policy to contain London was soon recognized. People—both in and out of town and regional planning—widely acknowledged the problem of office concentration and the urgency of the new controls. Mr. Henry Brooke became the Minister early in 1957, and, although not championing the cause as Mr. Sandys had, he tended to support the policy, his periodic pronouncements reaffirming the Ministry's stand.

The Town and County Planning Association has also been active in urging office decentralization. It sponsored a significant conference in July, 1958, proposing a regional approach and positive

* See also p. 119 above for quotation expressing the change in policy by the London County Council.

lures to encourage firms voluntarily to decentralize their offices.[18] The Association followed this up by appointing a study committee. As a consequence of this committee's activity, the Association in March, 1962, issued a compact, informative report, *The Paper Metropolis*. The Association claims credit for helping to bring a climate of acceptance for office decentralization, but it is difficult to weigh the Association's relative influence in this regard.

In January, 1960, a motion presented in the House of Commons proposed that the Government extend the industrial development certificate scheme to office development, but it was not passed. The Minister opposed such an extension, arguing that office buildings, unlike factory buildings, are usually put up by developers for rental to others and, in advance of occupancy by these renters, it would be difficult to know whether the occupation should be permitted.[19] The Minister also sent letters during November, 1960, to about 200 large London firms, requesting that they explore the possibility of decentralizing their office staffs.

The Ministry and the London County Council have, then, both displayed initiative as they faced up to the problem of office development. The Ministry, acting both formally and informally, affirmed the policy of preventing undue concentration in London, interpreted this as including the control of excessive office construction in central London, and urged the London County Council to undertake a survey of the evolving situation as a basis for firmer implementation measures. The London County Council, with its strong political leadership and excellent technical staff, was already becoming sensitive to the problem. It evolved the main modifications in control and, after consultation with the Ministry, put them into effect. Despite diverse and powerful political and developmental pressures, the London County Council acted with resourcefulness and firmness.[20]

The Impact of Changing Central-Government Policies

Many of the most important changes in national policy have been directed toward town planning throughout England and Wales and, to a significant degree, toward substantive ends other than those of town planning as such. Many of these changes have significant implications for the planning of the London Region, but their impact has often been somewhat indirect.

Various amendments to the Town and Country Planning Act during the 'fifties, although directed toward planning generally, have affected planning for the London Region. These amendments have tended to weaken planning and to place increased reliance on the market mechanism. It has become more expensive to procure land for public use and more difficult to channel the strong initiative passed on to private developers.[21]

High in importance are the varied aspects of fiscal policy and fiscal control. The character of subsidies for housing, the form in which block grants are made available to local governments, the outlook toward major highway construction programs, the ways in which the rating system* are maintained or altered—these and other policies, reflecting the economic health of the nation and the dominant political philosophy, have contributed to the strengthening or weakening of town and regional planning.

The central government continues to be highly influential through its own capital expenditures and through its control of private capital investment. The determination, for example, to concentrate or deconcentrate the construction of major governmental office buildings may have had profound—though, to date, unstudied—impact on the growth and spatial patterning of London. The decision to relax or to enforce more tightly the location of industrial structures bears importantly on the London situation.

Recommendations of the Royal Commission

During recent years no single organization has been charged with planning the London Region and with comprehending and taking into account the implications of various trends and policies as they bear on the Region. Largely because of this deficiency, a Royal Commission on Local Government in Greater London was appointed in December, 1957, to explore the situation. Chaired by Sir Edwin Herbert, it was directed "To examine the present system and working of local government in the Greater London area; to recommend whether any, and if so what, changes in the local government structure and the distribution of local authority functions in the area, or in any part of it, would better secure effective and convenient local government. . . ." [22]

After nearly three years of study, visits to most of the local au-

---

* *Rates* in Britain comprise a form of *property tax,* as Americans use the term.

thorities within the Review Area (slightly larger than the Greater London Conurbation),* and an exhaustive series of hearings, the Commission presented its final report in October, 1960.[23] While the Commission had some dozen governmental functions to examine, it is no coincidence that town and country planning was the first function listed and that it absorbed more of the Commission's discussion than any other. The Commission hinged its most telling arguments for a reorganized government within the Review Area on the urgent need responsibly to revise planning policy for Greater London. The Commission was deeply concerned that Abercrombie's regional plan needed continuing reexamination and, as necessary, formal review and modification.

In summarizing the postwar situation, the Herbert Commission explained that "present policy is enshrined in the Greater London Plan as accepted and modified in the Minister's Memorandum" [24] and that there has been no satisfactory mechanism for any comprehensive modification of Greater London Plan policy. The Commission asserted that the nine development plans covering the Review Area "only add up to a plan for Greater London insofar as it was known in advance that a development plan was unlikely to receive approval by the Minister if it conflicted in any substantial degree with the Greater London Plan. . . ." [25] And, it concluded: "No single body, whether within central government or within local government, is charged with the responsibility for making continuous surveys of land availability, population movements, housing requirements, traffic problems, industrial and commercial development, and the many other matters which affect the Review Area as a whole. No body therefore is charged with the duty of constantly watching and assessing the effect of changing circumstances on the Greater London Plan, which is still accepted as the basic conception in planning." [26]

The report showed that present arguments for the *status quo* build on two assertions: (1) The Greater London Plan is still fully adequate as a policy carrier and does not need serious reconsideration. (2) Such studies as may be necessary to review and to reconsider Greater London Plan policies require the initiative of the central government. The Commission carefully considered these assertions and found them untenable.

* See pp. 74-75 above.

The presuppositions of the Greater London Plan are by no means being realized, the Commission found. In the growth of its economy and its resident and working population, Greater London has shown a far greater vitality than was envisaged in the plan. Commercial developments were not accurately anticipated. The transportation measures proposed by the plan have not been carried out, and congestion has materially worsened. The Commission concluded with this strong statement:

We have no hesitation in finding as a fact that the presuppositions of the Greater London Plan require early reconsideration, and that this can only be done, so far as the Review Area is concerned, by some body which has the statutory duty of examining the Review Area as a whole and planning accordingly. It will clearly have to be the duty of such a body to have a properly organised intelligence staff. . . . It is nobody's business to collect [needed information], analyse it, keep it up-to-date and find out what is really happening or is likely to happen in Greater London. . . .[27]

The Commission went on to assert that the body charged with keeping the equivalent of the Greater London Plan up to date should be within local government, rejecting "the view of the local planning authorities [favoring present governmental organization] that their business is simply to implement government policy as laid down in the Minister's Memorandum of 1947 and that if the central government want that policy changed it is for central government to take the initiative." [28] The Commission explained that in the early 'forties the Ministry necessarily initiated the advisory plans because no satisfactory framework for local plan preparation existed. But the situation had materially changed. There was a system of development plans by which local authorities could plan. And the Ministry had taken on various appellate functions. In the Commission's words: "We do not see how the Minister could properly, having regard for his duties under the 1947 Act, commission what in effect would be a review of existing development plans, express his opinion on such a review, and at the same time preserve his quasi-judicial position." [29]

That Greater London had become so distinctively large and complex did not seem to the Commission to vitiate its fundamental right to maintain self-government. But what form of self-government? This is the crucial question with which the Commission was confronted. Sir Edwin Herbert and his colleagues considered four major solutions: (1) central government may assume responsibility for certain functions; (2) *ad hoc* authorities may be created to handle particular functions; (3) consultation among local authorities and between their officers can provide a mechanism for dealing with problems; and (4) some form of local authority with a geographic area at conurban or metropolitan scale is needed. The Commission concluded in favor of the fourth.

In the Commission's recommendations for reorganized local government, the primary unit would be a new structure, a Greater London Borough. Each such borough would have a population between 100,000 and 250,000. In most instances, a new borough would consolidate two or three existing boroughs or urban districts. The Greater London Borough scheme would keep local government "close to the people" while providing units large enough to handle functions effectively and to attract competent professional officers. These new boroughs, 52 in number, were to handle housing, personal health, welfare and children's services, environmental health (other than refuse disposal), roads (other than main roads), and libraries.

The scheme also called for creation of a Council for Greater London supplementing the boroughs. This Council would cover the Review Area (with slight modifications), comprising the main built-up portions of Greater London and extending well into the Metropolitan Green Belt. To this new level of local government would be assigned "functions which can only be or can be better performed over a wider area [than the borough]." [30] The Council would serve as planning authority and education authority, with responsibility for policy formulation, while the executive work would fall mainly to the boroughs. Other Council functions would include main roads, traffic management, refuse disposal, and fire and ambulance services. Concurrent or supplementary functions would include housing, provision of parks, open spaces, and cultural and entertainment facilities, main sewerage and sewage disposal, and land drainage. The Council would be elected, with one member for each of the 109 parliamentary divisions within the Council's area.[31]

As Professor W. A. Robson and other informed critics have

shown, the Royal Commission's reform proposals reflect the logical extension of principles of local government long in existence, particularly the arrangements by which the administrative County of London was itself created for what was in 1888 relatively as large an area as is now being proposed for the Greater London Council.[32] The political correspondent for *The Times* put it succinctly: "The conviction grew inside the commission that if London does not reorganize its local government, then local government in London may have to give way in vital respects to central government. So it is that they feel the apparent revolutionary form of their report expresses no more than the historic process of change in modern terms." [33]

With respect to town and country planning, the Royal Commission

discerns three basic elements . . . each of which requires a different type of administration. These are:

(i) The need to preserve and improve local amenity, which is essentially a local function;

(ii) the need to plan for Greater London as a whole, which should be the function of some authority acting for the whole of the Review area, and

(iii) the need to hold the balance in terms of national policy between each region, which is properly the function of the Minister.[34]

The Council for Greater London would manage the second function and be responsible for the continuing analysis and the periodic revision of the policy initially formulated in the Greater London Plan. The Commission concluded—indeed, virtually assumed—that the preparation and periodic revision of one development plan for the Greater London area would provide the full equivalent of keeping the Greater London Plan under revision. There may well be a question as to whether the development plan, as a type of plan, is adequate for this task of major policy revision—a problem we shall discuss in detail shortly.

The Greater London Council would also act upon all applications for the extraction of minerals. The Council would have direct jurisdiction over a central area of London, the exact geographic limits to be determined. In special cases the Minister would have power to require that applications be referred to him.

The boroughs, on the other hand, would consider all other applications for planning permission. Under policy established by the Council's development plan, the boroughs would administer planning control. If an application were to involve a departure from the development plan, it would, at the determination of the borough, be forwarded for consideration by the Council.

Governmental Reorganization: Subsequent Developments

It is not surprising that the Commission's report evoked strong reactions. In the Commission's own words, each of the major political parties "was quite legitimately thinking in terms of electoral advantage." [35] The London Labour Party in the counties of London and Middlesex has, for example, remained adamantly opposed to the reorganization, for it would displace the London County Council, a Labour stronghold, and the political mix of the proposed Greater London Council would probably be such that, over time, some rotation of parties in power might come to pass.

While some critics were upset because they have felt the Commission went too far, others have argued that the Commission by no means went far enough. Some have been convinced that regional problems in the larger area around Greater London—perhaps embracing most of South-Eastern England—were not adequately met by the Commission's proposals. A committee of the Town Planning Institute stated that regional planning (along with a regional authority or government) was needed rather than the local governmental Council for Greater London.[36] The Greater London Group of faculty members of the London School of Economics and Political Science, whose earlier memoranda had been highly influential as evidence to the Royal Commission, suggested that the Greater London Council "should be associated with the Home Counties in a joint planning board which would work in close cooperation with the regional offices of Government departments." [37]

The size and number of the proposed Greater London Boroughs also elicited reactions. Many local authorities, representing historically important communities, have expressed strong resistance to a forced amalgamation with nearby local areas. Some critics, including the faculty Greater London Group, have claimed that the boroughs would be too small to function as fully competent political and administrative units and too numerous to make for as simple a coverage within Greater London as they judged desirable. They have expressed fears that functions outstandingly handled by the London County Council and its competent staff would by no means be equally well carried out by a dispersed set of smaller local authorities. What, for example, would happen to the distinctive competence that has come to be traditionally associated with the London County Council's Architect's Department? [38]

After careful study of the Royal Commission report and of the views of the local authorities and other commentators, the Government issued a White Paper in November, 1961, declaring its support, in broad principle, of the Commission's recommendations.[39] The Government added certain qualifications to its support, however. First, the boroughs ought to be larger, with a minimum population of about 200,000, and hence fewer. Second, a special education authority should cover roughly 2 million residents in central London, while outside of this central area education would be the direct responsibility of the new boroughs. The Government further expressed the view that the Greater London Council's powers with respect to planning and housing ought to be fairly strong, including powers to supplement borough councils' powers to carry out comprehensive redevelopment and to arrange for overspill housing.

Still further study by the Ministry of Housing and Local Government and recommendations by four town clerks from outside the London Region have resulted in Government support, as of August, 1962, for a revised grouping of 32 London Boroughs.[40] As shown in Figure 9, this proposed pattern[41] excludes several outer districts that had been part of the Royal Commission's Review Area.* The Minister also announced that the Government proposed to adopt the present area of the Administrative County of London as the central education area.[42]

The urgency of dealing with changing conditions and of peri-

---

* The original Review Area contained about 840 square miles; this was reduced to about 760 square miles in the Royal Commission's recommendations for the Greater London Council area; another 130 square miles were deleted by a Ministry announcement in May, 1962. Thus, the current proposal is for a Greater London Council to encompass about 630 square miles, only three-fourths of the initial Review Area.

FIGURE 9

THE PROPOSED GOVERNMENTAL STRUCTURE FOR GREATER LONDON

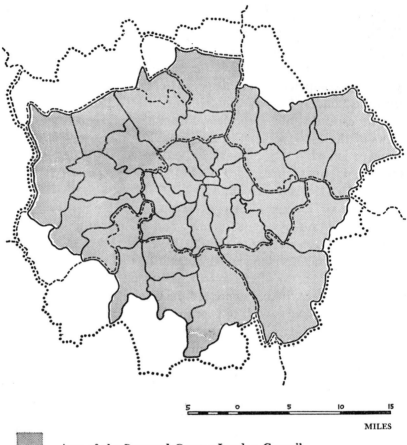

MILES

Area of the Proposed Greater London Council
Proposed London Borough Boundaries
Review Area of the Royal Commission on Local Government in
    Greater London
Existing County Boundaries

odically modifying the development policy guiding the growth
and rebuilding of Greater London has been clearly recognized by
the Royal Commission and by the Government in its subsequent
consideration of the Commission's report. Following up on its as-
sertion that it aimed "to make it possible for the new authorities
to be elected in the autumn of 1964, and to take over from the

existing authorities in April, 1965," [43] the Government, in December, 1963, introduced the London Government Bill into Parliament. Judging from the character of debates following its initial readings, the legislation seemed destined to move through without serious opposition.

PART III. Implications and Conclusions

Chapter 7

■
■   *Metropolitan Containment*
■   *as Policy*

The past twenty years have provided a drama in which, relentlessly, a firm set of ideas as to how Greater London should develop has been pitted against amazingly vigorous and essentially
unanticipated forces of growth and change. It is as if a strait-laced,
inner-directed Boston matron brought up in the New England of
yesterday were determined to "stick it out" amidst contemporary
kaleidoscopic transformations. But whereas the lady, if she prefers,
can disregard most of the main changes and settle for controlling
her own reactions and preserving a congenial immediate social environment, the Greater London Plan and the other advisory plans
have been expected to provide valid and practicable policy, by no
means disregarding the mainstream of things.

The Vitality of the London Region

London's continuing functional importance—as the seat of
the central government, as the locus of the finance-insurance-head-
quarters offices complex, as the dominant port, as an impressive
center for a set of expanding industries, as a transportation and
communications hub, and as the province of many professional
and highly specialized activities (art, law, medicine, etc.)—has
meant increased employment opportunities and, correspondingly,
a growing, though suburbanizing, resident population. Added to
this have been a disproportionately high demand for housing, a
lively interest in moving to the suburbs, a greatly increased ownership of automobiles, and an improved suburban railway service
—thus providing the essential ingredients for an "exploding
metropolis."

Examined more closely, the triggering of this expansion has

been the selective growth of particular activities, with consequent employment opportunities and relentless competition for favored geographic sites. Office-type enterprises have flourished, creating unprecedented demand for space in central London. A substantial number of thriving manufacturing firms have built new plants in outer London, particularly in a burgeoning ring outside of the Metropolitan Green Belt. For many reasons, including the impetus of wartime evacuation from central London, the outward movement of households has proceeded, largely voluntarily, at a pace that has fully matched the most visionary hopes of the decentrists and the targets of the Greater London Plan formulators.

This vigor has demonstrated the distinctive advantage of a great metropolitan community: that it can spark, service, and absorb unanticipated bursts of expanding activity. For the metropolis, if functioning effectively, can furnish the specialized technical assistance, the capital, the labor force, the many and varied services required, and often, a major part of the market. The metropolitan advantage lies particularly in the ready availability of facilities and services, offering what may technically be termed "external economies." But such spontaneous and market-oriented growth by its very nature is extremely difficult to forecast. In retrospect, it is not surprising that projections of modest or little growth for the Greater London Plan Region formulated in the early 'forties have proved quite unrealistic.

But evidences of this vigor also remind us that the same tendencies toward concentration in London and the surrounding region that were so central to the Barlow Commission years ago are still present. A reconvened Barlow Commission might find it important to focus on employment in much broader terms than it initially used. No one can deny the reality and, depending upon one's philosophy, the possible imbalance of the London Region's overwhelming concentration of specialized and headquarters activity, expertise, and talent.

Prospects for Future Growth

If the late 'thirties and early 'forties harbored a climate in which economic and demographic projections were, as it subsequently turned out, unduly low, the current period of considerable growth gives rise to forecasts for the next two or three decades that suggest anything but a static future.

Projections for the future have, in fact, tended to rise as each recent year has come along. In 1955 the Registrar General's office forecast for England and Wales 46.0 million persons as of 1970 and 46.4 million as of 1995; by 1960 these projections had risen to 48.0 million for 1970 and 55.6 million for the year 2000; and by the end of 1961, 58.3 million were forecast for forty years later.[1] In six years the forecast for the end of the century has risen by nearly 12 million.

Projections for the London Region (and particularly for the probable volume of overspill to the Regional Ring beyond the Conurbation) are now considerably higher than they were a few years ago, and we may anticipate reasonably lively growth during the next twenty years. In order to communicate something of the scale and pace of the growth likely to confront planners responsible for the London Region, we have assembled, and sought to make plausibly consistent internally, a set of projected population figures for component parts of the London Region and for England and Wales. We do not know all of the precise assumptions upon which the published sources have relied. Nor have we attempted to analyze possible alternative projections according to the mix of assumptions used. The rough magnitudes of possible growth follow:[2]

	Millions of Persons			
	1960	1980	Increase, 1960–1980	1980 Index (1960 = 100)
Administrative County of London	3.2	3.0	−0.2	94
Conurban Ring	5.0	5.0	—	100
Greater London Conurbation	8.2	8.0	−0.2	98
Regional Ring	4.2	6.2	2.0	148
London Region	12.4	14.2	1.8	115
Rest of South-Eastern England	5.1	5.3	0.2	104
South-Eastern England	17.5	19.5	2.0	111
Rest of England and Wales	28.3	30.9	2.6	109
England and Wales	45.8	50.4	4.6	110

This table suggests that 2 million (or 42 percent) of England and Wales' 4.6 million projected increase may be expected to fall within the outer ring of the London Region, giving the Region as a whole a probable rate of growth (15 per cent) in excess of that for England and Wales (10 per cent). These projections apparently assume that national policy will not effectively hold down the growth of the London Region.

Granting the relative magnitude of this projected growth of the London Region, it may be helpful to realize that even this increase is noticeably less than that currently projected for large American metropolitan regions:[3]

	Millions of Persons			
	1960	1980	Increase, 1960–1980	Percentage Increase, 1960–1980
London Region	12.4	14.2	1.8	15
New York Metropolitan Region	(1955) 15.1	(1975) 20.8	(1955–75) 5.7	(1955–75) 38
Chicago Consolidated Metropolitan Area	6.8	9.1	2.3	33
Los Angeles Standard Metropolitan Statistical Area	6.7	11.3	4.6	70

This suggests, of course, that the United States may be facing metropolitan growth and planning problems even more serious than Britain's.

Employment in the London Region is projected to increase at a rate at least as great as that for population, with a continued selectivity in migration such that the economically active age groups are attracted to and held by the Region.[4] The formation of households will, if anything, continue to outrun population increase. The consequent demand for housing units will be great: a net increase of more than 400,000 housing units within the Region will be needed and, including replacement housing, this figure jumps to an expected 1.5 million new housing units by 1980.[5]

Growth in the Regional Ring beyond the Conurbation may be expected to absorb some 250 square miles (160,000 acres) into urban use. The Ministry estimated, as of late 1960, that only three years' supply of developable residential land, as provided for in the Region's development plans, was still available. Only a fifth of this was within the Conurbation's limits.[6]

Doctrine for Planning London: Current Status and Tests

In the face of these prospects for vigorous growth, what is the current status of that planning doctrine which, exemplified in the Greater London Plan, featured containment as a policy bulwark?

On the surface, at least, the doctrine appears to remain firmly held, with stalwart support. The official affirmations are reinforcing. But in the face of London's pattern of growth, which tends to invalidate some of the underlying assumptions behind the advisory plans, serious questions arise. How flexible and ambivalent can doctrine for planning be? To what extent is it polite double-talk to continue to reaffirm such doctrine when changing conditions force significant reinterpretations?

The doctrine for planning Greater London assumed conditions of an idealistic, socialistic context within which strong public enterprise and positive planning were expected. The last decade has brought a decided shift in climate. Private-development and market decision-making forces have come back into considerable ascendancy, and the anti-planning political blocs have made inroads. Doctrine has been undermined by the erosion of major legal and fiscal features at the heart of the planning machinery established in the 'forties.

There has been no slackening in support of the principle that town planning's task is to bring about the best possible living conditions. British town planners and planning officials generally agree that this depends, in turn, on the maintenance of relatively low residential densities as well as the full provision of community facilities, open space, and well-designed housing. Density controls are supported in principle and are generally being maintained in practice. Certain increases which appeared to be realistic were recommended in the County of London's five-year review of its development plan, but these were somewhat balanced by other proposed reductions in densities. We may expect the County to achieve the full goals of residential deconcentration envisaged in the advisory plans.

Planned overspill remains a central feature of planning doctrine, and recent estimates suggest that it will be a far more serious problem than was earlier estimated. Additional government-supported new towns are being favored, although for other parts of Britain rather than for the already well-to-do London Region. No additional new towns around London have been initiated by the Government, and Hook was disapproved. The government has been supporting the expanded-town program, and, as we have recounted, progress is being made at last. More may also be forthcoming by way of privately financed equivalents of new towns.

The Metropolitan Green Belt is conscientiously supported with Ministerial statements and directives attesting to this portion of the doctrine. With the apparent blessing of the Ministry, several local planning authorities have recently submitted formal proposals for the generous outward expansion of those parts of the Green Belt falling within their respective jurisdictions.[7]

After a period of some possible relaxation during the middle 'fifties, the Board of Trade has, in the past several years, been enforcing with vigor the principle of redistributing industrial employment to areas of high unemployment. Thus, in the interests of plugging economic underdevelopment in some parts of Britain, industrial employment continues to be shunted away from London.

As the problem of increasing office employment in central London was grappled with during the mid-'fifties, the conviction that this growth should be halted came to be translated into formal policy and to be actively implemented. The supporting rationale was that control had already been implicitly stated in Barlow doctrine, even though restriction of office employment had not been separately articulated. We have thus witnessed the rise of virtually new doctrine under the guise of already expressed doctrine and policy. That central employment should be held down is, of course, clearly consistent with the strong decentrist tone of the overall doctrine.

The rebuilding and thinning out of central areas is still accepted as doctrine, and the cumulative record of redevelopment has its impressive aspects. Within Britain, however, loyal friends of planning appear discouraged that it has not received fuller financial support and has therefore fallen behind expectations.

We earlier made the point that doctrine and official policy may be closely related, but there may also be discrepancies between general acceptance of ideas and their full implementation. The Metropolitan Green Belt has been both accepted and fully carried into effect; the new towns have been accepted, were initially implemented, but subsequently have no longer been vigorously pursued; the removal of people from the London Region and from South-Eastern England to other sections of Britain has enjoyed considerable doctrinal acceptance, but has never been fully put into effect, except for the necessarily limited controls of the Board of Trade. Implementation requires methods, financing, and political leadership.

These reinforcing facets of doctrine, accepted into the form of tradition and built into official policy, currently face severe tests. Is the rising trend of employment in central London to be countenanced? Is the expansive growth of the residential suburbs (and exurbs) of the London Region to be encouraged? Is the Metropolitan Green Belt, including current proposals for its outward widening, to be firmly maintained in the face of heavy residential development into the Ring beyond it? Are increasingly numerous long-distance commuter trips from suburban residences to inner London to be accepted?

The experiences the London Region has been undergoing have important implications not only for its future experience, but also for the planning of metropolitan regions in the United States and in other countries. These will become more evident at the end of this chapter and in the subsequent discussion of institutional mechanisms by which changing circumstances might be taken into account.

London's Containment in the Light of Postwar Developments

The containment idea, like the key piece that must be fitted into a three-dimensional wooden puzzle to keep the other pieces from falling apart, is intricately enmeshed in the planning doctrine of the advisory plans for Greater London:* containment must be achieved for several other planning goals to be realizable; various presuppositions about demographic and economic trends must hold up for the containment concept to be readily feasible; the containment idea provides a salient link among national, regional, and local levels of planning. But containment can be achieved only if consistent and rigorous governmental controls are maintained to keep dynamic pressures for growth and change under control.

Containment both has and has not been a successful central concept for fashioning planning policy for London. The containment concept has proven successful as it has been applied to the older, central, solidly urbanized portion—the Greater London Conurbation proper. The containment concept has been unsuccessful, however, as it has been applied to restraining the growth of the London Region as a whole; but this failure has not been the failure of containment itself so much as a matter of its not being wholeheartedly formulated and pursued at this regional scale. To the degree that this idea of containing the London Region has been taken seriously, it has, moreover, undoubtedly misdirected attention away from the challenge of guiding London toward a realistic new metropolitan regional spatial pattern.

Interpreting containment as applying to the Conurbation couples the idea positively with the redistribution of resident population to the Regional Ring beyond the Green Belt or to other sections of Great Britain. This interpretation permits a dynamic approach to recognizing and guiding the total growth of Britain while striving to hold in the growth of the mother Conurbation.

Some town planners and observers in Britain have maintained that containment has been mainly a physical planning concept and that it has applied properly only to the Greater London Conurbation. They have contended that it was this main urbanized part of London within the Metropolitan Green Belt that was being contained, not the Greater London Plan Region.[8] According to this view, the overspill of population and employment from within the Conurbation to that part of the Region beyond the Green Belt and the growth of this outer part was to be expected and could not imply any lack of success of the containment policy. Such an

---

* See diagram (Fig. 3) and the section on doctrine in chapter 4.

interpretation permits a dynamic expectation of growth in other sections of Britain, too, while growth of the London Conurbation is restrained. This pattern of containing the mother city and colonizing new cities dates back at least to the Greeks.

Insofar as the containment idea has been interpreted as being a matter of restraining the lateral growth of the Conurbation, it has contributed to the maintenance of commendably high residential development standards and to the provision of a remarkably fine surrounding belt of open countryside. A broad Green Belt is visibly in being, is generally being held inviolate, and, without question, is introducing a direct control resulting in the reduction of additional suburban sprawl. Bombed-out and slum sections of inner London have been rebuilt to high community-planning standards. Residential densities and population have been held down within the Conurbation. London, to its great credit, has avoided the brutally high densities characterizing some postwar housing in New York. The growth of manufacturing employment within the Conurbation has been restrained. The British can be justifiably proud of these achievements. Certainly no American metropolis can point to any comparable record of purposeful physical planning and persistent accomplishment in carrying out this planning.

Such an interpretation, applying containment merely to the Conurbation, now seems to have been overly literal. For behind the Greater London Plan and importantly related to Government policy pronouncements over the years has been a far more significant carry-over from the Barlow Commission—the rationale that jobs and people were to be distributed from the Greater London Plan Region as a whole to other parts of Britain.[9] In this spirit, there is every logical reason to include the Region, and not only the Conurbation, as the unit to be contained. The idea of restraining the growth of the entire London Region has, however, involved serious difficulties which have overlain and inevitably obfuscated the planning for metropolitan London. In particular, three interconnected difficulties have never been successfully resolved: the complementarity between social-economic planning at the national level and physical planning at the local (or, potentially, the metropolitan) level has not been fully understood and implemented; the interweaving of policy and assumption has proved ambiguous; a continuing focus on London as a compact city has been at the expense of recognition of the forces, at work in all western industrial nations, for more loosely structured, multi-centered metropolitan regions.

Even the most vigilant attention to the physical containment of the London Conurbation cannot also bring about the controlled limitation of regional growth, short of full and coordinated national controls. These were envisaged in the minority report of the Barlow Commission, and were sought and in part attained in national legislation dealing with the distribution of employment, but remain incompletely developed. And in the current political climate they are likely to remain so. True, the Board of Trade specifically stated in its written evidence to the Royal Commission on Local Government in Greater London that "it has been the Government's policy to seek to limit the expansion of the London region as a whole and to effect dispersal within that area." [10] The Board also reported that it had sought to restrain manufacturing firms from entering, or expanding within, "the Greater London Area [slightly more extensive than the Greater London Plan Region] or, indeed, the south-eastern corner of the country generally." [11] And yet, in that same written evidence, the Board included a table showing that of 160,000 industrial employees in firms that, from 1945 to 1958, have moved out of "the metropolitan area" (apparently the Conurbation), 43,000, or 27 per cent, moved to London new towns or other parts of the Greater London Plan Region; 32,000, or 20 per cent, moved to other parts of South-Eastern England; and only 59,000, or 37 per cent, moved to development areas, and 26,000, or 16 per cent, to other parts of the United Kingdom.[12]

No full integration of national planning efforts and local physical planning policies has ever been achieved. The national concern for halting the drain from, and counteracting serious conditions facing, depressed communities in provincial sections of the country has been generally consistent with the proposals of the London advisory plans and with subsequent planning measures, but there remain serious gaps. No fully positive plan for guiding the larger London Region has ever been developed and, lacking this, there has been no closure between questions of internatal spatial organization of the Region and the national policy implications.

Too, there have been out and out differences in interests that have not been resolved. The vigorous promotion of the eight proposed new towns in outer London was bound to compete with a national interest in encouraging migration to northern England or to Scotland. The sustained economic growth of the London Region, contributing in certain positive ways to Britain's wellbeing, has not lent itself readily to piecemeal decentralization to other areas.

Similarly, there has been no full and consistent resolution of the relation between assumption and policy in the way containment has emerged as idea and policy. Stemming from the Barlow Commission, control of the distribution of industrial employment was accepted as a policy matter of great import. But since from a strictly physical planning vantage point the fundamental issues regarding and the prospects for controlling employment distribution were jurisdictionally out of bounds, the question had to be dealt with in terms of an assumption that the controls would be effectively maintained. It then also followed as an assumption that population for the Greater London Plan Region would not rise above the prewar level. In contrast to such assumptions, however, restraint of urban sprawl was recognized as a policy objective of the Greater London Plan.[13] Yet what is treated as assumption at one point slips disconcertingly over into policy at another moment. The Royal Commission report in 1960, for example, picked up what in the Greater London Plan had been treated as assumptions and firmly stated: "The underlying principle was that the population of the Greater London Plan Region would not increase above the 1938 level. . . . An indispensable pre-requisite for this . . . was control of the number of jobs available . . ."[14] And yet on the very next page of the same report the ideas that population and employment were to be held constant were termed "presuppositions" (tantamount to assumptions). It makes for very different notions of the planning task whether the control of employment can be taken as a valid assumption or whether it remains an active part of what one must seek to control. Even the deft phrasing, "accepted ultimate population" and "target population,"[15] delightfully evades whether targets of this order are to be assumed or to be purposefully worked toward.

To those who think of containing London in the more restricted sense of holding in the Conurbation, the notion of London as a single great city with its monolithic structure around a traditional dominant center is particularly congenial. To those who view containment in broader regional terms the question of spatial structure of the entire region also looms. One answer is merely to add a number of new or expanded towns for accommodating overspill. Another, and one we shall develop in greater detail below, would seek a pattern that more fully recognizes the potentials for outer growth within the London Region and seeks actively to channel this rather than relying on assumptions that the region will not grow beyond designated levels.

Factual evidence by no means leads to similar interpretations by all observers. Some find the current situation depressing, for they feel that great opportunities have been lost by ineffective and even contradictory public controls and initiative. For decentrists who are more flexible in their outlook there remain promising possibilities, providing the present trends are fully recognized and a broader regional planning is somehow put into effect.[16] Centrists tend to believe that too much low-density peripheral growth is being allowed, indeed even encouraged, and hope for higher densities within the Conurbation. Two schools of containment are theoretically possible and may work against each other, although the labels may be other than containment and the positions far from pure. One school favors holding down densities at all costs, and Sir Frederic Osborn has undoubtedly served as the most vigorous spokesman for this position. The other school holds for lateral containment and a more urban, higher-density pattern of flats within the area contained.

What Next? Same, Modified, or New Doctrine?

It could be irresponsible or even cavalier to propose planning definitive solutions for metropolitan London. It is not inappropriate, however, to discuss some considerations that deserve to be more fully taken into account, and to indicate possible directions that at least merit exploration.

In a situation in which possible change in doctrine is under consideration, it is difficult to disentangle problems of substance from those of political strategy. Hard-won controls and gains, however far from perfect, are cherished dearly; needs for change are all too readily minimized for fear that to admit them might open wedges for general opposition to planning or introduce new divisions among the planners and their allies. Fortunately (as we shall treat further in chapter 8), the British have an institutional knack of achieving an evolving consensus, and this tradition would seem to make some approach via modification a natural procedure, without calling excessive attention to the change contemplated.

In general terms, the policies—including that of containment—applied to the main Greater London Conurbation do make sense; and, subject to normal reviews taking changing conditions into account, they can be maintained with a full sense of continuity. Certainly the culturally important features of inner London's physical environment deserve to be preserved and enhanced. The tremendous fixed capital investment in the Conurbation's physical base must be fully relied on. Fortunately, the County of London, the City Corporation, and the other planning authorities in the Conurbation have demonstrated a mature capacity to introduce improved standards of residential and community development. The extremely thorny problem of the private car in central London requires ingenious and positive planning. Other problems, too, will confront the Greater London Council when it takes over its new responsibilities for preparing and periodically revising a development plan for its Conurban jurisdiction.

On the other hand, existing planning doctrine as it applies to the Regional Ring outside of the Conurbation seems less than adequate. Even worse, in important ways it may be downright confusing and misleading. Its preservationist spirit and garden-city traditionalism ought to give way to fully positive, comprehensive planning for the growth and change that will mark London's evolving adaptation to the world around it. If British planners were to take this challenge seriously, they might contribute new leadership in the planning of metropolitan fringe areas, just as they provided forceful and inspiring leadership during the early and mid-'forties. For the problem that confronts London is also a serious problem in America, and may well become an equally critical problem in other high-standard countries. Some experience from the United States might be tapped, particularly in creating outlying shopping centers and in dealing with the automobile. But no example of a fully comprehensive approach to building full new regional arrangements is available. In California, for example, suburban areas are expanding at dizzying rates, but there is serious question as to how fully adequate these new environments will prove in the decades to come.

The planning doctrine to date has contributed a not unimaginative interlocking of green-belt, overspill, new-town, and expanded-town approaches. These make good sense so far as they go. But they have not provided any full determination to plan for entire sectors of the outer fringe. Larger subregional centers have not been planned, transportation connections have not been integrated with other developments, and, because of underestimates of the growth to be accommodated, the potential scale of development has not been openly faced up to.

These shortcomings are closely related to the ways in which existing doctrine may be proving detrimental. First, it perpetuates an idea that it is mainly the monolithic, central city within the Green Belt that is important, and therefore treats the outer developments merely as overspill from the main city. And, while the new-town approach certainly has sought to achieve this outer development on a whole-community basis, it goes about this in terms of smallish new cities. Second, doctrine as it stands continues to infuse an idea that the growth of the London Region is somehow to be held down, so that, as if magically, this would wish away the problem. Here the facts must be faced. Either the British do mean business on holding down London and South-Eastern England or they do not. If they do—and this calls for a responsible analysis of alternatives—they must then invoke far more comprehensive national planning measures. The coöperation of all central government departments will be required. Or, to accommodate London's natural vitality and to recognize that it may be to Britain's benefit to encourage newly conceived regional development—again, assuming an analysis of the benefits and costs of alternatives—it may prove better to modify this part of containment policy. Better yet, an evolutionary modification could follow from an expanded emphasis on positively planning for the whole outer-London Regional Ring.

This also raises a serious question as to the political responsibility for planning for the Region outside the Green Belt. Even the proposed reorganization to create a Greater London Council with direct responsibilities for preparing and keeping up to date a development plan for its geographic jurisdiction will not get to the heart of the problem as it relates to the Regional Ring. Whether the counties that will encircle the new Greater London Council area will be able to handle the task cannot be known. Past experience suggests, however, that a guiding regional plan would be required before the separate counties would be able to act with full responsibility to meet regional as well as local needs.

Some Possible Modifications

Just as the distinctive and traditional features of London's main, older portions should be as fully respected as feasible, planning policy for the Regional Ring should respect and build from existing conditions and currently accepted new-town and expanded-town approaches. And, while it might have been quite possible to have approached the green-belt need in a rather different way—possibly greater emphasis on green wedges with intervening fingers of urban development, better to recognize various radial transportation routes—as things now stand the present Metropolitan Green Belt should be accepted as an outstanding accomplishment and future plans should fully incorporate it as a distinctive feature.

Several criteria deserve consideration and might enhance the review and modification of advisory plans and associated governmental policies, particularly as they apply to the Regional Ring:

a. *Accommodation of growth.* It must be assumed, in line with current understanding of the situation, that growth in outer London will be of great significance (probably some 2 million additional residents in the twenty years to 1980). This consideration stands in obvious contrast to earlier assumptions that population and employment in the London Region were likely to grow only slowly or perhaps not at all.

b. *Increasing reliance on automobile.* Upsetting as this may be to many tradition-minded persons, automobiles will inevitably continue to gain in use. This will particularly be the case for suburban areas. Hopefully, public transport can provide the main transportation into central London, but, for trips within outer London and recreational trips to more distant points, the auto will become the prevalent mode. (Many California suburban areas have reached the point where more families have two or more cars than only one car. We do not foresee this level of automobile ownership for suburban London, but trends for the auto's far greater ownership and use are impressive.)

c. *Appeal of the suburban home with private garden.* Reflecting British cultural tradition for the home with a garden, the continuing demand for suburban homes is likely to be strong. This contrasts to earlier traditions prevalent in some Continental countries favoring higher-density urban flats. The pull toward the suburban home, coupled with increasing reliance on the automobile, spell low-density, diffuse outer residential developments.

d. *Increasing use of larger-scale, less-local facilities.* From both consumption and distribution viewpoints, there appear to be advantages to larger stores, chain-organized services, and more specialized offerings in both outer and central sections of the metropolis. This rationalization may, for a time, be seriously at odds with the British traditions of small, local shops and services, even though large and specialized stores are already an integral feature of central London. But, in the long run, these features may help to provide the fullest opportunities for metropolitan residents to draw upon the resources of the metropolitan region (or, at least, of their sector of the region). Doctrine promoting community and neighborhood units notwithstanding, the metropolitan region of tomorrow will be challenged to accommodate more, longer, and more complexly patterned trips and contacts.

e. *Opportunities for full hierarchies of service centers within each sector of the Regional Ring.* Outer London will increasingly need many levels of activities and services, ranging up to the subregional level. Planners have the opportunity to provide pleasant, efficient settings for these. Specially planned subregional centers may be called for, supplementing the new-town and expanded-town centers already being developed at a smaller scale.

f. *Bolstering the transportation system in outer London.* In addition to present transportation lines, most of which have been designed to provide for trips into central London and which need improvements in their own right, a full transportation system for serving the Regional Ring and for providing for extensive movement within and among outer areas is urgently required. This system will necessarily tie in with and help to stabilize the various main outlying centers. The mix between automobiles and public transport in this outer system remains to be determined.

If we assume that outer growth of the London Region is to be openly planned for and that restraining the growth of the overall Region is no longer appropriate, then the function, character and geographic pattern of the Metropolitan Green Belt and other open space should be carefully reëxamined. The recent proposals for extending the Green Belt much farther out, while consistent with the doctrine of containing the Region as well as the Conurbation, are scarcely helpful in permitting outer areas to be readily linked with the main Conurbation. Indeed, it would be most inappropriate to widen the Green Belt. The Green Belt has a most useful function, to be sure, as priceless open space in the metropolitan region; but it should remain just that—preserved space for the visual and active enjoyment of metropolitan residents and a device for breaking up unduly monotonous solid urban development.[17] Some outward strips or wedges of green area might be extended into particularly picturesque portions, such as the Chiltern Hills, but not so much solid extension of the main Green Belt as additional reserved open space.

Some additional new towns may prove to be most desirable, although they could perhaps be appropriately conceived as clusters related to new subregional centers. Perhaps two or three outer communities should be built or expanded with goals of a quarter-million or more population.[18] It may also be important to think of particular parts of these newly developed outer sections as suitable for higher-than-ordinary suburban densities. Just as compactness within new towns has preserved a greater amount of outlying open space, so compactness in new regional cities could provide a very full mix of housing types as well as greater contrasting open space. The problem here becomes one of public versus private open space.*

To supplement the planning for central London with a bold, new vision of the metropolitan region, with fully functioning,

---

* In the United States the pressures, in line with heavy dependence upon the play of the private market, have seemed disproportionate for privately owned space, such as surrounds each house.

high-quality planned outer development—thus supplanting the incomplete image of small, semi-isolated new towns beyond a formidable green belt—could, with proper leadership, mark the latest in the great eras of London's historical growth.

Lessons for American Metropolitan Planning

What is to be learned from the efforts to apply a containment policy in planning Greater London? What can American planners, in particular, find that is relevant and applicable to their own situations?

The London planning experience holds up a mirror to American planners so that they may better identify some of their own biases. In contrast to the English situation, American planners are inclined to accept metropolitan growth as natural; to place great faith in investment in transportation, particularly highways for automobiles; to consider very high densities and considerable congestion at the center as not unnatural; to accept low-density, single-family home suburban development patterns; and to emphasize local, grassroots planning and to remain suspicious of regional and national planning. Most American planners, despite their convictions that cities at a more precise scale are to be planned, probably do not seriously consider the idea of firmly controlling the *main* patterns of metropolitan growth as these reflect the interplay of many private development decisions and decentralized and diverse public policies and capital investments.

London planning also provides a powerful reminder that a mature and integrated set of policies as to regional distribution and metropolitan patterns may provide an essential component in any system for urban planning. The British understandably wonder how Americans can possibly plan for a large urban area if there are no strong ideals as to desirable patterns of development and no firm regional-level policy guidance. They see the American system as so accepting of compromises and so open to pulls and hauls from varied political interests that they wonder how we get any plan carried out at all.

The American is able, moreover, to witness results in London. The best are outstanding. The Green Belt has been boldly put into effect and presents exceedingly pleasant countryside, uncluttered by outdoor advertising and relatively free from the scatter and sprawl of suburban building. The new towns are stirring examples of how clustered communities can be shaped in the suburbs. They embody standards and qualities which, linked with the system of overspill, suggest other possibilities for development not necessarily in a strict new-town pattern, but adaptable to American needs.

Overspill as a planning mechanism should prove of particular interest to American planners. With the siting of new housing projects for low-income and minority-group residents in central cities in America virtually stymied because of strong neighborhood resistances, overspill arrangements into selected suburban or outer areas could prove helpful (although serious new resistances in the suburbs would inevitably have to be overcome, too). While the administrative and fiscal arrangements employed by the English are different from those that might be relied upon in the United States, these experiences and arrangements are worthy of examination.

Additionally, Americans interested in, or responsible for, metropolitan governmental restudy and possible reorganization can gain a lesson in mature governmental review from the hearings and report of the Royal Commission on Local Government in Greater London.

The Greater London planning case also provides an object lesson in the relentless force of growth. It demonstrates that containment, even if implemented by a set of controls far more powerful than those currently available in the United States, is extremely difficult to achieve. And, considering that the growth rates for most American metropolitan areas exceed that for Greater London, this spells out even further difficulties.

Finally, we must remember the responsibility, in cross-cultural comparisons and borrowing, for understanding how different governmental-social contexts may make an idea that has had considerable merit in its own situation less directly applicable in other countries. The British system depends upon a much greater place for central government than is customary in the United States. The scale of things in Britain is such that typically central government is able to deal directly with local government (as might an American state). The British system relies heavily on compensation to property owners who give up development rights;

the United States depends upon a greater reliance on police power via zoning. The latter approach is sometimes inadequate; for example, it is all but impossible in the United States to create large public green belts. English planning also reflects and ties in with a strong tradition of executive-administrative discretion.

The overwhelming dominance of London in Great Britain, if we may once again emphasize the point, has no direct counterpart in the United States. The pluralistic competition and division of function among America's largest metropolitan areas has no British equivalent. The pace of growth is slower in Britain. These factors certainly have relevant bearing on the appropriateness of a philosophy geared to Britain's level of growth in contrast to a philosophy that might be most appropriate in the United States.

Chapter 8

Doctrine and Change

The institutional arrangements by which continuity of policy and adaptation to changing conditions are balanced are, in a sense, the keystone to successful planning. How do potential new approaches for planning Greater London get introduced, agitated, and tested? How are new ideas discussed and, ultimately, accepted or rejected? What relative amounts of initiative and responsibility are assumed by the various parts of the whole mechanism by which the planning for this great Region is carried out?

Authority and Consensus in Britain

The British clearly respect continuity and tradition. This may lead the American observer to the view that the British are disdainful of making changes, but this would be an unwarranted interpretation. As Watson has put it, "unreflective [foreigners] are inclined to write off the country as a kind of animated museum. No greater mistake could be made. The stability of British life by no means implies rigidity or an inability to adapt new ideas. The romantic reverence for the past conceals, and perhaps facilitates, a marked capacity to keep up with the times . . ." [1] But, granting willingness to introduce change, what are the conditions under which and the manner in which adaptation may be expected to take place?

The social and governmental structure in Britain places strong emphasis upon influential and authoritative leadership, both in and out of government. Pronouncements by governmental leaders

provide bases for affirming or modifying policy, and prospective
major policy changes may be explored, recommended, and perhaps
introduced in specially authorized ways, as by Royal Commission
reports or governmental White Papers. Leadership from private
circles is also significant (*e.g.,* see the account of the Town and
Country Planning Association below). For deliberate change to
be effective it must secure the blessing of the Establishment—the
institutional web reinforcing governmental authority—so that the
change is "legitimatized."

Change in Britain is often handled artfully—as if it were not
really change. Continuity is maintained by periodic reaffirmation
of policy and by explicit assertions that the situation is covered by
existing policy. And yet, at the same time, changing conditions
force fresh interpretations. When the government machine is operating at its smoothest, shifts in policy assume the character of a
continuous flow, and we can perhaps best term this process one of
adaptive consensus. Evolving agreement reflects respect for authority and for governmental leadership. Over and beyond official
and conscious decision, much depends upon an expectation that
shared agreement will prevail. "[Much] more in England is done
by subconscious influence than by conscious decision, much more
by ambient feeling than by indentifiable conspirators, such as the
word 'establishment' suggests. The power of the Establishment,
such as it is, comes not from the fact that a dozen people impose
their will on the rest of us but from the fact that there is in all of
us a degree of establishment-mindedness—that we feel it right that
the opinions of such persons should have attention paid to them." [2]

Perhaps the British are so attuned to the many and subtle variations in their society that they underestimate their sense of agreement. But a non-British observer, viewing the scene as an an-
thropologist might, senses a remarkable degree of consensus, a
respectability attaching to this consensus, and a conviction that
agreement paves the way for getting on with carrying it out. In
Eckstein's words, "there has in fact existed in Britain a consensus
on general policy, shifting political conflict to matters of technique
and detail, that is, matters generally dealt with by administrative
departments." [3]

Leadership rests firmly with government and lay leaders. Within
established organizational frameworks, specialists tend to be sub-

ordinated to lay political leaders and to a special class of administrators. Heavy responsibilities are deliberately entrusted to men
who are amateur with respect to the function in question. It is
held that this brings a breadth of viewpoint not available to the
professional specialist from a single field.[4] Two types of amateurs
would seem to have been particularly instrumental in the case of
the planning for London. First are those formally within government—notably the administrative class of the higher civil service
in the central government and the council committees at the local
level. Second are influential leaders of associations given over to
propagandistic and watchdog roles.

The administrative class, numbering some 2,500, comprise an
elite of amateurs.[5] But if its members are amateurs with respect
to the various subject fields to which they may be assigned, collectively they constitute a profession of remarkably high status—
ranking above most of the specialist professions with which they
may be dealing. These officers, assigned to the various ministries,
quite literally serve as guardians of the continuity and consistency
of policy as they codify, amend, and reinterpret official versions of
doctrine. These higher civil servants are responsible, in behalf of
their respective ministers, for evolving and defending the full web
of official pronouncements comprising policy. Protocol calls for
most communications between ministers and particular technical
officers to proceed via administrative officers. This offers the administrative officer an opportunity to exercise his own judgment in
reviewing and possibly rewording the communication as it moves
through his hands.

Outside the system of formal government, it is the spokesman
for the recognized professional or interest group whose reactions
tend to be sought and listened to. This situation follows from a
tradition of strong reliance on the formal association, whose leaders, with the advice of a small handful of trusted senior colleagues,
are characteristically authorized to speak out on behalf of the entire association. One recent observer has emphasized "a persistent
'corporatism' in British social attitudes . . . a conception of society as consisting primarily not of individuals but of sub-societies,
groups having traditions, occupational and other characteristics in
common." [6]

This system places the individual member, and especially the

younger or dissenting member, in a position of considerably limited potential influence. "Young Turks" may have some difficulty,
and iconoclasts may be singularly devoid of an official audience.
Conversely, the senior and presumably the more conservative members of associations may come to have undue influence. Associations traditionally representative of particular interests and led by
solid, influential persons are likely to retain a distinct edge, for
they tend to be accepted more readily by the Government in con-
sultations and at hearings.[7]

Fierce loyalty to pragmatic approaches and disdain for the theoretical mark British approaches to policy decisions. By sharing
essential agreement as to goals, leaders in Britain claim they can
concentrate on getting things done to implement these goals. Some
British feel that Americans talk too much about the big "theoretical" alternatives at the expense of getting on with the job. Consistent with the influence of the nonspecialist administrative officer,
social scientific and analytic approaches in any strength may be
conspicuously lacking. One critic has gone so far as to assert that
"British society to-day exhibits a greater unwillingness to discover,
to collect and to face up to the social facts of life than at any time
during the last hundred years. . . . Indeed, as the potentialities
of the social sciences widen, the barriers to their effective utilization seem to become more formidable. Thus the paradox of better
means to social knowledge and less inclination to use it." [8]

What are the prospects for rational—and, as relevant, scientific
—analysis of alternatives in the face of such traditionalism and
amateurism? In a country that has in various technical research
undertakings shown an impressive record, it may be expected that
social and behavioral scientists will in the future be invited to
make greater contributions. Yet, for various reasons, we should not
be surprised at continuing, serious resistance in Britain to a fuller
acceptance of social scientific investigation.[9]

The Guardians and Innovators of Planning Doctrine

Town planning in Great Britain, like city planning in the
United States, is simultaneously a governmental activity, a profession, and a social movement. The formation and potential
modification of town and regional planning doctrine is bound to
be a mixture of political determination, professional exploration

and pronouncement, and the lobbying influences of lay special-interest groups.

The distinction between planning doctrine and public policy in Britain is by no means sharply drawn. Policy inevitably expresses doctrine to a considerable degree; in literate Britain this is clearly the situation. Some steps in doctrinal reasoning may not, however, be fully indicated in public policy pronouncements.

The central government has a major responsibility for policy formulation in regard to town planning. Pressures to maintain a semblance of clarity and consistency of policy may belie the welter of competing points of view actually at work. Political pressures are exerted to incorporate compromises and to achieve statements of sufficient breadth and ambivalence to attract diverse supporting interests. And, in the best British tradition that government shall act to protect the public interest, great trust has been placed in public officials—with the full expectation that they will be scrupulously dedicated and incorruptible.

Except for an initial period in the life of the then Ministry of Town and Country Planning when some extremely capable professionals filled technical (and even some administrative) posts, a more orthodox situation has come to prevail. Within the Ministry, the professional town planners ("technical officers") are somewhat under the shadow of administrative officers. Each technical officer has an administrative officer as his counterpart, and certain administrative officers stand in positions higher than any of the technical officers and distinctly in the line of communication between the Minister (with his immediate aides) and the technical officers. While it may well be that technical officers are given full opportunities to initiate proposals for change and are able to work closely with administrative officers in personally putting forth their views, the total ministerial apparatus is geared to putting all proposals through a politically sensitive screening. Understandably, few proposals for change move through without substantial modification, and some may be emasculated.

The situations within various local planning authorities vary, but it appears that, by and large, the technical planning officers at the local level have much greater opportunity openly to express their professional judgments. The town planning committee is always in charge, and with a vigorous chairman and supporting membership may take a certain initiative, but is more likely to go along with the planning officer's recommendations while he, in turn, seeks to be ever-sensitive to the committee's general outlook. Only in relatively rare instances must planning officers go through their council clerks (roughly the equivalent of the administrative officers in the Ministry).

We have already suggested that a dynamic process of consultative give and take temper the Ministry's formal policy supervision of the local planning authority. In a formal sense, the Ministry is responsible for maintaining continuity in planning policy and in recommending periodic modifications. As things work out, considerable initiative for change actually comes from the livelier of the local planning authorities, with the informal support of the Ministry. On many matters, however, the Ministry takes the lead, as in urging or requiring local authorities to undertake particular surveys or to adopt modifications in plans.

Town planning doctrine has tended, in important respects, to cut across party lines. Some party differences are evident, however. The Labour party has tended to support broad and concerted application of planning controls, a reasonably strong plan, and related programs of governmental housing. It favors a climate for planning that might, in turn, foster change. But if the Labour party were to come back into power during the next several years, its leaders might fall back to the task of carrying out doctrine firmed up during the 'forties rather than undertaking striking modifications. The Conservative party tends to support conservationist measures and—whether openly stated or not—to go along with a lessening of governmental planning powers. Indirectly it has favored a market-achieved spatial pattern rather than a planned one.[10] But Conservative party members also support the maintenance of the Green Belt and the preservation of traditional London features.

We might expect considerable initiative for modification in planning doctrine to come from the town planning profession itself, preceded by research-minded and experience-based examination and testing of alternative approaches. It has, however, remained for selected nonprofessional organizations and their leaders —neither town planners nor governmental officials—to provide some of the most important exploration and to promote potentially important new or revised ideas and approaches. No single influence has been more significant than that of the British garden-city movement, which has evolved into a broader decentrist movement.[11] This movement, predating town planning proper and adapting its own philosophy and propagandist efforts to take into account emerging conditions, has consistently been ready with a substantive philosophy congenial to British values and has proved amazingly influential in shaping fundamental aspects of town-planning doctrine. Since the Greater London Plan so faithfully mirrored the movement's precepts, the Town and Country Planning Association has naturally continued to provide support for those portions of doctrine promoting containment and planned dispersal.

No other single group (with the possible exception of work within the Ministry that because of its semiconfidential character is not publicized) is currently more active in exploring the implications of recent developments. Peter Self, as chairman of the Association's executive committee, and Wyndham Thomas, as director, are spearheading current reviews of underlying trends and their projection into the future, and are actively formulating and propagandizing proposed revisions in doctrine. A number of influential town planners have been coöpted to participate actively in Association affairs and to serve on study committees. While decentrist interests remain paramount, the Association's spokesmen exhibit a marked adaptability in taking prospective change into account.[12]

The Association, drawing upon trend data developed by A. G. Powell and others in the London Technical Branch of the Ministry, has led in calling attention to the nature of the outward residential growth beyond the Green Belt. What is required, the Association concludes, is a scale of planning not currently provided—in effect, regional planning. In addition to new towns and expanded towns, which the Association continues to support, there is a need, its leaders claim, for regional centers, some of which might be a considerable distance from London. They are exploring the feasibility of regional development corporations for initiating comprehensive efforts in the new outer London Region.

The Association has also taken the lead in exploring the possibilities for the decentralization of offices to sites in outer London. This supplements the Ministry's and the London County Council's own efforts in holding down the amount of office space built in the center.

Also effective currently is the coalition of faculty members of the London School of Economics and Political Science, under the chairmanship of Professor W. A. Robson, which since 1958 has been organized as the Greater London Group. In addition to submitting influential evidence before the Herbert Commission, the Group has continued to explore the implications of the Commission's recommendations and to fashion its own further proposals as to how Greater London and the London Region may best be governed and planned. The Group, numbering more than a dozen members, represents divergent outlooks, yet maintains a singularly important overlapping membership with the Town and Country Planning Association. Professor Robson is also a member of the Association's Council, Mr. Self is chairman of its Executive Committee, and Professor Wise has been heavily relied upon as a speaker at recent Association conferences. The Association's director, in his important work, is, in turn, closely in touch with the Group. Peter Self's excellent *Town Planning in Greater London,* published in the spring of 1962 as Number 7 in the series of Greater London Papers, provides an exceedingly clear statement, emphasizing the need for a more general plan and a broader regional approach as supplementing a development plan to be maintained by the Greater London Council. His approach, and indirectly the work of the larger Group, is fully complementary and congenial to the parallel study and propagandistic campaign of the Town and Country Planning Association.

The contributions of the Greater London Group—essentially in tune with those currently emerging from the Association—may be fairly appraised as constructively revisionary within the general spirit of the Barlow-Abercrombie-decentrist doctrinal framework. Although the Group rejects any diehard maintenance of present political structure, it has maintained a well-informed, respectable, and positive approach.

All in all, one gains the strong impression that the doctrine crystallized by the advisory plans has remained relatively unchallenged. More accurately put, perhaps, a continuing pragmatic and administrative drive to carry out what has proved to be an essentially congenial doctrine has absorbed the main energies. The

British have presumably judged this to be more appropriate and more positive than shunting off undue efforts to challenging basic doctrinal tenets.

The Town Planning Profession

The character of the leadership provided by the town planning profession also weighs significantly in the planning scene. To what degree and in what ways does the profession contribute to doctrinal review and innovation? Examination of the Town Planning Institute and its membership, the professional's sphere of maneuver within government, and the professional educational programs offers insight into the professional role.

Despite town planning's importance as a governmental activity for some 50 years, town planning as a profession in Britain is both young and still relatively low in status. It was only in 1959 that the Queen granted a charter to the Town Planning Institute (the TPI), and it will be some years, no doubt, before it may achieve the status of a royal institute. In line with the British pattern of influence, the Institute's leaders may have been highly concerned with gaining respectability and status for the Institute, even at the cost of holding back on some outspoken support for planning policies that might prove unduly controversial.

The TPI confines its efforts primarily to the managerial aspects of the profession (*e.g.*, administering examinations, holding professional meetings, etc.) and generally, but not always, tries to avoid undue involvement in broad doctrinal and political questions. The town planner appears to maintain a view of himself as a technical professional. This reflects the close association with other "technical" professions and takes into account the degree to which important larger aspects of doctrine and policy flow from laymen and amateurs as an integral part of the governmental process, rather than from the planning professionals. It inevitably reflects, too, the relative unimportance of social scientific outlooks within the profession.

The town planner as a professional often finds himself boxed in, so to speak, and may have to fight for territory within which his own distinctive judgment is recognized as prevailing. He holds no monopoly on the top technical planning positions in local government. We have already pointed out that, except in the counties, planning officers may serve under other officers or may bear the labels of other professions (*e.g.*, engineer or surveyor). In 42 of the 83 county boroughs, as of a recent count, the man serving as planning officer was not even a member of the TPI.[13] In the Ministry of Housing and Local Government the town planner as technical officer may be readily overruled and subtly influenceable by a senior profession of administrative officers (this is the customary situation vis à vis other professionals, too). And, on many town planning matters, it is other associations—the Town and Country Planning Association, the Civic Trust, the Council for the Preservation of Rural England, etc.—that seem to be speaking forth and establishing spokesmanship on behalf of planning. This situation implies no lack of capacity on the part of British town planning professionals. But any profession that is so seriously hemmed in may be forced into a somewhat defensive stance. The profession may feign a more solid basis in knowledge and doctrine than may actually be justified. And where systematically acquired and tested knowledge is not more readily available, doctrine may come to be unduly relied upon in its stead.

Because a large proportion of TPI members—about 73 per cent as of 1959—are also members of one or more other professional associations, some division of allegiance is inevitable. For example, Sir William Holford, the distinguished Professor of Town Planning, University College, University of London, recently served as President of the Royal Institute of British Architects. The more senior members of the Institute and those in leadership positions are more prone to such multiple memberships than are the younger members. The tabulation on page 169 illustrates the situation (the first three rows show the situation among selected leaders; the final four rows cover broader membership).[14]

The most prevalent other memberships for town planners are in the professions of architecture (45 per cent of TPI members), engineering (21 per cent), surveying (12 per cent), and landscape architecture (2 per cent).* In general, the architecture, engineering, and surveying interests are evenly distributed among older members of the TPI. But among TPI members admitted within

---

* These tabulations are restricted to these "brother" professions and do not include other fields such as geography or economics, although, for the past several years, degree holders in these two fields have been eligible to take TPI examinations.

| | TPI Membership | | Percentage Distribution | | |
	Number	Per Cent	With at least 2 other memberships	With 1 other membership	With no other membership
Council of the TPI, 1959	37	100	22	73	5
Past Presidents, TPI, 1951–59	10	100	20	70	10
Principal Planning Officers or higher, MHLG, 1959	8[15]	100	—	88	12
TPI membership, 1959 (10% sample)[a]	*270*	*100*	*7*	*66*	*27*
Became members, 1939 and earlier	44	100	11	78	11
Became members, 1940–1949	105	100	12	75	13
Became members, 1950–1959	121	100	2	53	45

[a] This 10 per cent random sample was taken from the *Yearbook of the Town Planning Institute* (cited in note 14). Only Members and Associate Members were included. Retired Members, Legal and Legal Associate Members, and Students were excluded. The numbers refer to the sample, and, by definition, total figures would be roughly ten times the sample.

the past 10 years there has been a distinct falling off of accompanying engineering and surveying memberships. This is shown on page 170.

There has been no uniform, distinctive, or rigorous single educational and examinational path into the profession. Traditionally, members of the TPI have not held college degrees or diplomas, but have entered by professional examination. Also, typically, they have been members of other professions, as described above, which qualification has exempted them from the TPI intermediate examination, so that they have had only to pass its final examination. This is changing, for university and college programs in town planning are well established and growing and completion of such courses offer exemption from the TPI final examination. Exemp-

	TPI members also members of other professions[16]		Percentage Distribution of Other Memberships[a]			
	Num-ber	Per Cent	Archi-tecture	Engi-neering	Survey-ing	Land-scape Archi-tect
Council of the TPI, 1959	35	95	38	46	22	11
Past Presidents, TPI, 1951–59	9	90	60	20	20	10
Principal Planning Officers or higher, MHLG, 1959	7	88	50	25	13	—
TPI membership 1959 (10% sample)	*197*	*73*	*45*	*21*	*12*	*2*
Became members, 1939 and earlier	39	89	36	36	25	2
Became members, 1940–1949	91	87	51	31	13	3
Became members, 1950–1959	67	55	43	8	10	—

[a] The percentage of "other members" usually adds to more than the percentage in the total column because of multiple other memberships. All footnotes for previous table also apply.

tion from the intermediate examination is also granted to graduates in economics and geography, with the latter entering the field in significant numbers during the past 10 years. According to a 1960 survey of 61 county planning departments, 17 per cent of nearly 1,800 technical staff members held university degrees, and in some of the largest departments this percentage exceeded 30.[17] (Most of the planning programs have offered diplomas rather than degrees, but the current picture as to numbers of diploma holders is obscure.) The great bulk of the degree holders were less than 28 years of age and had entered planning departments since 1955; more than half secured their first degrees in geography and less than 10 per cent in planning. Of the 297 college graduates, only 110 held TPI memberships.

We have suggested that the profession, represented by the TPI, has for various reasons not played a vigorous role in agitating new ideas. Even so, we might expect to find a spirit of exploration and intellectual forcefulness spreading from the planning schools and through the rise of graduates to important positions. This does not, however, seem to be the case. Most of the students are part-time, already working during the day in planning departments or other professional offices. A number come from outside Britain and return without contributing directly to the British planning scene. A considerable body of students from other professions, particularly architecture, may be augmenting their other professional interests rather than dedicating themselves fully to planning. There is also a serious question whether the large county planning offices, now so typical, are providing fully attractive opportunities for promising young graduates. Many excellent people are lured into architecture, where the demand is brisk, or into other fields rather than into the planning profession and into governmental planning activity.

Outstanding features and contributors within the various schools can be identified, however. The faculty of the Department of Civic Design, University of Liverpool, has a record of editing the *Town Planning Review,* and has recently contributed a review of British town planning, *Land Use in an Urban Environment.* The program at King's College, University of Durham, continues to elicit favorable reactions, and the *Planning Outlook* attests to considerable exploratory spirit. Lewis Keeble, associated with the Department of Town Planning, University College in the University of London, is recognized as a lively and independent critic of contemporary planning. Also in University College, the Centre for Urban Studies, under Mrs. Ruth Glass' guiding hand, has carried through valuable research. But, taken as a whole, the volume and depth of research associated with the planning schools is not such as to spark the interest of able students or to bolster the profession's reputation for knowledge building.[18]

The political leaders, the government bureaucrats, and the amateurs have, it appears, retained much initiative that might have been assumed by the town planning profession. Given the present state of affairs, it appears unlikely that new sources of dynamic intellectual leadership are likely to emerge from the profession's institutional structure.

*Unitary Plans, Adaptive Consensus, and
Development Forces*

The Greater London Plan and the County of London Plan
were unitary plans; each portrayed a single desirable physical-
spatial pattern toward which future development was to be directed. Each plan proposed a stabilized end-to-be-sought pattern
as designed by planning teams, after these teams had posited the
assumptions that forces for growth would not be unduly disruptive
and that a strong system of planning controls could and would be
maintained.

It is no coincidence that Sir Patrick Abercrombie was an architect and a landscape architect as well as a town planner. It is also
significant that of the twelve other key staff members working on
the two plans, nine were architect-planners (of whom three were
also landscape architects), only one was an engineer-planner and
one a surveyor-planner, and not one was a social scientist.[19] In
these advisory plans, the end product was the spatial pattern of
physical environment that was to be achieved. Social scientific considerations were not ignored, but neither the political economy in
its broad operation nor the implementation measures and stages
were dealt with or outlined with any thoroughness.

Abercrombie was a shrewd leader of the teams. He saw to it that
already agreed-upon or emerging policies were artfully respected,
his plans merely checking the feasibility of accommodating them
within a correlated pair of spatial plans. Most important, Abercrombie was a highly influential man, certainly acceptable to the
elite keepers of the consensus. The Abercrombie plans portrayed
a deceptively simple picture of what was to be accomplished, putting ideas on a direct, genteel level and avoiding complex considerations that might diminish such appeal.*

The plans' greatest force was in communicating a set of inter-
related ideas, fashioning them into a doctrinal package. The plans
achieved something of the importance of Royal Commission reports, despite the professional makeup of their makers. They were
authoritative pronouncements of a direction in which London
should be guided, pronouncements called for by the central government and produced by a master.

---

* See also notes 1 and 2, chapter 3.

Under these auspicious conditions the plans were sympathet-ically received and seriously considered. The Greater London Plan in particular provided a basis for high-level response and policy affirmation. But once this began to appear, the Greater London Plan—despite its initial architectural-planner, unitary character—came to be absorbed into a political and administra-tive process within central government that, by its very nature, was essentially adaptive in character. The original unitary spatial features provided the basis for a seeming unity of doctrine furnish-ing a rough profile of desirable directions and of environmental conditions to be sought. But the plan has not been imposed *in toto;* only selective features have been firmly insisted upon. Other features have been modified, and some (such as those dealing with transportation) have been almost totally dropped. Rather than providing the monolithic basis for guidance envisioned by the architect-planners and some benevolent socialists, the plan and its policy have guided but part of the range of forces at work in developing London.

With the passage of the all-embracing 1947 Act, planning in Britain became a major function in local government and a highly significant responsibility of central government. What had been entrusted to the professionals in the Ministry in the exploratory, reforming mid-'forties came to be pulled back into more orthodox political-administrative circles. As town and regional planning be-came more important, the political process by which modifications are deliberated made inroads on plan revision which, by profes-sional inclination, might have been maintained in more unitary form. Establishment-maintaining administrative officers came to play an increasingly important role, but their sense of preserving consistency in policy by no means respected the architect-planner's sense of coherent whole.

Even the technical approaches to town planning and the char-acter of the plans relied upon shifted as the advisory plans gave way to development plans. The development plans were less uto-pian, less grand schemes seeking to formulate and communicate main ideas as to desirable directions for future development. They were, rather, practical devices for looking ahead to probable pat-terns of growth and for working out appropriate responses in the form of public improvements and controls over private development. Thus, the technical content of plans and the pervasive philosophy surrounding the use of plans altered as development plans became prevalent.

The advisory plans, with the passage of time, have also received increasingly competitive impact from market forces. In contrast to the initial socialistic climate in which it was assumed that major initiative and responsibility for development would rest with central government, the climate in recent years has increasingly passed initiative back into the hands of private investors and developers. The mutual adjustment of supply and demand has tended to supplant a preconceived spatial pattern as a main determinant.

Viewed in these terms, we have a triangular set of relationships:

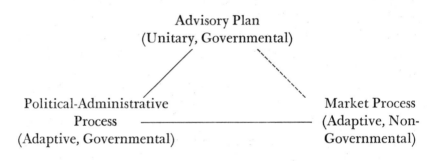

The political-administrative process by which policy is initiated, maintained, modified, or discarded proves to be of central importance for British town planning. It mediates, so to speak, between the advisory plans and the market process. It shares with the plan a governmental responsibility and focus; it shares with the market process an adaptive character. The relation between the advisory plan and the market process is shown on the diagram by a broken line, which indicates that they share characteristics only indirectly. The market process is inherently nongovernmental and essentially adaptive, thus contrasting on both counts with a unitary plan.

The evidence suggests that, on the whole, the *adaptive consensus* that is fashioned by the processes and structure of British central government has been too powerful an alternative for the *unitary town or regional plan.* Adaptive consensus reflects the operational mode of a cabinet-type government, permits effective use of the administrative class and adjustments to changing circumstances (such as may be brought about by market trends), and yet preserves a semblance of continuity and symbolically reaffirms that policy is already covering a new situation. But it would be inaccurate to speak of adaptive consensus as a Trojan horse that was brought in to defeat the unitary plan idea. Rather, it has been the other way around. The governmental system, with its stress on consensual leadership, was in existence all the time. Into this was introduced the idea of a plan for guiding London's future. The architect-minded planners who led the attack were familiar with designing for a fixed, end-product pattern. They were far less conversant with the politics of metropolitan planning and with the prospects for unanticipated forces of growth and change. Nevertheless, they had a strong hand in formulating the development plan concept, and thus contributed to a practical way of phasing relatively precise improvements.

It now appears that if the professional planners had wanted to preserve a greater say in periodically restudying the advisory plans from a broad regional (or metropolitan regional) vantage, they should have concentrated on recommending a framework within which they as professionals might have been brought more fully into the process. With very capable professionals holding down important positions within the Ministry following the war, the professionals may have felt that they would be able to maintain an influential role. If so, they underestimated the power of the established governmental forces—the higher civil service, "the Treasury boys," and the traditional channels for authoritative pronouncement—which came so completely to dominate their advice. Perhaps, too, they failed to reckon with adaptive influences in their own midst; for surveyors and engineers may be more inclined to go along with adaptive approaches and processes than are architect-planners.

They might also have paid much more attention to the need for research to bolster professional recommendations for regional planning and to developing concepts of governmental organization suited to metropolitan planning.

Regional Planning for London: Whose Responsibility?

As things now stand, the central government has committed itself to set up a new system of government for London. The

bulk of the London Conurbation—in all, some 630 square miles
—is to be brought under the joint control of a Greater London
Council and a set of primary governmental units, Greater London
Boroughs. The Royal Commission has specifically conceived of the
area to be encompassed by the new government as "a great city"
rather than "a metropolitan region." [20] This proposed two-layer
system of government reflects an extension of local governmental
principles and is to be understood as a form of local government.

Treating the proposal as an adaptation of local government,
as the Royal Commission has done, makes great sense. It suggests
to citizens and to local political leaders that this large area is still
their own direct responsibility, that it is but an expansion of the
outwardly spreading Conurbation, and that it is deliberately designed to offset too much government from the top.[21]

But—as we have taken pains to indicate—commuting and other
functional ties with inner London are spreading to a rapidly growing and increasingly important regional fringe. Once we include
this larger region—and reckon on its further growth in the future
—we tend to pass beyond local governmental jurisdiction and
into regional or central governmental domain. Three main alternatives of governmental responsibility for this large region seem
possible. Local governments can collaborate, but short of formal
regional authority. In such collaboration, the services of the Ministry of Housing and Local Government could be available. Local
governments may be more willing to accept a modicum of central-
government guidance than to see their own responsibilities in-
vaded by a metropolitan or regional government.[22] A second possibility is for a regional authority to assume responsibility. Such
a proposal was presented in the London Planning Administration
Committee's 1949 report and has recently been supported by the
Town Planning Institute.[23] Or, finally, the central government
can take upon itself the direct responsibility for planning the
larger London Region. This arrangement would presumably be
organized within or around the Ministry of Housing and Local
Government. Such a scheme may be justified on grounds of London's unique national importance.*

---

* The MHLG is alleged to be engaged in preparing a statement regarding the
development policy for the London Region, implying initiative in the direction of
this third alternative. It is likely that a significant report on this subject will
be issued in the autumn of 1963.

We shall not presume to recommend a best governmental organization for this critical task. But suggesting a number of considerations that deserve to be taken into account may be in order. It would seem, for example, that regional planning for a large metropolitan region should be reoriented to focus more directly on functional relations and their implications for a desirable spatial patterning of the metropolis and its immediate hinterland. British regional planning to date has tended to deal mainly with the distribution of population and economic activities, short of identifying the dynamic web of linkages among activities and the whole process by which development takes place.

It would then follow that metropolitan regional planning would necessarily require a continuing major program of policy-oriented research dedicated to gaining, and translating into the form of planning recommendations, the fullest possible understanding of how the metropolitan region is growing and what the impact of alternative major policy proposals would probably be. Much of this research would relate to central London and to other portions of the Conurbation, but the larger Region deserves comprehensive consideration.

Closely related is the urgency of the fullest possible coördination between land-use planning and transportation planning. Here the best examples of the large American metropolitan transportation studies cannot be disregarded.[24] We are moving rapidly to the point where the possible impacts of hypothesized bundles of public policies, such as might result from specific plans, can be studied by simulation techniques. Such analysis rests mainly on the very great advances in theoretical approaches to metropolitan development, corresponding mathematical models or constructs, and the availability of advanced computer technology for running through what would otherwise be prohibitively costly and time-consuming mathematical manipulations.[25]

There is nothing magical in research using theoretical models, nor do research findings per se determine action. The decisions are fundamentally political, and must rest with responsible governmental leaders—in the final analysis, with elected officials. Yet the wise use of scientific knowledge aids in the exposure of critical variables to be considered, in the identification and study of likely policy alternatives, and in selecting the most effective methods of achieving desired goals. In the exigencies of war and in various spheres of industrial production, the reliance by the British on scientific research and the most sophisticated methods of rational decision making have been among the world's finest examples of applied science. The problems of urban growth also call for the most thorough analytic approaches that can be mustered. The fine tradition of political decisions by elected and administrative amateurs can well be buttressed by fully professional and scientific approaches.

In the partnership between government and the town planning profession, both share heavy responsibilities for leadership. Town planning as a governmental activity remains within the context of political deliberation and decision, and modifications of the governmental organization for planning and of major substantive approaches to planning are clearly the continuing responsibility of government and its leaders.

As was intimated earlier, it seems that the town planning profession must itself assume stronger intellectual leadership in Britain. It must particularly focus on developing a convincing associated research arm and it must encourage far more vigorous educational programs. These, incidentally, are by no means newly stressed conclusions. The Schuster Committee clearly sought attraction to the profession of first-class minds, improved and broadened educational opportunities, and greatly expanded provisions for continuing research.[26] Professor Rodwin earlier identified the weakness in town planning research as the Achilles heel of British town planning.[27]

Very great responsibility rests with the planning schools. If any segment of the total institutional framework of town and regional planning represents a unique opportunity it is the professional department or school. Here should be a cutting edge, a frontier of what is being learned about cities and metropolitan regions and what can be known about the impact of particular policies and plan ideas on their development. And here should be posed exciting problems to which the best talents of able researchers from other fields will be drawn.

All of this suggests that the planning schools deserve to be considerably strengthened. They should expand their faculties, drawing in persons with varied practical and theoretical interests—

economists, sociologists, geographers, and political scientists. They should be in full contact with regional science, operations research, and transportation engineering; with newer branches of mathematics and statistics applicable to the construction and testing of theoretical models dealing with urban development. Research should be intimately related to course work, so that students become fully conversant with the spirit and methods of scientific research. Students must come to appreciate (and some to specialize in) the connections between town and regional planning and various other fields of inquiry. In particular, the planning school should provide a bridge between the profession and the full resources of the larger university within which the school is set.

The Schuster Committee recommended that the Town Planning Institute develop a section for conducting research, and that it apply for governmental financial assistance. In view of the British pattern of corporatism, this might be an appropriate step. The gain of placing this research close to the association representing the profession and its membership might be offset, however, by diverting these research activities from the broader university setting of inquiry. Research could too readily come under the conservatism of the Institute's senior leadership, rather than representing the freer and the more independently critical climate of a school separate from the Institute. A competition of ideas should be fully encouraged.

Within the British context, a national research center for town and regional planning might provide a workable arrangement, perhaps within the Department of Scientific and Industrial Research and parallel to the Building Research Station, thus providing a governmental facility of high competence. Such a center could maintain liaison with the Ministry of Housing and Local Government, with the Town Planning Institute, and with various town planning schools. It might allow pooled resources to be used to best advantage. While the United States gains by the pluralism of diverse centers,[28] it might be more realistic in Britain to put greater emphasis on a single one. It would be sound to encourage such a center to concentrate on research and to stop short of preparing plans or recommending specific policy.[29] The center might seek chiefly to improve the understanding of what people need or want by way of an urban environment, how urban development takes place, how large urban areas function, and what consequences are likely to result from given public policies. Comparative analyses of alternative policies should rank high in priority.

The governmental unit most directly responsible for planning for the larger London Region must itself be given financial support and encouragement for a major, continuing study of the Region; and something like this in the form of an Intelligence Department was envisaged by the Royal Commission. It should be able to attract a highly qualified team of planners and researchers, and should have funds for contracting for additional research. This work ought to range from the documentation of past trends to the examination of likely future developments to the fashioning of ways of predicting the probable impacts of particular planning approaches.

London is a great and very special metropolis. It deserves the most thoughtful guidance. This, in turn, calls for a quality of understanding and an examination of possible alternatives regarding its future that will not be achieved short of a concerted effort of unusually high quality. In dealing with this great metropolitan region, intuitive and amateur judgments will by no means suffice. Required is a framework that will introduce the best that human intellect can discover about the needs and values of its residents, the development forces at work, the most efficient bases of public policy leverage for guiding metropolitan growth, and the implications of proposed planning approaches.

London deserves a most sensitive balance between continuity and change. Much must be respected and preserved. Yet the situation also calls for an adaptive willingness to change, led by a town and regional planning mechanism within which men of sound judgment are able to draw on a ready knowledge of whether the measures they recommend are in fact likely to bring about the results they hope to achieve.

Appendix

DEVELOPMENT PLANS AND FIVE-YEAR REVIEWS

| Planning Authority | Development Plan | | First Five-Year Review Submitted |
	Submitted	Approved by MHLG[b]	
Within Greater London Plan Region			
Administrative County of London	December, 1951[a]	March, 1955	March, 1960
Middlesex	June, 1952	June, 1956	—
Hertfordshire	December, 1952	December, 1958	—
Essex	March, 1953	September, 1957	—
East Ham County Borough	December, 1952	May, 1956	—
West Ham County Borough	December, 1952	May, 1956	—
Kent			
Part A (Main)	March, 1952	January, 1958	—
Part B (N.W.)	August, 1953	December, 1958	—
Surrey	March, 1953	May, 1958	—
Croydon County Borough	June, 1951	June, 1954	—·
Buckinghamshire	December, 1951	October, 1954	—·
Within London Region Defined by MHLG			
Berkshire	July, 1951	April, 1953	September, 1960
Hampshire	June, 1952	June, 1955	August, 1961

[a] Dates refer to the initial main development plan and to the first review of the county map. Numerous amendments have been submitted and, for most of the Home Counties, town maps as well as county maps are submitted. None of the first five-year review plans has been approved by the MHLG.

[b] MHLG stands for Ministry of Housing and Local Government (see also key to abbreviations, p. 189).

TABLE A2

PERMANENT HOUSES COMPLETED, ENGLAND AND WALES, 1934–1960
(Annual Averages, Selected Periods)

| Period | Total[a] | | For Local Housing Authorities and New Town Corporations | | For Private Owners | | For Others[b] | |
	Number	Per Cent	Number	Per Cent	Number	Per Cent	Number	Per Cent
1934–38	334,000	100.0	69,100	20.7	264,900	69.3[c]	[c]	[c]
1941–44	42,500	100.0	15,400	36.4	27,100	63.6[c]	[c]	[c]
1945–49	111,700	100.0	84,200	75.2	25,200	22.7	2,200	2.1
1950–54	228,300	100.0	169,800	74.9	45,700	20.0	12,700	5.1
1955–58	265,600	100.0	138,300	52.1	119,100	44.8	8,100	3.1
1959–60	259,300	100.0	101,300	39.1	154,300	59.5	3,700	1.4

SOURCE: Adapted from Central Statistical Office, *Annual Abstract of Statistics 1961* (London: HMSO, 1961), Table 60.

[a] Because of rounding, figures may not add to totals.

[b] For families of police, prison staffs, armed forces, and various other services, and for certain housing associations.

[c] For the first two time periods the data "For Others" not separately available and included with "Private Owners."

TABLE A3

Employment in Selected Sections of the London Region, in South-Eastern England, and in England and Wales, 1948–1960

	Employment (in thousands)[a]				Percentage Distribution				Increase in Employment (in thousands)				Percentage Distribution of Employment Increase				Indexes of Employment Growth (1952 = 100)		
	1948	1952	1956	1960	1948	1952	1956	1960	1948–1952	1952–1956	1956–1960	1952–1960	1948–1952	1952–1956	1956–1960	1952–1960	1948	1956	1960
Central Area[b]	n.a.	1,229	1,316	1,402	n.a.	6.6	6.7	7.0	n.a.	87	86	173	n.a.	10.4	16.2	12.6	n.a.	107	114
Rest of County	n.a.	1,335	1,353	1,365	n.a.	7.1	7.0	6.8	n.a.	18	12	30	n.a.	2.1	2.3	2.2	n.a.	101	102
Administrative County of London	2,464[c]	2,564	2,669	2,767	13.6	13.7	13.7	13.8	100	105	98	203	19.3	12.5	18.5	14.8	95	104	108
Rest of Conurbation	1,753	1,838	1,847	1,827	9.6	9.8	9.4	9.1	85	9	−20	−11	16.4	0.9	−3.8	−0.8	96	100	99
Greater London Conurbation[d]	4,217	4,402	4,516	4,594	23.2	23.5	23.1	22.9	185	114	78	192	35.7	13.6	14.7	14.0	96	103	104
Rest of London Region	n.a.	889	1,108	1,310	n.a.	4.8	5.7	6.5	n.a.	219	202	421	n.a.	26.1	38.1	30.8	n.a.	125	147
London Region[e]	n.a.	5,291	5,624	5,904	n.a.	28.3	28.8	29.4	n.a.	333	280	613	n.a.	39.7	52.8	44.8	n.a.	106	112
Rest of South-Eastern England	n.a.	2,021	2,076	2,069	n.a.	10.8	10.6	10.3	n.a.	55	−17	38	n.a.	6.6	−3.2	2.8	n.a.	103	102
South-Eastern England[f]	n.a.	7,312	7,700	7,963	n.a.	39.1	39.4	39.7	n.a.	388	263	651	n.a.	46.3	49.6	47.6	n.a.	105	109
Rest of England and Wales	n.a.	11,386	11,836	12,103	n.a.	60.9	60.6	60.3	n.a.	450	267	717	n.a.	53.7	50.4	52.4	n.a.	104	106
England and Wales	18,180	18,698	19,536	20,066	100.0	100.0	100.0	100.0	518	838	530	1,368	100.0	100.0	100.0	100.0	97	104	107

SOURCES: Published reports, especially various issues of the Ministry of Labour *Gazette*, and unpublished figures from the MHLG, except where otherwise noted.
a "Employment" includes unemployed, but excludes employers and persons working on own account.
b Those labor exchanges representing the City, Westminster, Holborn, Finsbury, and parts of St. Pancras and St. Marylebone.
c *Administrative County of London Development Plan 1951: Analysis*, p. 64.
d This is the London part of the Ministry of Labour London and South-Eastern Region, and is not the exact counterpart of the Conurbation. For all figures except 1960, see *Report of the Royal Commission of Local Government in Greater London 1957–60*, pp. 292–294.
e As defined by the London Technical Branch (Research Section), MHLG. See A. G. Powell, "The Recent Development of Greater London," *Advancement o Science*, XVII (May, 1961), esp. map on p. 82.
f The London and South-Eastern, the Eastern, and the Southern standard regions. Figures before 1960 have been adjusted to take into account boundary changes in the Southern region.

TABLE A4

THE POPULATION FOR SELECTED SECTIONS OF THE LONDON REGION, FOR SOUTH-EASTERN ENGLAND, AND FOR ENGLAND AND WALES, 1931–1961

	Population (in thousands)[a]							Percentage Distribution						
	1931	1939	1948[b]	1952	1956	1960	1961	1931	1939	1948[b]	1952	1956	1960	1961
Central Area[c]	545	488	382	380	365	350	377	1.4	1.2	0.9	0.9	0.8	0.8	0.7
Rest of County	3,852	3,525	2,957	2,983	2,908	2,844	2,843	9.6	8.5	6.9	6.8	6.5	6.2	6.2
Administrative County of London	4,397	4,013	3,339	3,363	3,273	3,194	3,180	11.0	9.7	7.8	7.7	7.3	7.0	6.9
Conurban Ring	3,819	4,734	4,943	5,001	4,997	5,016	4,972	9.6	11.4	11.6	11.3	11.2	10.9	10.8
Greater London Conurbation	8,216	8,747	(8,320) 8,282	8,364	8,270	8,210	8,152	20.6	21.1	(19.2) 19.4	19.0	18.5	17.9	17.7
Regional Ring	2,457	2,791	3,170	3,417	3,744	4,156	4,308	6.1	6.7	7.4	7.8	8.4	9.1	9.3
London Region[d]	10,673[f]	11,538	11,452	11,781	12,014	12,366	12,460	26.7	27.8	26.8	26.8	26.9	27.0	27.0
Rest of South-Eastern England	4,046	4,333	4,574	4,841	4,968	5,156	5,231	10.1	10.5	10.7	11.0	11.1	11.3	11.3
South-Eastern England[e]	14,719	15,871	16,026	16,622	16,982	17,522	17,691	36.8	38.3	37.5	37.8	38.0	38.3	38.3
Rest of England and Wales	25,233	25,589	26,724	27,333	27,685	28,233	28,475	63.2	61.7	62.5	62.2	62.0	61.7	61.7
England and Wales	39,952	41,460	(43,296) 42,750	43,955	44,677	45,755	46,166	100.0	100.0	100.0	100.0	100.0	100.0	100.0

	Increase in Population (in thousands)ᵍ						Percentage Distribution of Population Increaseᵍ					
	1931–1939	1939–1948ᵇ	1948–1952ᵇ	1952–1956	1956–1961	1939–1961	1931–1939	1939–1948	1948–1952	1952–1956	1956–1961	1939–1961
Central Areaᶜ	−57	−106	−2	−15	−28	−151	−3.8	−8.2	−0.2	−2.1	−1.9	−3.2
Rest of County	−327	−568	26	−75	−65	−682	−21.7	−44.0	2.2	−10.5	−4.3	−14.5
Administrative County of London	−384	−674	24	−90	−93	−833	−25.5	−52.2	2.0	−12.6	−6.2	−17.7
Conurban Ring	915	209	58	−4	−25	238	60.7	16.2	4.8	−0.6	−1.7	5.1
Greater London Conurbation	531	(−427) −465	(44) 82	−94	−118	−595	35.2	(−23.3) −36.0	(6.7) 6.8	−13.2	−7.9	−12.6
Regional Ring	334	379	247	327	564	1,517	22.2	29.3	20.5	45.9	37.7	32.2
London Regionᵈ	865	−86	329	233	446	922	57.4	−6.7	27.3	32.7	29.8	19.6
Rest of South-Eastern England	287	241	267	127	263	898	19.0	18.7	22.2	17.9	17.5	19.1
South-Eastern Englandᵉ	1,152	155	596	360	709	1,820	76.4	12.0	49.5	50.6	47.3	38.7
Rest of England and Wales	356	1,135	609	352	790	2,886	23.6	88.0	50.5	49.4	52.7	61.3
England and Wales	1,508	(1,836) 1,290	(659) 1,205	712	1,499	4,706	100.0	100.0	100.0	100.0	100.0	100.0

SOURCE: Figures except 1931 are mid-year estimates, compiled from various published sources, mainly Registrar General's *Statistical Review of England and Wales* (various years) and *Annual Estimates of the Population of England and Wales and of Local Authority Areas 1961*.

ᵃ The figures for 1931 and 1939 are resident population and are roughly comparable with the figures for the years 1952 through 1961, which are home population, including members of the armed services, merchant seamen, and certain other persons if within the country. All percentages and ratios computed. 1952 and 1961 are the most reliable estimates, for they reflect adjustments from the 1951 and 1961 censuses.

ᵇ The figures for 1948 are resident *civilian* population and are not directly comparable with the figures for the other years. The only available published 1948 figures for resident population are shown in parentheses. For the Greater London Conurbation, the civilian population was 0.5 per cent less than the resident population; for England and Wales, it was 1.3 per cent less. Because of noncomparability, the population increase columns for 1939–48 and 1948–52 must be viewed with caution. Direct 1939–52 comparisons are more valid.

ᶜ The City, and Finsbury, Holborn, St. Marylebone, St. Pancras, and Westminster metropolitan boroughs.

ᵈ Footnote c, Table A3, also applies here. Subsequent analyses have suggested adding the Basingstoke urban and rural districts to the Region, but to maintain comparability of definition, we have excluded these throughout.

ᵉ Footnote f, Table A3, applies.

ᶠ This is for civilian population only. From the London Technical Branch (Research Section), MHLG as published in the Centre for Urban Studies, *Statement of Evidence to the Royal Commission on Local Government in Greater London* (London: Centre for Urban Studies, University of London, December 4, 1959), Table 1, p. 29.

ᵍ For increases and percentage distribution of increases for 1939–52 and 1952–61, and for indexes of increase with bases, respectively, of 1939 and 1952, see Table 9, p. 96.

TABLE A5

AVERAGE ANNUAL PERCENTAGE INCREASES IN POPULATION FOR SELECTED
LONDON RINGS, FOR SOUTH-EASTERN ENGLAND, AND FOR
ENGLAND AND WALES, 1931–1961[a]

	1931–1939	1939–1948[b]	1948–1952[b]	1952–1956	1956–1961
County of London	−1.1	−1.9	0.2	−0.7	−0.6
Rest of Conurbation	3.0	0.5	0.3	[c]	−0.1
Greater London		(−0.5)	(0.1)		
Conurbation	0.8	−0.6	0.2	−0.3	−0.3
Regional Ring	1.7	1.5	1.9	2.4	3.0
London Region	1.0	−0.1	0.7	0.5	0.7
South-Eastern England Ring	0.9	0.7	1.5	0.7	1.1
South-Eastern England	1.0	0.1	0.9	0.5	0.8
Rest of England and Wales	0.2	0.5	0.6	0.3	0.6
England and Wales		(0.5)	(0.7)		
	0.5	0.3	0.4	0.4	0.6

[a] These percentage increases were computed by dividing the percentage increase for each longer period by the number of years in the period, and are not true annual rates of increase.

[b] The 1948 figures are for civilian population and the figures for the other years are for home (or equivalent) population. This seriously affects the 1939–1948 and the 1948–1952 rates as they have been computed. Only for the Greater London Conurbation and for England and Wales do we have corresponding home population counts available, and the average annual percentages using these are shown in parentheses. In general, the 1939–1948 percentages are too low, and the 1948–1952 percentages are too high, but we do not know by how much.

[c] Less than 0.1 per cent.

TABLE A6

(Based on a 10 per cent sample of membership)

		Period in which gained Associate Membership in the TPI		
	Total	1939 and earlier	1940– 1949	1950– 1959
	Number in the 10 Per Cent Sample[a]			
All TPI Members	270	44	105	121
TPI Members with no other professional memberships	73	5	14	54
TPI Members with at least one other membership	197	39	91	67
	Percentage Distribution (All TPI Members = 100.0 Per Cent)			
All TPI Members	100.0	100.0	100.0	100.0
No other memberships	27.0	11.4	13.3	44.6
At least one other membership[b]	73.0	88.6	86.7	55.4
RIBA only	42.2	31.9	45.7	43.0
RIBA + a third membership	2.9	4.5	5.7	—
ICE or I Mun. E only	16.7	27.3	23.8	6.6
Above + a third membership	4.7	9.1	6.7	1.7
RICS only	5.9	15.9	3.8	4.1
RICS + a third membership	6.0	9.1	9.5	6.0
ILA only	1.1	2.3	1.9	—
ILA + a third membership	0.4	—	1.0	—
	Percentage Distribution (All Other Memberships = 100.0 Per Cent)			
RIBA	56.5	36.4	52.4	75.4
ICE or I Mun. E	26.9	36.4	31.1	14.5
RICS	14.8	25.0	13.6	10.1
ILA	1.9	2.3	2.9	—

Source: From *Yearbook of the Town Planning Institute 1959–60* (London: TPI, November, 1959).

[a] Only Members and Associate Members included in the sample. Retired Members, Legal and Legal Associate Members, and Students excluded. In each case, the absolute number refers to the sample, and total membership would be approximately ten times this figure.

[b] The full names of the other professional associations are:

> RIBA—Royal Institute of British Architects
> ICE—Institution of Civil Engineers
> I Mun. E—Institution of Municipal Engineers
> RICS—Royal Institution of Chartered Surveyors
> ILA—Institute of Landscape Architects

Notes

Abbreviations Used in Notes

AJ — *Architects Journal*
AR — *Architectural Review*
GPO — (U. S.) Government Printing Office
HLG — (The Minister of) Housing and Local Government
HMSO — Her (or His) Majesty's Stationery Office
JAIP — *Journal of the American Institute of Planners*
JTPI — *Journal of the Town Planning Institute*
LCC — London County Council
LGGL — (Royal Commission on) Local Government in Greater London
LGP — (Minister of) Local Government and Planning
LSE — London School of Economics and Political Science
MHLG — Ministry of Housing and Local Government (1951–   )
MLGP — Ministry of Local Government and Planning (1951)
MTCP — Ministry of Town and Country Planning (1943–1951)
TCP — (Minister of) Town and Country Planning
TCP — *Town and Country Planning* (journal published by the TCPA)
TCPA — Town and Country Planning Association
TPI — Town Planning Institute
TPR — *Town Planning Review*

Notes to Chapter 1
Introduction: Focus and Context
(Pages 3–26)

[1] Scholarly opinion is divided as to whether Rome's population exceeded a million. For a summary of divergent estimates, see Arthur E. R. Boak, *Manpower Shortage and the Fall of the Roman Empire in the West* (Ann Arbor: University of Michigan Press, 1955), p. 6. Also Jérôme Carcopino, "Rome and the Antonines," in *Golden Ages of the Great Cities* (London and New York: Thomas and Hudson, 1952), pp. 30–31, where he argues that Rome must have passed the million mark in the second century.

[2] Concern for checking London's growth is by no means new. Rasmussen provides a fascinating chapter featuring Queen Elizabeth's proclamation in 1580, charging her subjects "to desist and forbear from any new buildings of any house or tenement within three miles from any of the gates of the said city of London . . . and also to forbear from letting or setting, or suffering any more families than one only to be placed, or to inhabit from henceforth in any house that heretofore hath been inhabited." Steen Eiler Rasmussen, *London: The Unique City* (London: Jonathan Cape, 1937), p. 68. See also pp. 63–75.

[3] *Doctrine,* as we use the term, shares some of the characteristics of *ideology,* but seems less pretentious and hence more readily applicable to the straightforward character of town planning as a governmental and professional activity. For an excellent discussion of the functions and determinants of doctrine in a governmental planning context, see Philip Selznick, *TVA and the Grass Roots: A Study in the Sociology of Formal Organization* (Berkeley and Los Angeles: University of California Press, 1953), esp. pp. 8–16, *passim.*

[4] William Ashworth has provided a thorough account of town planning's history up to the early 'forties: *The Genesis of Modern British Town Plan-*

ning: A Study in Economic and Social History of the Nineteenth and Twentieth Centuries (London: Routledge and Kegan Paul, 1954). See also Peter Self's lucid analysis of recent developments in *Cities in Flood: The Problems of Urban Growth* (2d ed.; London: Faber and Faber, 1961). William A. Robson's classic *The Government and Misgovernment of London* (2d ed.; London: George Allen and Unwin, 1948) furnishes a history of the evolution of government and planning in Greater London.

[5] William A. Robson, "London," in Robson (ed.), *Great Cities of the World: Their Government, Politics and Planning* (London: George Allen and Unwin, 1954), pp. 259–260. By permission of George Allen and Unwin, the Macmillian Co. of New York, and the author.

[6] Robson, *The Government and Misgovernment of London,* p. 28.

[7] See General Register Office, *Census, 1951, England and Wales: Report on Greater London and Five Other Conurbations* (London: HMSO, 1956), pp. xii–xix. The term *Greater London* was introduced as early as 1881, and essential comparability as to territorial definition has been maintained since. The full phrase *Greater London Conurbation* was not adopted until the 1951 census.

[8] For a listing of its constituent units, see footnote d, Table 1. This Region includes certain cities—notably Portsmouth, Southampton, Bournemouth, Brighton and Oxford—sufficiently large and remote from London to suggest their exclusion from a London Region. But using complete counties permits documentation of broad trends from 1801 onward. For postwar trends (in chap. 5) we shall rely on other regional definitions, for this particular region is no longer used for census or planning purposes.

[9] General Register Office, *Census of England and Wales, 1931: General Report* (London: HMSO, 1950), p. 32.

[10] Robson, *The Government and Misgovernment of London,* pp. 42, 45; J. H. Forshaw and Patrick Abercrombie, *County of London Plan* (London: Macmillan, 1943), p. 168.

[11] Catherine Bauer, *Modern Housing* (Boston: Houghton Mifflin, 1934), esp. pp. 122–123.

[12] Alec Johnson, *This Housing Question* (London: Lawrence and Wishart, 1954), pp. 21–22.

[13] *Report of the Royal Commission on the Distribution of Industrial Population,* Cmd. 6153 (London: HMSO, January, 1940), p. 67.

[14] See Bauer, *op. cit.,* part I; Lewis Mumford, *The Story of Utopias* (New York: Boni and Liveright, 1923), pp. 196–211. On the evolution of anti-urbanism in Great Britain, see Ruth Glass, "Urban Sociology in Great Britain: A Trend Report," *Current Sociology,* IV (No. 4, 1955), esp. 14–19.

[15] Ashworth, *op. cit.,* chap. V.

[16] Reissued with slight revisions as *Garden Cities of To-Morrow* (2d ed., 1902; 3d ed., 1922; as edited by F. J. Osborn, 1945).

[17] Ashworth, *op. cit.,* p. 164. A number of books on town planning written from 1905 to 1930 were essentially tracts on the garden-city idea. See, for ex-

ample, C. B. Purdom (ed.), *Town Theory and Practice* (London: Benn Brothers, 1921).

[18] For a longer account of the rise and influence of the Association, from which this section has drawn, see D. L. Foley, "Idea and Influence: The Town and Country Planning Association," *JAIP,* XXVIII (February, 1962), 10–17.

[19] Howard, *op. cit.* (Osborn edition), p. 142 and diagram on p. 143.

[20] The best general sources on planning for London include TPI, *Report on Planning in the London Region* (London: TPI, 1956), esp. chap. 2; *Report of the Royal Commission on Local Government in Greater London, 1957–60,* Cmnd. 1164 (London: HMSO, October, 1960), pp. 67–82, 312–313; Robson, *The Government and Misgovernment of London,* pp. 175–191, 403–420; C. B. Purdom, *How Should We Rebuild London?* (2d ed.; London: J. M. Dent and Sons, 1946), esp. pp. 125–131.

[21] W. Loftus Hare, "The Green Belt—Its Relation to London's Growth," *Journal of the Royal Institute of British Architects.* XLIV (May 8, 1937), 678–679; Purdom, *op. cit.,* p. 126.

[22] See Mr. Niven's obituary, *JTPI,* XXVIII (January-February, 1942), 89.

[23] Presented in a paper to the Royal Institute of British Architects' Town Planning Conference of 1910. See Hare, *op. cit.,* pp. 679–681; Purdom, *op. cit.,* p. 91.

[24] As presented in student project, Department of Town Planning, University of London, Spring, 1960.

[25] Hare, *op. cit.,* pp. 680, 682; Purdom, *op. cit.,* p. 126.

[26] Purdom, *op. cit.,* p. 126; for the diagrammatic plan, see Purdom (ed.), *Town Theory and Practice,* facing p. 32.

[27] Personal interview, Miss J. Tyrwhitt.

[28] Greater London Regional Planning Committee, *First Report* (London: Knapp, Drewett and Sons, December, 1929), p. 14.

[29] *Ibid.,* pp. 16–17, and diagrams facing these two pages.

[30] See particularly the map and plan, Greater London Regional Planning Committee, *Second Report* (London: Knapp, Drewett and Sons, March, 1933), facing p. 72.

[31] Hare, *op. cit.,* pp. 680, 683.

[32] A. T. Edwards, *A Hundred New Towns?* (London: J. M. Dent, 1944). Also other editions.

[33] Robson, *The Government and Misgovernment of London,* p. 427.

[34] *Ibid.,* pp. 184–185; Hare, *op. cit.,* pp. 683–685; Purdom, *How Should We Rebuild London?,* pp. 127–129.

[35] *Report of the Royal Commission on the Distribution of Industrial Population,* esp. pp. 40–50, 164–170.

[36] *Ibid.,* p. 202.

[37] *Ibid.,* pp. 201–202.

[38] *Ibid.,* p. 206.

[39] *Ibid.,* pp. 81–83, 155.

[40] *Ibid.,* pp. 58–66.

[41] Personal interview, Sir Frederic J. Osborn.

[42] See also the thoughtful essay by Harold F. Dorn, "Pitfalls in Population Forecasts and Projections," *Journal of the American Statistical Association,* XLV (September, 1950), 311–334.

[43] Patrick Abercrombie, *Greater London Plan 1944* (London: HMSO, 1945), Appendix 6, p. 191.

[44] Ladislas Segoe *et al., Local Planning Administration* (1st ed.; Chicago: Institute for Training in Municipal Administration, 1941), pp. 83–84. Similar projections were also provided in National Resources Committee, *Problems of a Changing Population* (Washington, D. C.: U. S. GPO, May, 1938).

[45] Richard M. Titmuss, *Problems of Social Policy* (London: HMSO and Longmans, Green, 1950), pp. 256–257.

[46] *Ibid.,* pp. 299, 322, 324.

[47] *Ibid.,* p. 330. Professor Titmuss explains that damage in this case included minor damage such as broken windows.

[48] *Ibid.,* pp. 239, 273.

[49] *Ibid.,* pp. 102–103, 355, 434.

[50] *Statistical Abstract for London, 1937–46* (London: LCC, 1948).

[51] Herbert Finer, "Post-War Reconstruction in Great Britain," *The Canadian Journal of Economics and Political Science,* VIII (November, 1942), 494. Also see William A. Robson, *The War and the Planning Outlook* (Rebuilding Britain Series, No. 4; London: Faber and Faber, 1941).

[52] Good general discussions are provided in British Information Services, *Post-War Planning in Britain: Unofficial Post-War Planning 1939–1943* (New York: British Information Services, [1943?]); Eugene C. Kent and Felix J. Samuely, "Physical Planning: A Method of Comparative Analysis on Four London Plans," *AJ,* C (August 19, 1944), 99–114; Purdom, *How Shall We Rebuild London?* pp. 133–135, 284–285. We are also indebted to Miss Jacqueline Tyrwhitt for a personal interview.

[53] See *AJ,* XCVII (June 10, 1943), 375–376, 379–384. The main review here is by G. M. K(allman).

[54] "The R. A. Plan for London," *AJ,* XCVI (October 22, 1942), 264–270. "The R. A. Plan" (by a Town Planner), *AJ,* XCVII (January 7, 1943), 7–8; also *AJ,* XCIX (May 18, 1944), 367–370.

[55] Arthur Korn and Felix J. Samuely, "A Master Plan for London: Based on Research Carried out by the Planning Committee of the M.A.R.S. Group," *AR,* XCI (June, 1942), 143–150. Lionel Brett, "Doubts on the Mars Plan for London," *AJ,* XCVI (July 9, 1942), 23–25. "Mars Plan for London," *loc. cit.,* pp. 19–20.

[56] Excellent accounts of this period are to be found in Robson, *The Government and Misgovernment of London;* Finer, *op. cit.,* pp. 493–513; F. J. Osborn (ed.), *Planning and Reconstruction* (London: Todd Publishing Co., 1946), "Planning Legislation and Policy," pp. 261–318, "The Planning Act 1944, and National Policy" (by Lord Balfour), pp. 75–94; Catherine Bauer, "Planning is Politics . . . but are Planners Politicians?", *Pencil Points,* XXV (March, 1944), 66–70, also in *AR,* XLVI (September, 1944), 81–82; and Catherine

Bauer, "Toward a Green and Pleasant England?: Critical Review of English Publication on Postwar Planning," *Pencil Points,* XXV (April, 1944), 78 *ff. passim.* Factual material in this section drawn from these sources will not be footnoted further.

[57] Minister of Reconstruction, *Employment Policy,* Cmd. 6527 (London: HMSO, May, 1944).

[58] Minister of TCP and Secretary of State for Scotland, *The Control of Land Use,* Cmd. 6537 (London: HMSO, June, 1944).

[59] Herbert Morrison, *Government and Parliament: A Survey from the Inside* (2d ed.; London: Oxford University Press, 1959), p. 247.

Notes to Chapter 2
The Advisory Plans and Their Main Ideas
(Pages 26–50)

[1] LCC, Minutes of Proceedings, July 13, 1943, p. 138.

[2] LCC, Report of the Town Planning Committee on "County of London Plan," June 11, 1945 (approved by the Council, July 17, 1945), p. 1.

[3] *Ibid.,* p. 8.

[4] J. H. Forshaw and Patrick Abercrombie, *County of London Plan* (Prepared for the LCC; London: Macmillan and Co., 1943). J. H. Forshaw was Architect to the LCC, and it was within his department that the staff work was conducted.

[5] Patrick Abercrombie, *Greater London Plan 1944* (London: HMSO, 1945).

[6] Corporation of London, *Reconstruction of the City of London* (London: B. T. Batsford, 1944).

[7] The plan report is most readily available as Part 5 of Corporation of London, Improvements and Town Planning Committee, *The City of London: a Record of Destruction and Survival* (London: Architectural Press, 1951).

[8] Personal interview with Mr. Ronald J. Sharpe, the only member of the team preparing the County of London Plan still on the staff of the LCC's Town Planning Division as of 1959.

[9] Advisory Committee for London Regional Planning, *Report to the Minister of Town and Country Planning and Report of the Technical Sub-Committee* (London: HMSO, 1946).

[10] See also Robson, *The Government and Misgovernment of London* (2d ed.; London: George Allen and Unwin, 1948), pp. 490–491.

[11] *Ibid.,* p. 490.

[12] *Hansard,* March 5, 1946, cols. 189–192; also reprinted, MTCP, *Greater London Plan: Memorandum by the Ministry of Town and Country Planning on the Report of the Advisory Committee for London Regional Planning* (London: HMSO, 1947), p. 14.

[13] *Hansard,* November 19, 1946, cols. 692–693; MTCP, *op. cit.*

[14] Although British town planning has introduced social goals with greater self-consciousness than has American city planning, there has remained some

tendency for town planning to seem technical in its nature and purposes. Purdom pleaded the case for placing highest priority on social goals, stating: "The urgent needs in town-planning are not the solution of architectural or engineering problems, but the establishment of forms of direction and control. . . . The technical questions are soluble or disappear when social aims are decided upon. In short, we have to pass from the subconscious stage of city growth, which has hitherto inhibited creative town-planning, into the sphere of defined social policy. . . . Without a clear vision of what we want our cities to be, firmly held in the mind and affections, the cities of tomorrow will repeat the past and make impossible the new life of the future. . . ." C. B. Purdom, *Britain's Cities Tomorrow: Notes for Everyman on a Great Theme* (London: King, Littlewood and King, 1942), pp. 5–6, 8.

[15] This emphasis on living conditions has been expressed and reaffirmed in various ways. Reviews of the County of London Plan by several Americans have emphasized that housing considerations were given first priority. "The County of London Plan," *AR*, XCVI (September, 1944), 77–82, 83–86.

Desmond Heap stated: "Indeed, I think one may say that the whole object of planning is the preservation and improvement of existing amenities and the creation of new ones." "Planning—A Lawyer's Reflections," *JTPI*, XXX (March-April, 1944), 105.

In a talk at about the time the County of London Plan was being released, J. H. Forshaw said: "The main aim of town planning is to secure the health and welfare of the people in their homes, at work, and in their leisure. . . . Proper sanitary conditions, amenity and convenience are the three-fold objectives of the Town Planning Acts of 1909 onwards." "Town Planning and Health," *JTPI*, XXX (November, December, 1943), 14.

Citing Geddes, the McAllisters suggest that the essential rationale is to "plan for the family. . . . From the home, the planner reaches out to all those manifold activities which characterise human life. . . ." Gilbert and Elizabeth McAllister, *Town and Country Planning; A Study of Physical Environment: The Prelude to Post-War Reconstruction* (London: Faber and Faber, 1941), pp. xxi, xxii.

[16] P. 12.

[17] Particularly in the White Papers, *Employment Policy*, Cmd. 6527 (London: HMSO, May, 1944), and *Distribution of Industry*, Cmd. 7540 (London: HMSO, October, 1948).

[18] See J. R. Jarmain, *Housing Subsidies and Rents* (London: Stevens and Sons), pp. 10 ff.

[19] *County of London Plan*, esp. p. 83.

[20] "The Planning of New Towns and the Re-planning of Old Ones," *JTPI*, XXV (January, 1939), 86.

[21] Extracts from Patrick Abercrombie's talk in Scotland reported in *JTPI*, XXIX (November-December, 1942), 47.

[22] *County of London Plan*, pp. 32–33, 115; *Greater London Plan 1944*, pp. 33–35. Dashes indicate that densities were not specified in the Plans.

[23] See MHLG, *The Density of Residential Areas* (London: HMSO, 1952),

Tables 4 and 10; and Lewis Keeble, *Principles and Practice of Town and Country Planning* (2d ed.; London: Estates Gazette, 1959), esp. pp. 197–203.

[24] *County of London Plan,* pp. 32–33.

[25] For example, "The County of London Plan," *AR,* XCVI (September, 1944), 77–82, 83–86.

[26] Cf. Robson, *op. cit.,* pp. 478–479; Lewis Mumford, "Lewis Mumford on the Future of London," *AR,* XCVII (January, 1945), 3–10, reprinted as "The Plan of London" in Mumford (ed.), *City Development* (New York: Harcourt Brace, 1945), pp. 198–240.

[27] The main references to new-town proposals in the *Greater London Plan 1944* are pp. 12–15, 20, 33–37, 49–50, and 160–165; to green belts, pp. 8, 11–12, 26, 30, and 35–36.

[28] Abercrombie showed his own philosophy in a talk in 1942: "What is to be the limitation of size of a satellite town? My own view is that there must be a definite maximum. . . . In my opinion, a population of 30,000 to 60,000 will provide a perfectly adequate number of people necessary to support the various institutions, social and cultural, in the town. . . ." Excerpts from an address in Scotland, *op. cit.* (footnote 21), p. 47.

[29] *Greater London Plan 1944,* p. 108.

[30] The choice was also narrowed by the consensus that population was not expected to grow: ". . . we appear to be almost at the end of the rise in population and . . . only an exceptional rise in the birth rate can prevent a decline." Robert H. Mattocks' presidential address to the TPI, in *JTPI,* XXVIII (November-December, 1941), 4. "The age of expansion has come to an end . . . Population expansion is coming to an end." Quoted from E. A. Gutkind, *Creative Demobilisation,* in book review, *JTPI,* XXIX (July-August, 1943), 215.

[31] Steen Eiler Rasmussen, *London: The Unique City* (London: Jonathan Cape, 1937), pp. 403–404.

[32] Abercrombie himself was strongly influenced by garden-city ideas; as early as 1933 he stated: "There seems to be general agreement that after towns have reached a certain size some form of satellite devolution is desirable. . . ." *Town and Country Planning* (1st ed.; London: Home University Library: Thornton Butterworth, 1933), pp. 122–123.

[33] Ministry of Works and Planning, *Report of the Committee on Land Utilisation in Rural Areas,* Cmd. 6378 (London: HMSO, August, 1942), p. 47.

[34] For a recent discussion of the traditional circular vs. the linear plan, see Josephine P. Reynolds, "The Plan: The Changing Objectives of the Drawn Plan," chap. 6, in Department of Civic Design, University of Liverpool (ed.), *Land Use in an Urban Environment: A General View of Town and Country Planning,* a special issue of *TPR,* XXXII (October, 1961–January, 1962), 175–179.

[35] See Reynolds, *op. cit.,* Figure 23, p. 177. F. Longstreth Thompson, in his plan for the Liverpool area, recommended compact radial spurs with green wedges between them and argued the case for this pattern. See *Merseyside Plan 1944* (London: HMSO, 1945), p. 5, and his talk, *JTPI,* XXXI (March-

April, 1945), 95. Various members of the TPI took issue with Thompson's proposals. *Ibid.,* pp. 105–106.

[36] An unsigned review of the County of London Plan said: "There is a choice to be made but, if this was fairly stated it would not be 'Do you prefer a house and garden to a flat,' but 'Do you prefer a flat in London with plenty of grass and open space and the amenities of city life to a house and garden in a satellite town, some fifty miles from London, with little or no domestic help and very limited amenities.'" *JTPI,* XXX (September-October, 1943), 236.

An editorial in *AJ:* "The real difference between Mr. Osborn and us is that, while Mr. Osborn wants to force 1½ million people to leave London, in order to provide material for additional garden cities, we want to arrange things so that as many as possible of those who wish to remain where they are can do so in comfort." *AJ,* XCI (February 3, 1944), 96.

Whether most people want private gardens is a matter of opinion, suggests Thompson. "It is probably true that the majority of English people would prefer to have a garden if they could do so and at the same time enjoy the advantages of living in a large city. But the two things are plainly incompatible; and the large city is still the magnet that attracts the great bulk of the population." Thompson, *Merseyside Plan 1944,* p. 16.

[37] We have not dwelt on other criticisms of new towns. Ling, for example, felt that the new towns were sited too close to London, becoming mere dormitories. Arthur Ling, "Plans—Problems of Realisation," *JTPI,* XXXII (May-June, 1946), p. 132. Heap expressed concern that the new towns may not be large enough to provide the full "social amenities of town life." *Op. cit.* (footnote 15), p. 107.

[38] See Ling, *op. cit.,* esp. p. 131.

Notes to Chapter 3
Doctrine Affirmed by the Plans
(Pages 51–58)

[1] Jacqueline Tyrwhitt has asserted: "The London plans enunciate in simple and dramatic form the most generally accepted lines of solution for the problems of the amorphous metropolitan area of the twentieth century. . . . [They] represent a crystallization of planning theory. They bring together, in authoritative form, all the symbols that have become stereotyped cliches and figure in every planning scheme in almost every country, whether the plan is to remodel a huge metropolitan area or to build a new village." "Opening Up Greater London . . . ," *National Municipal Review,* XXXVII (December, 1948), 592.

[2] Tyrwhitt: "The two plans do not contain any new or radical philosophy or planning patterns. Decentralization, new towns, green belts, ring roads, have all formed part of the planner's jargon since the days of Ebenezer Howard. . . . [T]here is no doubt that the popularity of the scheme as a whole

is due to the simplicity of its concepts and the fact that each of its main features has already received some popular sanction." *Ibid.*, 592–593.

[3] This draws upon Foley, "British Town Planning: One Ideology or Three?" *British Journal of Sociology*, XI (September, 1960), esp. 211–213. See also footnote 3, Chapter 1, above.

[4] *Ibid.*, pp. 224–227.

[5] It is possible, nevertheless, that doctrine which is widely accepted and, as a general principle, given official recognition still may not be fully implemented by Parliament and by governmental leaders. Examples will be furnished in chap. 7. On this point we are indebted to Dr. Nathaniel Lichfield.

[6] The reader may ask whether there is *a* doctrinal theme. Two main lines of argument may be directed against our interpretation. It can be contended that the advisory plans were too eclectic—reflecting compromise solutions to divergent pressures—to be dominated by any single theme. It can also be argued at a semantic level that we seek to encompass too much within our term, containment, and that we are really dealing with separate versions—containment$_1$, containment$_2$, containment$_3$, etc.—that only tenuously hold together as one. We admit a potentially subjective element in our interpretation, but stand by this interpretation as identifying the essence of the plans' philosophic basis and the crux of the resulting policy package.

[7] This distinction between unitary and adaptive as ideal-type approaches has been more fully developed in Foley, "An Approach to Metropolitan Spatial Structure," in Melvin M. Webber *et al.*, *Explorations into Urban Structure* (Philadelphia: University of Pennsylvania Press, 1963).

[8] We were tempted to identify certain of the substantive features of the advisory plans for London as unitary in spirit, since the plans stressed a single main center, a pyramidal density pattern and a radial circulation scheme reinforcing this center, and a circular metropolitan green belt—features that relate to a static and isolated conception of a community, in contrast to the dynamic, interconnected view of a community more characteristic of the adaptive approach. But on reflection we became convinced that the substantive pattern was not inherently unitary; the MARS plan, with very different substantive features, was, for example, also prepared in a unitary spirit, architect-planner conceived and depicted a future spatial pattern as goal.

Notes to Chapter 4
Carrying Out the Plan: Governmental Machinery
(Pages 61–79)

[1] Since the legislation and the system for land use planning in Scotland are somewhat different, they are not included.

[2] Prior to 1951, known as Minister of Local Government and Planning (1951), of Town and Country Planning (1943–51), of Works and Planning (1942–43).

[3] See Minister of LGP, *Town and Country Planning 1943–1951: Progress*

Report by the Minister of Local Government and Planning on the Work of the Ministry of Town and Country Planning, Cmd. 8204 (London: HMSO, 1951), pp. 22–23.

⁴ For explanations of development plans, see Charles M. Haar, *Land Planning Law in a Free Society: A Study of the British Town and Country Planning Act* (Cambridge: Harvard University Press, 1951), pp. 56–70; and B. J. Collins, *Development Plans Explained* (London: HMSO, 1951). We are indebted to these sources.

⁵ Charles M. Haar, "Planning Law: Public v. Private Interest in the Land and the 1959 Act," chap. 4, in Department of Civic Design, University of Liverpool (ed.), *Land Use in an Urban Environment: A General View of Town and Country Planning*, a special issue of *TPR*, XXXII (October, 1961–January, 1962), 96.

⁶ See Mr. Megarry's comments on this point, in Charles Haar (ed.), "Proceedings of Comparative Seminar on English and American Land Use Controls" (Mimeographed draft, May, 1961, pp. 54–55. Forthcoming in revised form, Harvard University Press.)

⁷ Some variation may be permitted. The Administrative County of London Development Plan for 1951, for example, used: first period, 5 years after approval of plan; second period, the following 12 years; third period, from 17 until 50 years from the approval of the plan. Many public projects, particularly roads, would be shown only if their financing were ensured, however, and this has greatly shortened the future period to which these features of the plans extend.

⁸ See Peter Self, "Town Planning in the United States and Britain: I. Law and Organization," *TPR*, XXV (October, 1954), 172.

⁹ Lewis Keeble, *Principles and Practice of Town and Country Planning* (2d ed.; London: Estates Gazette, 1959), p. 286.

¹⁰ Town and Country Planning Act, 1947, sect. 12.

¹¹ Town and Country Planning (Use Classes) Order, 1950 (S. I. 1950/1131), modifying an earlier 1948 Order with twenty-two classes.

¹² Ruth Glass and J. A. G. Griffith have questioned whether even the Minister has possessed "the elementary information" about the extent, character, and effects of development control as it has been practiced. *Minutes of Evidence taken before the Committee on Administrative Tribunals and Enquiries, Twenty-First Day* (London: HMSO, 1956), paragraph 21 of their memorandum, p. 975.

¹³ This £300 million was an estimate in 1948, and the actual valuations five years later rose to some £350 million.

¹⁴ Peter Self, *Cities in Flood: The Problems of Urban Growth* (1st ed.; London: Faber and Faber, 1957), p. 152.

¹⁵ The following discussion draws mainly on the excellent discussion of compensation and betterment in Haar, "Planning Law . . . ," *op. cit.*, pp. 106–114.

¹⁶ This paragraph relies on Minister of LGP, *op. cit.*, pp. 38–49, and Haar, *Land Planning Law in a Free Society*, pp. 129–146.

[17] We have not attempted to spell out the details. For some years the central government granted for war-damage projects up to 90 per cent of the loan charges for the first five years, and up to 50 per cent for the next 55 years. Later this became 50 per cent throughout, and then was abandoned when this form of grant was absorbed into block grants to local authorities.

[18] Regarding the organization for building new towns, see esp. Minister of LGP, *op. cit.*, pp. 120–136.

[19] See *Report of the Ministry of Housing and Local Government for the period 1950/51 to 1954*, Cmd. 9559 (London: HMSO, August, 1955), pp. 69–72.

[20] See the Board's statement in Royal Commission on LGGL, *Memoranda of Evidence from Government Departments* (London: HMSO, 1959), pp. 158–160.

[21] See also D. N. Chester, *Central and Local Government: Financial and Administrative Relations* (London: Macmillan, 1951) and R. M. Jackson, *The Machinery of Local Government* (London: Macmillan, 1958), esp. chap. 10.

[22] British Information Services, *Town and Country Planning in Britain*, I.D. 920 (Revised ed.; New York: British Information Services, July 1959), p. 14.

[23] In addition to the Greater London Conurbation, the Royal Commission Review Area includes three municipal boroughs, five urban districts, and three rural parishes on the periphery. The largest of these were Romford Municipal Borough with 115,000 and Watford Municipal Borough with 74,000 persons as of 1959.

[24] *Report of the Royal Commission on Local Government in Greater London, 1957–60*, Cmnd. 1164 (London: HMSO, 1960), pp. 39–41.

[25] *Greater London Plan 1944* (London: HMSO, 1945), pp. 183–184.

[26] MTCP, *Report of the London Planning Administration Committee 1949* (London: HMSO, 1949), esp. pp. 13–18. Also, see William A. Robson, *The Government and Misgovernment of London* (2d ed.; London: George Allen and Unwin, 1948), pp. 494–495.

[27] MTCP, *op. cit.*, pp. 16–18.

[28] Interview with Professor Percy Johnson-Marshall.

[29] Keeble, *op. cit.*, p. 287.

[30] As the Royal Commission report has suggested, "The present machinery is so confused that it is difficult even to put down on paper a description of what it is, let alone how it works." *Op. cit.*, p. 110.

[31] One board and a single staff have been responsible for both Welwyn Garden City and Hatfield New Towns. Each of the other new towns has its own board and staff.

Notes to Chapter 5
Carrying Out the Plan: Programs, Trends, and Results
(Pages 80–116)

[1] See G. D. H. Cole, *The Post-War Condition of Britain* (London: Routledge and Kegan Paul, 1956), esp. chaps. 4–6.

[2] See A. G. Powell, "The Recent Development of Greater London," *Advancement of Science,* XVII (May, 1960), 77; Central Statistical Office, *Annual Abstract of Statistics 1961* (London: HMSO, 1961), esp. Tables 146, 147, 151.

[3] Since the British census term *private dwelling* includes as one criterion "separate access to the street or to a common landing or staircase to which the public has access," it excludes many situations (*e.g.,* resulting from conversions of large older homes) in which rooms do not qualify. See discussion in J. B. Cullingworth, *Housing Needs and Planning Policy* (London: Routledge and Kegan Paul, 1960), esp. pp. 6–7, 29–33.

[4] Sources for tabulation: *Annual Abstract of Statistics 1961,* Table 231; U. S. Department of Commerce, *Historical Statistics of the United States* (Washington, D. C.: U. S. GPO, 1960), p. 462; U. S. Department of Commerce, *Statistical Abstract of the United States* (Washington, D. C.: U. S. GPO, 1961), p. 558.

[5] P. 5.

[6] A rather comprehensive study, roughly contemporaneous with the advisory plans was, for example, carried out by Homer Hoyt, *The Economic Status of the New York Metropolitan Region in 1944* (New York: The Regional Plan Association, Inc., 1944). Hoyt restricted his projection, however, to the first year following the war, assumed to be 1946.

[7] Among the best recent reviews of trends in and problems confronting Greater London are Wyndham Thomas, "The Growth of the London Region," *TCP,* XXIX (May, 1961), 185–193; Peter Self, *Town Planning in Greater London* (London: LSE, 1962. Greater London Papers, No. 7); A. G. Powell, *op. cit.;* J. B. Cullingworth, *op. cit.;* TPI, *Report on Planning in the London Region* (London: TPI, 1956); R. W. G. Bryant *et al., The Face of Britain: A Policy for Town and Country Planning* (Reprinted from *Socialist Commentary,* September, 1961); and *Report of the Ministry of Housing and Local Government for the Year 1956,* Cmnd. 193 (London: HMSO, June, 1957), section on "London Regional Planning," pp. 60–76.

[8] Even the Royal Commission on LGGL, backed by the best technical assistance of Ministry officers, could show no comparable statistics earlier than 1948, and cautioned about some since 1948. The Commission's report stated: "Lack of suitable statistics makes it impossible to compare changes in employment in the main sub-divisions of the Greater London Region or to compare conditions before and after the war." *Op. cit.,* p. 293. And the Barlow Commission before it had great difficulty in mustering statistics that would show accurately what had been happening.

[9] See particularly Wyndham Thomas, *op. cit.,* pp. 186–187; also "The London Region and the Development of South-East England: 1961 to 1981," *TCP,* XXIX (June, 1961), 225–233. The Greater London Group, under the chairmanship of William A. Robson, has concluded that an areal definition of a London region even broader than that being used by the MHLG may be needed. MHLG has within the last year or so reorganized its technical officers so as to focus more attention directly on a broad South-Eastern England region.

[10] Thomas, *op. cit.*, p. 190; R. W. G. Bryant *et al., op. cit.*, pp. v-vi.

[11] A fascinating question arises: Why this separate and exclusive focus on industrial employment? A contemporaneous critique spotted this, in the course of reviewing the County of London Plan: ". . . by appearing to base a policy of decentralization on industry alone the whole problem of checking London's growth is oversimplified and distorted in a way that is unrealistic and dangerous. . . . Industry . . . gives employment to a mere 743,473 [i.e., 28 per cent] out of a total of 2,618,392 people employed in the County." *AR,* XCVI (September, 1944), 85.

[12] Powell, *op. cit.*, p. 78.

[13] F. J. McCulloch, "The Social and Economic Determinants of Land Use," chap. 1 of *Land Use in an Urban Environment: A General View of Town and Country Planning,* a special issue of *TPR,* XXXII (October, 1961–January, 1962), 14–15. He shows that from 1945 to 1952 only 47 per cent of industrial floor space was allowed to locate in the fortunate regions of middle and southeastern England, but that from 1953 to 1959, 60 per cent of the space was granted such permission.

[14] See Pragma's comments, *JTPI,* XLVII (March, 1961), 55.

[15] See E. A. Powdrill, "Administrative County of London Development Plan. First Review 1960," *JTPI,* XLVI (December, 1960), 295–297.

[16] Thomas, "The Growth of the London Region," *op. cit.*, p. 185.

[17] Dame Evelyn Sharp, "Development Trends and the Development Plans" (Address to the National Conference of the TCPA; mimeographed, October, 1959), p. 4.

[18] Thomas, *op. cit.*, p. 188.

[19] "The London Region and the Development of South-East England: 1961 to 1981," *TCP,* XXIX (June, 1961), 227.

[20] Powdrill, *op. cit.*, p. 296. (Quotation in previous sentence, same source.)

[21] *London Statistics 1950–59* (London: LCC, 1961), Table 142.

[22] R. W. G. Bryant *et al., op. cit.*, p. iii.

[23] Unfortunately, we have been forced to compute much of our population data from raw census sources as published. Thus we have not been able to benefit, except indirectly, from the most comprehensive analyses of postwar trends carried out by technical officers in the MHLG using refined civilian population figures not published and treated as confidential. Nor have we been able to take advantage of certain technical data adjustments that can be made in the Ministry. On this difficulty in obtaining clear, comprehensive statistics, see also J. B. Cullingworth's observations, *op. cit., passim.*

[24] *Ibid.*, p. 83. In general, Cullingworth's discussion of the planning policy for Greater London and of its implementation is excellent, and we have drawn heavily upon his book. See *ibid.*, chap. 8.

[25] Public construction—Hatfield New Town with an increase of 13,000 and several LCC out-county estates accommodating an estimated 84,000—is known to have accounted for about 14 per cent of this Ring's increase from 1938 to 1961. We lack figures on housing construction by other governmental units.

[26] Cullingworth, *op. cit.*, chap. 2; Louis Winnick, *American Housing and Its Use* (New York: John Wiley, 1957), chap. 8.

[27] Cullingworth, *op. cit.*, p. 15.

[28] *Administrative County of London Development Plan 1951: Analysis* (London: LCC, 1951), p. 46. The same section also states: "Assuming that: (a) the provisions of the London School Plan will be carried out, (b) four acres of open space per 1,000 population will be provided, (c) industry will be reduced, and (d) redevelopment will take place to modern standards at the zoned densities, it is estimated that there will be sufficient land in the Administrative County to accommodate ultimately about 3¼ million people. . . . The ultimate figure of about 3¼ million must not . . . be taken as a rigid figure but rather as one on which to base calculations. London is a place of constant movement, change, and redevelopment and it is impossible to fix a target figure which is to remain forever stable."

[29] *Ibid.*, p. 29.

[30] From Table 6 above. This corresponds to the figures published by the MHLG in its 1956 annual report, p. 74, and used by Cullingworth, *op. cit.*, p. 82.

The TPI in its *Report on Planning in the London Region* (1956), p. 15, used as the point of comparison with the development plan forecasts the ultimate population envisaged in the *Greater London Plan: Memorandum by the Ministry of Town and Country Planning on the Report of the Advisory Committee for London Regional Planning* (London: HMSO, 1947). This provides a total "ultimate population" of 9,891,400—109,000 higher than we have used based on the Ministry's 1956 annual report. This suggests that even in the space between the Greater London Plan's submission and 1947, the government had accepted some likely increase in target population. Since the 1947 Memorandum included certain incomplete estimates, this may also have been an unstable figure from which to work.

[31] Administrative County of Surrey, *Development Plan 1953: Report and Analysis of Survey, Part I The County Map* (1953), para. 320; *Development Plan: Written Statement* (Approved 1958), p. 6.

[32] Buckinghamshire County Council, *County Development Plan (First Five-year Review): The County: Report and Analysis of Survey* (Mimeographed, 1959), p. 8.

[33] For 1971 forecasts, see TPI, *op. cit.*, Table 1, p. 15; also letter dated April 1, 1960, from A. F. Holt, Borough Engineer and Surveyor, County Borough of Croydon.

[34] *Administrative County of London Development Plan. First Review 1960: County Planning Report*, Vol. 1 (London: LCC, 1960), p. 157.

[35] *Housing Londoners . . . The Part Played by the London County Council* (London: LCC, 1961), inside of front cover.

[36] The Stepney-Poplar comprehensive development area material has been drawn from various plans and reports by the LCC. There seems to be no published crosstabulation showing the change from prewar land uses to existing or to proposed land uses.

[37] Paul Brenikov, "The Conurbations," in *Land Use in an Urban Environment* . . . , *op. cit.*, p. 62.

[38] See *Greater London Plan 1944* (London: HMSO, 1945), Maps 5 and 10.

[39] See TPI, *op. cit.*, pp. 41–42.

[40] Since this text was written, the MHLG has published a handsome little booklet, *The Green Belts* (London: HMSO, 1962), explaining in words and pictures the nature of green belts as they have been developed. London's Green Belt is described on pp. 11–21.

[41] Unpublished study map from the MHLG. Also first five-year reviews of development plans for Berkshire and Buckinghamshire. Subsequently, the MHLG has published a map showing proposed extensions. *Ibid.*

[42] We are particularly indebted to Daniel R. Mandelker, an American professor of law. His book, *Green Belts and Urban Growth* (Madison: University of Wisconsin Press, 1962) unfortunately appeared only after this part of our manuscript had been written.

[43] The percentage of appeals allowed for all cases settled rose from 34 per cent in 1948 to a high of 54 per cent in 1954 and has steadily declined to 29 per cent for 1960. Lewis Keeble, "Planning at the Crossroads," *JTPI*, XLVII (July-August, 1961), footnote 9, p. 191; and recent annual reports of the MHLG.

[44] See Cullingworth, *op. cit.*, pp. 110–114; Derek Senior, "Speculation in Land Values," *Manchester Guardian*, October 16, 1959. This will be discussed further in chap. 7.

[45] *TCP*, XXX (January, 1962), 26–29.

[46] Thomas, *op. cit.*, p. 185.

[47] *TCP*, XXX (January, 1962), 27, 32.

[48] Thomas, *op. cit.*, p. 185, estimated nonfactory employment as of December, 1960, to be 35,000 in the London new towns.

[49] *Reports of the Development Corporations for the Period ended 31st March, 1958* (London: HMSO, 1958), p. 155.

[50] R. W. G. Bryant *et al.*, *op. cit.*, p. xii.

[51] Since this was written, the Minister of HLG has asked Harlow and Stevenage new towns to study the possibility of expanding their populations to 140,000 each. *TCP*, XXX (August-September, 1962), 325–326.

[52] *Planning of a New Town* (London: LCC, 1961).

[53] Neville Borg, "Overspill: A Short Study of the Essentials," *JTPI*, XLVII (May, 1961), 120.

[54] "Comment by Pragma," *JTPI*, XLVII (January, 1961), 2–3.

[55] Powdrill, *op. cit.*, p. 297. See also "Expansion of Country Towns," *TCP*, XXX (November, 1962), 439–444.

[56] Adapted from *Greater London Plan 1944*, pp. 32–38.

[57] Powell, *op. cit.*, p. 80.

[58] Our calculations. New towns: 228,000 times .80 = 182,000, based on Thomas, *op. cit.*, p. 185. LCC estates: 19,600 housing units in estates built outside conurbation times 3.6 estimated population per housing unit = 106,-000, based on *Housing Londoners* . . . , *op. cit.*, p. 9. Expanded towns: 2,900

homes to $1960 \times 3.6 = 10{,}500$, based on *ibid.*, p. 13. Private development: Estimated by multiplying 180,000 for 1952–58, by 1.58 (the ratio in England and Wales of private houses built in 1945–1960 to houses built in 1952–1958) = 285,000.

[59] "Planning and Reconstruction: The Data Required," *JTPI*, XXIX (May-June, 1943), 141–148.

[60] P. 59.

[61] P. 64.

[62] *Statement of Evidence by the Centre for Urban Studies to the Royal Commission on Local Government in Greater London* (London: Centre for Urban Studies, University College, December 1959), p. 14.

[63] *Ibid.*, Table 5, p. 35.

[64] From Table 7.

Notes to Chapter 6
Modifying Major Plans and Policies
(Pages 117–135)

[1] See also Table A1, listing, for each local authority, the dates of submission and approval of the initial development plan, and date of submission of the first five-year review.

[2] See particularly MHLG, "First Review of Approved Development Plans" (Circular 9/55, March 2, 1955).

[3] Dame Evelyn Sharp, "Development Trends and the Development Plans" (Address before the 1959 National Conference of the TCPA; mimeographed, 6 pp.), p. 1.

[4] MHLG, "The Review of Development Plans" (Circular 37/60, August 25, 1960).

[5] *Administrative County of London Development Plan: First Review. Statement* (London: LCC, 1960), p. 3.

[6] E. A. Powdrill, *Vocabulary of Land Planning* (London: The Estates Gazette, 1961), p. 21.

[7] Lewis Keeble, *Principle and Practice of Town and Country Planning* (2d ed.; London: The Estates Gazette, 1959), p. 285.

[8] Much of the next two sections is adapted from Foley, "Controlling Office Development in London: a Case Study of Central Local Government Relations" (typescript).

[9] Royal Commission on LGGL, *Minutes of Evidence,* 68 (London: HMSO, 1960), p. 2842.

[10] *Administrative County of London Development Plan: First Review, 1960. County Planning Report* (London: LCC, 1960), p. 143. "Information is not complete either about the office floor space in the Central Area in 1939 or about the office floor space destroyed during the war." *Ibid.*

[11] See D. H. Crompton, "The Daylight Code: Some Notes on the Form of Control of Space about Buildings," *TPR,* XXVI (October, 1955), 155–164.

[12] Unfortunately, from a research viewpoint, memoranda of this type tend to be confidential, are not openly available to persons from outside the Ministry, and cannot be precisely cited.

[13] W. F. Manthorpe, "The Limitation of Employment in Central London with Particular Reference to Employment in Offices," *Journal of the Royal Institute of Chartered Surveyors*, XXXIV (November, 1954), 389–399.

[14] For Minister's letter of March 7, 1955 and the reaction by the LCC's Town Planning Committee, see LCC Minutes, March 15, 1955, pp. 128–135.

[15] See *Report of Proceedings, Annual Conference, Association of Municipal Corporations 1955*, pp. 47–51; *JTPI*, XLII (April, 1956), 99–100.

[16] LCC Minutes, July 17, 1956, pp. 409–411.

[17] LCC Minutes, July 16, 1957, pp. 444–446.

[18] See TCPA, *Office Location in the London Region: Report of a Conference at the Royal Festival Hall on Thursday, 24 July, 1958* (Mimeographed, 36 pp.).

[19] Letter from Professor W. A. Robson, February 14, 1962.

[20] There has also been some criticism of both the MHLG and the LCC for not putting more of a halt to the growth of offices and office employment in central London. It is evident that major—and honest—differences in outlook have been involved: differences as to the respective place of private development and of governmental control, and as to the most desirable spatial organization for metropolitan London. In any event, the Ministry and the County found themselves pitted against forces of very great strength and momentum.

[21] On this see especially H. R. Parker, "Finance: The Effects of Government Policies on Land Use and Building Development," chap. 5 in Department of Civic Design, University of Liverpool (ed.), *Land Use in an Urban Environment: A General View of Town and Country Planning*, a special issue of *TPR*, XXXII (October, 1961–January, 1962), 125–150.

[22] *Report of the Royal Commission on Local Government in Greater London, 1957–60*, Cmnd. 1164 (London: HMSO, October, 1960), p. 1.

[23] Royal Commission report, *op. cit.*, p. 83.

[24] *Ibid.*

[25] *Ibid.*, p. 82.

[26] *Ibid.*

[27] *Ibid.*, p. 90.

[28] *Ibid.*, p. 91.

[29] *Ibid.*, p. 92.

[30] *Ibid.*, p. 192.

[31] The Royal Commission Report stated that there were 115 such constituencies. *Ibid.*, p. 217. Professor Robson has subsequently shown this to be 109 constituencies. See his "Reform of London Government," *Public Administration*, XXXIX (Spring, 1961), 66. A succeeding white paper stated there would be about 110 constituencies. *London Government: Government Proposals for Reorganisation*, Cmnd. 1562 (London: HMSO, 1961), p. 7.

[32] Robson, *op. cit.* (footnote 31), esp. pp. 59–62.

[33] *The Times,* October 20, 1960.

[34] L. J. Sharpe, "The Report of the Royal Commission on Local Government in Greater London," *Public Administration,* XXXIX (Spring, 1961), 79.

[35] Royal Commission Report, *op. cit.,* p. 58.

[36] "The Report of the Royal Commission on Local Government in Greater London," *JTPI,* XLVII (May, 1961), 139–140.

[37] "Comments and Criticisms on the Planning Proposals of the Royal Commission on Local Government in Greater London 1960" (mimeographed [August, 1961?]), p. 4.

[38] See, for example, "Farewell, L C C!" *AJ,* CXXXIV (December 6, 1961), 1091–1092.

[39] *London Government: Government Proposals for Reorganisation.*

[40] MHLG, "The New Shape of London" (Mimeographed release, August 8, 1962); MHLG, *London Government: The London Boroughs* (London: HMSO, 1962); and accompanying maps.

[41] Announcement by the Minister of HLG, May 17, 1962.

[42] Announcement, May 3, 1962.

[43] *London Government: Government Proposals for Reorganisation,* p. 12.

Notes to Chapter 7
Metropolitan Containment as Policy
(*Pages 139–158*)

[1] Registrar General's returns. See also the provocative discussion by Cynthia Lonsdale, "After the Census," *TCP,* XXX (September, 1961), 377–379.

[2] This is a composite adapted from the following sources: Registrar General's projections; Wyndham Thomas, "The Growth of the London Region," *TCP,* XXIX (May, 1961), 188; TCPA, *The Paper Metropolis: A Study of London's Office Growth* (London: TCPA, 1962), esp. pp. 18–20, 57; and a technical memorandum from the MHLG. Since the fullest data on which to face projections are available only within the Ministry, the researcher without full access to confidential Ministry studies cannot be certain that he is fully *au courant.* Fortunately, our published sources are recent and have apparently benefitted from information furnished by the Ministry, although some undoubtedly relied, at least in part, on pre-1961 census figures and estimates.

A paper by J. R. James, Chief Planner, MHLG, presented after our table had been prepared, suggests that the additional impact of net migration may well take the total increases for 1961–1981 to 5.9 million for England and Wales and to 2.6 million for South-Eastern England. "City Regions" (presented to the TPI Summer School, August, 1962).

[3] Barbara R. Berman, Benjamin Chinitz, and Edgar M. Hoover, *Projection of a Metropolis: Technical Supplement to the New York Metropolitan Region Study* (Cambridge, Mass.: Harvard University Press, 1960), esp. p. 70;

D. J. Bogue and D. P. Dandekar, *Population Trends and Prospects for the Chicago-Northwestern Indiana Consolidated Metropolitan Area: 1960 to 1990* (Chicago: Population Research and Training Center, University of Chicago, March, 1962), pp. 3, 27; Population Study Committee, Research Department, Los Angeles Chamber of Commerce, *Impact of Future Population Growth . . . : Projections from 1960 by 5 Year Intervals* (Los Angeles: Los Angeles Chamber of Commerce, May 1961), p. 6.

[4] MHLG technical memorandum. Further information about projected distribution of employment within the Region is unavailable.

[5] Thomas, *op. cit.,* p. 189. Also, source cited in previous footnote.

[6] Thomas, *op. cit.,* p. 192. Also, MHLG sources.

[7] Whether these proposals for green-belt extensions will, in fact, be fully supported by the MHLG has become unclear. A report by the MHLG, published after our text was written, states: "At the time of writing none of these [proposals for extensions] have been finally approved, except for a small area round Ascot, though the Minister has announced his intention to approve an extension of the belt in Buckinghamshire." MHLG, *The Green Belts* (London: HMSO, 1962), p. 11. One informant has suggested that approval of these extensions was unlikely.

[8] For example, in recent correspondence Derek Senior has explained: "I, as a layman closely involved in planning, always took it for granted that it was the continuously built-up areas of the overgrown conurbations that the planners (as distinct from the vested interests, including the majority of the Scott Committee) wanted to contain. . . . I can't prove, of course, that the Abercrombies and their governmental supporters thought at the time of containment always in relation to the continuous conurbation and never in relation to the urbanised area, population or employment capacity of the Greater London region. Since population and employment were assumed to be broadly stabilised, there was just no occasion for practical planners and administrators to make the distinction."

[9] Gordon Stephenson, an influential town planner and a member of the team preparing the Greater London Plan, supported this in his contemporary comments: "One of the principal aims of the [Greater London] Plan is to discourage the further growth of industry and population within the London Region, and to provide for their better distribution and grouping. [Professor Abercrombie] allows for no increase of population in the Region but he provides for a considerable shift of population and industries from the congested inner areas to new towns or enlarged existing communities in the other areas." "Review of Britain's Town Planning and the Greater London Plan, 1944," *JAIP,* XI (April-June, 1945), 14.

[10] Royal Commission on LGGL, *Memoranda of Evidence from Government Departments* (London: HMSO, 1959), p. 159.

[11] *Ibid.*

[12] *Ibid.,* p. 160.

[13] *Report of the Ministry of Housing and Local Government for the Year 1956,* Cmnd. 193 (London: HMSO, June, 1957), p. 61.

[14] *Report of the Royal Commission on Local Government in Greater London, 1957–60,* Cmnd. 1164 (London: HMSO, October, 1960), p. 83.

[15] MTCP, *Greater London Plan: Memorandum by the Ministry of Town and Country Planning on the Report of the Advisory Committee for London Regional Planning* (London: HMSO, 1947), table headings, pp. 4, 15.

[16] Peter Self and Wyndham Thomas in their various publications represent this flexible decentrist position. The TCPA would seem to be veering toward this exploratory outlook from a previous greater insistence on a few elementals. Self, in a recent paper not under TCPA auspices, has even suggested higher densities at various points within the Conurbation—a position seldom if ever previously advocated by the Association itself. Peter Self, *Town Planning in Greater London* (London: LSE, 1962. Greater London Papers, No. 7.), pp. 14–16.

[17] Since this was written, we have seen Maurice A. Ash's similar comments about the Green Belt in his *The Human Cloud: A Reconsideration of Civic Planning* (London: TCPA, May, 1962), esp. pp. 22–23.

[18] Footnote 51, chap. 5, also applies. For a fuller development of this point and certain other points in the present chapter, see also Foley, "Some Notes on Planning for Greater London," *TPR,* XXXII (April, 1961), 53–65.

Notes to Chapter 8
Doctrine and Change
(Pages 159–180)

[1] William Watson, "The Managerial Specialist," *Twentieth Century,* CLXVII (May, 1960), 413. A foreigner's reaction is expressed in the title of Muriel Beadle's recent book, *These Ruins Are Inhabited* (Garden City: Doubleday, 1961).

[2] Christopher Hollis, "Parliament and the Establishment," in Hugh Thomas (ed.), *The Establishment* (London: Anthony Blond, 1959), p. 181.

[3] Harry Eckstein, *Pressure Group Politics: The Case of the British Medical Association* (Stanford: Stanford University Press, 1960), p. 19.

[4] See Lord Balniel, "The Upper Class," *Twentieth Century,* CLXVII (May, 1960), 430–431.

[5] These men have traditionally been drawn mainly from Oxford and Cambridge (and strongly from the Classics), tend to belong to the best clubs, and, if they do well, may fully expect honors, including the possibility of knighthood. They comprise "a highly organized and highly centralized directorate of amateurs and dilettantes" in a system which has come to undervalue specialized knowledge and technical skill. Goronwy Rees, reviewing Hugh Thomas (ed.), *The Establishment,* in *The Listener,* LXII (October 15, 1959), p. 641. See also R. K. Kelsall, *Higher Civil Servants in Britain* (London: Routledge and Kegan Paul, 1955), and W. J. M. Mackenzie and J. W. Grove, *Central Administration in Britain* (London: Longmans, Green and Co., 1957), esp. pp. 63–73.

[6] Eckstein, *op. cit.*, p. 24.

[7] On this point see Allen Potter, *Organized Groups in British National Politics* (London: Faber and Faber, 1961), esp. chaps. 9–12.

[8] O. R. McGregor, "Social Facts and the Social Conscience," *Twentieth Century,* CLXVII (May, 1960), 390.

[9] Although this may not be fully fair, we may contrast the situation in Britain as described by Thomas Balogh, "The Apotheosis of the Dilettante: The Establishment of Mandarins," in Hugh Thomas (ed.), *op. cit.,* pp. 83–126, with the recommendations by the President's Science Advisory Committee that the behavioral sciences be mobilized to measure the social impact of science in future America, regarding which see John Lear, "Summons to Science: Apply the Human Equation," *Saturday Review,* XLV (May 5, 1962), 35–39.

[10] For example: "Positive town and country planning should not make detailed economic decisions, but should provide the framework within which economic activity can take place in response to normal economic laws. . . . As Conservatives we are in favour of minimum government intervention in the economic field, and we believe that. . . . [economic] decisions should as far as possible be left to the free interplay of individual choice." Conservative Political Centre, *Change and Challenge* (1962), pp. 55, 12, as quoted in "Comment by Pragma," *JTPI,* XLVIII (May, 1962), 120.

[11] See Foley, "Idea and Influence: The Town and Country Planning Association," *JAIP,* XXVIII (February, 1962), 10–17.

[12] Examples of TCPA leaders' adaptability: "The London Region and the Development of South-East England: 1961 to 1981," *TCP,* XXIX (June, 1961), 225–233; *The Paper Metropolis: A Study of London's Office Growth* (London: TCPA, 1962); Maurice A. Ash, *The Human Cloud: A Reconsideration of Civic Planning* (London: TCPA, May, 1962).

[13] Gordon E. Cherry, "The Town Planner and His Profession," *JTPI,* XLVIII (May, 1962), 129.

[14] Our tabulation from listings in *Yearbook of the Town Planning Institute 1959–60* (London: TPI, November, 1959) and *Official Architecture and Planning Yearbook 1960* (London: Chantry Publications, 1960).

[15] Two additional technical officers were not members of the TPI, and for our purposes here were excluded. One of these, J. R. James, a Fellow of the Royal Geographical Society, has subsequently been appointed as Chief Planner and, even more recently, has become a member of the TPI.

[16] In each case is listed the number of TPI members also holding other professional memberships. The percentage represents this number compared with total TPI membership in the category.

[17] For this and other source data in this paragraph, see R. I. Maxwell, "The University Graduate in County Planning: A Survey of the Position in December 1960" (mimeographed, December, 1960).

[18] A recent bibliography of research pertaining to town and regional planning lists contributions from various university departments, but almost none from town planning departments in these universities. TPI, *Planning Re-*

search: A Register of Research of interest to those concerned with Town and Country Planning (London: TPI, 1961).

[19] Included Messrs. Stephenson, Coote, Macfarlane, Richards and Shepheard for the Greater London Plan and Messrs. H. B. Mackenzie, Dougill, Williams, Bellamy, Ling, A. Mackenzie, and Marshall for the County of London Plan.

[20] *Report of the Royal Commission on Local Government in Greater London, 1957–60,* Cmnd. 1164 (London: HMSO, October, 1960), p. 341.

[21] And, as Peter Self has stated, "Town Planning . . . is generally—and in my view rightly—regarded as an instrument for strengtheing the flagging sense of local community which still underlies local government institutions." *Town Planning in Greater London* (London: LSE, 1962. Greater London Papers, No. 7.), p. 5.

[22] This was illustrated repeatedly in reactions by local spokesmen in evidence to the Royal Commission. As the Commission declared in its final report, the counties and county boroughs argued "that the nine county and county borough plans, subject to the coordination of the Minister of Housing and Local Government, were all that were necessary." *Op. cit.,* p. 45.

It would seem to be in this spirit that nine county councils, three county borough councils, and the Borough Council of London agreed, in the autumn of 1962, to form a new "planning organization," the Standing Conference on London Regional Planning, for "the purpose of studying the principal planning issues affecting the area and recommending common policies to deal with them." Press notice of December 3, 1962. On the inappropriateness of such a mechanism, see "Comment by Pragma," *JTPI,* XLVIII (November, 1962), 284.

[23] See also chap. 5. Also TPI, "The Report of the Royal Commission on Local Government in Greater London," *JTPI,* XLVII (May, 1961), 139–140, and "London Government," *ibid.,* XLVIII (April, 1962), 101–102.

[24] Among current and recent examples are the Penn-Jersey Transportation Study of the Philadelphia area; the Chicago Area Transportation Study; the Los Angeles Regional Transportation Study; and the Pittsburgh Area Transportation Study.

[25] For one thoughtful summary see Melvin M. Webber, "Transportation Planning Models," *Traffic Quarterly,* XV (July, 1961), 373–390.

[26] MTCP; Department of Health for Scotland, *Report of the Committee on Qualifications of Planners,* Cmd. 8059 (London: HMSO, September, 1950).

[27] Lloyd Rodwin, *The British New Towns Policy: Problems and Implications* (Cambridge: Harvard University Press, 1956), pp. 187–201. He concluded: "Education and research are still weak points in contemporary British planning. The new planning responsibilities require, first, advanced planning education, and particularly strengthening in the social sciences; and, second, research and research mindedness to develop the concepts, methods, and knowledge of the profession." P. 201.

[28] Among the strongest of such research centers are the Institute for Urban Studies, University of Pennsylvania; the Joint Center for Urban Studies,

Massachusetts Institute of Technology and Harvard University; and Resources for the Future, Washington, D. C.

[29] Wyndham Thomas has suggested that a center for regional planning might be established and that it could be given "the task of producing (and constantly reviewing) a set of regional plans somewhat on the lines of the Abercrombie Greater London Plan." He argues that this might provide an authoritative and yet sufficiently independent basis for plan making. "Planning in the 1960's," *Political Quarterly,* XXXI (October-December, 1960), 472. This would, in our view, blur lines between research and policy recommendation that deserve to be respected.

Index

Index

Town and Country Planning Association, 15, 43, 46, 91, 125–126, 160, 165–166, 168
Town and Country Planning, Ministry of, 25, 29–32, 70, 77–78, 105, 163
Town planners and the town planning profession, 163–165, 167–172, 178–179
Town planning, 126, 162–171, 178–180; research, 177–180
Town Planning Institute, 124, 132, 167–171, 176, 179
Towns, industrial, 7, 11, 17–18
Transport, Ministry of, 62, 71–72, 76, 79
Transportation system, 152–153; planning for, 177

Unemployment: Barlow Commission findings, 17–20; insurance, 26; London, 17–18, 33–34; policies to deal with, 33–36, 84, 144; post-war trends, 80–81; South-Eastern England and other regions of England, 17–18, 33–34
Unitary approach to planning, 56–58, 172–175

United States. *See under* American
Unwin, (Sir) Raymond, 16, 42–43, 52
Urban districts, 74
Uthwatt Committee, 25–26

Wales. *See* England and Wales
War. *See* World War II
Washington, D. C., 6, 48
Watford, 106
Watson, William, 159
Welwyn Garden City, 14–15
West End, 91, 124–125
West Ham, 74–75
Winnick, Louis, 100
Wise, Michael, 166
Works and Buildings, Ministry of, 25, 27, 30
Works and Planning, Ministry of, 25
World War II, 18; bomb damage, 4, 22–24, 122; enforced moratorium on construction, 24, 122; evacuation from London, 23–24, 40, 97, 140; idealism re reconstruction plans, 24–26

Yorkshire, 7